RECLAIMING THE RAPTURE

RESTORING THE DOCTRINE OF THE GATHERING OF THE COMMONWEALTH OF ISRAEL

RECLAIMING THE RAPTURE

Restoring the Doctrine of the Gathering of the Commonwealth of Israel

by
Douglas Hamp
Chris Steinle

2017

Reclaiming the Rapture
Restoring the Doctrine of the Gathering of the Commonwealth of Israel

Copyright © 2017 by Memorial Crown Press

All rights reserved. This book or any portion thereof may not be reproduced or used in any manner whatsoever without the express written permission of the publisher except for the use of brief quotations in a book review or scholarly journal.

First Printing: 2017

ISBN: 978-0-9992048-0-1

ISBN-10: 0-9992048-0-7

Memorial Crown Press
Phoenix, AZ
www.memorialcrownpress.com

Ordering Information:

Special discounts are available on quantity purchases by corporations, associations, educators, and others. Contact the publisher for details.

U.S. trade bookstores and wholesalers: Please contact Memorial Crown Press by email: info@memorialcrownpress.com.

Cover art by Michael B. Steinle

Unless otherwise noted, Scripture quotations in this book are taken from *The Holy Bible, New King James Version*. Copyright 1982 by Thomas Nelson, Inc. Used by permission. All rights reserved.

CONTENTS

Introduction: What's Wrong with This Picture? 1
1 "Where's the Beef?" and "Where's the Verse?" 9
    "Where's the Beef?" 9
    Shadows 11
    Look, a Distraction! 11
    The Intimidating List 13
    Where is the Pre-Tribulation Rapture? 21
2 Coming Like a Thief in the Night 23
    The Thief in the Night in Second Peter 26
3 The Day of the Lord is the Second Coming 31
    Events Before the Day of the Lord 32
    Elijah 34
4 The Return of Jesus - Vignette 37
5 Unwinding Common Pre-Trib Assumptions 49
    Who Is Returning from Heaven with Jesus? 49
    What about the Church of Philadelphia? 51
    Will Christians Experience God's Wrath? 53
    The Mystical *Meta Tauta* 54
6 The Unmysterious Timing of the Rapture 57
    Isaiah 26:19-21 Resurrection/Rapture/Second Coming .. 59
    The Rapture (Gathering and Hiding Away) 60
7 Unmysterious Rapture Timing Verses 67
    Verses Affirming the Resurrection 67
    Rapture/Gathering Verses 68
    Resurrection/Gathering at Christ's Coming 76
    Resurrection Before the Rapture/Gathering 77

  Resurrection/Gathering at Last Trumpet/End of Days..77
  Resurrection and Indignation/Judgment on the Nations .78

8 First Century Expectations of the End of the Age ...83
  The Hope of the Pharisees 83
  The Afterlife in Modern Jewish Thought 88
  Christian Belief in the Resurrection 91

9 Revelation is Thematic - Not Chronological 95
  All the Mountains and Islands Flee Away 95
  Angels are Stars 100
  "And" versus "Then" in Revelation 103

10 Paul's Two Scheme Dimensional System 107
  Schemes, Forms, and Appearances 109
  Power, Resurrection, and Subjection..........................112
  The Rapture in Technical Terms–1st Corinthians 15...117

11 The Veil Between Heaven and Earth 127
  When Do the Heavens Pass Away? 127
  Heaven and Earth Fled Away......................................129
  There is a Veil Between Heaven and Earth 131
  The Two Veils 134
  We Are Like the Boy in the Bubble 135
  Adam and the *Adamáh* 136

12 The Veil -Vignette 139

13 Reclaiming the 1st Thessalonians Rapture Narrative 145
  The Coming of the Lord 147
  Translating the Rapture Verse......................................151
  Harpagēsometha 153
  What's Up with "Caught Up"? 161
  Where Do We Go from Here?...................................... 162

14 Tree of Life - New Body Transformation Vignette .. 167
15 Christ's Last Enemy and the Rapture 171
    Why the Lord Tarries 171
    Then Comes the End 175
    Daniel and the Thessalonians Connection.................. 177
16 Putting It All Together: What Happens
    on the Day of the Second Coming?...................... 187
    Rerferences 213

INTRODUCTION
What's Wrong with This Picture?

"Any story sounds true until someone tells the other side and sets the record straight." **Proverbs 18:17 TLB**

The Rapture was prophesied from Genesis to Revelation. That may come as a surprise to the millions of Christians around the world who have been taught that the rapture was not revealed until the New Testament. But did you know that famous Pre-Tribulation rapture authors and experts admit that there isn't a single verse that actually teaches a Pre-Tribulation rapture? Books such as *The Late Great Planet Earth* by Hal Lindsey, the *Left Behind* series by Tim LaHaye, as well as teachers like Chuck Smith of Calvary Chapel Costa Mesa, California, have greatly popularized the pre-tribulational rapture. "Pre-Trib" is the notion that at any moment Jesus will "catch up" (rapture) all true believers and take them to heaven to be with Him before the Tribulation begins. The stated need for the Pre-Tribulation rapture event, according to Pre-Tribulation teachers, is that the church has not been "appointed to wrath." The Great Tribulation is "God's wrath upon a Christ rejecting world"; therefore, God must remove His people before the commencement of the last seven years of human history.

Does the Bible actually state that the rapture will happen before the Great Tribulation? According to Jesus, speaking to His disciples concerning the end of the world, the rapture would occur *immediately **after** the tribulation of those days...he will send out his angels to gather his elect.* Matt. 24:29-31 According to Paul the apostle, the rapture happens in tandem with the return of Jesus, who spoke *concerning the coming of our Lord Jesus Christ and our gathering together to Him...* 2 Thess. 2:1 Jesus and the disciples don't indicate a removal of believers before the Great Tribulation at all. Rather, they tell us plainly that the rapture will occur *after* the time of the Great Tribulation.

And what is the purpose of the rapture? Is it simply to remove the church from the planet before the Great Tribulation (θλιψιν *thlipsin*)?

INTRODUCTION

Not according to Jesus. He stated that *in this world you will have tribulation* (θλιψιν *thlipsin*). *John 16:33* Jesus commended the ancient church of Smyrna saying, *I know your works, tribulation* (θλιψιν *thlipsin), and poverty (but you are rich)...* Rev. 2:9

According to the prophet Isaiah, the rapture's purpose is for God to *assemble the outcasts of Israel, and gather together the dispersed of Judah from the four corners of the earth.* Isa. 11:12

We believe it is time for us to rethink both the timing and purpose of the rapture. We see end times Bible prophecy akin to a 1000-piece jigsaw puzzle partially done. Many godly people have come before us and have spent a great deal of effort and time establishing the borders of the puzzle. Parts of the faces and the landscape are taking form, yet without the box cover showing the finished product. No one really knows how it ought to look entirely assembled.

Many of us have assisted in the effort to finish the puzzle; yet after carefully examining the remaining pieces and working for hours attempting to piece it all together, there are some pieces that simply will not fit. We cautiously conclude that some of the pieces already in the puzzle have been placed incorrectly; and sadly, the only way to make the entire puzzle to work is to remove a few key pieces and discover where they are really supposed to go.

We believe the timing of the rapture is a puzzle-piece incorrectly placed. Many times, teachers will begin with the assumption that the timing of the rapture is fixed and non-negotiable. They then demand that the rest of the end times scenario fit that assumption - very much analogous to our puzzle analogy, where people have a piece placed improperly. Until they realize the error in placing that piece, the puzzle will never completely be solved.

In this book we believe we must go back to the beginning to ask what the entire Bible teaches on the subject of the rapture. Both of us, Chris and Doug, are former believers in the pre-tribulational rapture scenario. I, Doug, remember from my earliest childhood going for walks and wondering if Jesus would come that day. I thought I was to be raptured up into His presence at any moment. When I became a professor at Calvary Chapel School of Ministry and Graduate School (in Costa Mesa, California), I taught the eschatology class and I taught the pre-tribulational rapture perspective as a foregone conclusion.

In 2008 I prepared a presentation called "There Will Be Signs." It became quite popular and I started going to many different Calvary Chapels sharing how many bad things were converging which seemed to line up with Scripture. I found as many things as I could to demonstrate that the world was falling apart, and quickly falling apart, because these signs could only be precursors to the imminent rapture of the church.

My realization of the complete lack of Scriptures did not strike me full force until I wrote a fictional account of the end times with the goal of only writing scenarios that I could identify in the Bible. I searched diligently and I could not find a definitive verse stating the timing of the rapture happening before the beginning of the seven year Tribulation. I was also a keynote speaker at many conferences where many of the top speakers were sharing their research. When I asked them where the verse was for the Pre-Tribulation rapture, no one could think of one. Everyone was convinced another expert knew where it was...yet we were the experts and none of us knew where to find the actual timing of the Pre-Tribulation rapture.

Because there are pieces that do not fit in the puzzle as it currently stands, when interpreted literally; figurative or allegorical interpretation is often used to make the pieces fit. The established placement of pieces is unfortunately considered unalterable, so relying on a "close enough" interpretation is accepted. However, I believe that there are some pieces that are incorrectly placed; and, once corrected, will lead to a new understanding of how the entire puzzle fits together. An understanding based on a more literal interpretation of Scripture.

The objective of this book will be to demonstrate primarily two things: 1) The purpose of the rapture scenario is to gather those who have been scattered abroad over the face of the earth. While that includes the body known as the church, it was prophesied throughout the entire Bible from Genesis to Revelation. 2) The event popularly called the rapture is comprised of a series of events: the resurrection of the dead, the transformation of the living, and the gathering of all of God's people.

INTRODUCTION

This connection between the rapture of First Thessalonians 4:17 and the gathering of Second Thessalonians 2:1 was the very issue that drew co-author Chris Steinle away from the Pre-Tribulation rapture position. If the rapture and the gathering were really two different events, wouldn't Paul have been more specific to make sure the Thessalonians didn't get their Days mixed up? These apparent references to the same day of Christ's coming led Steinle to a decade-long investigation to understand why the falling away and the revealing of the man of sin had to occur before Christ's return. Was Paul's chronology of end time events given solely by divine revelation? Or, was there a direct witness to these precursors in the Old Testament Scriptures?

The search for these answers prompted further questions about Paul's method of determining the timing of end time events. Why must the dead rise first - before the living are changed at Christ's coming? Jewish oral tradition suggests that the dead will be raised in the same condition in which they had died. Then the resurrected dead would be made whole in order to spend a final season on earth. Was Paul's statement that the dead must rise first based on his training as a Pharisee? Or, again, is there a verse that establishes the order of events at the resurrection of the dead?

Steinle became so fascinated with the Apostle to the Gentiles that he began to study Paul's life and way of thinking. He and his wife went to Greece and traveled the interior routes of Paul's missionary journeys. Then around 2002 they went on a Footsteps of Paul cruise with Chuck Smith to trace Paul's journeys by sea. Several years later Chris and his wife led their own "footsteps" tour to the sites in Macedonia and Achaia.

One night around the year 2011, as Steinle was drifting off to sleep and contemplating the fifteenth chapter of First Corinthians, the Lord revealed the significance of Christ's last enemy, death, in relation to other end time events. Further study led to the discovery of a complete logical system; a system that Paul might have used as the foundation for his eschatological passages. This logical framework is founded on certain prophetic Scriptures and can be shown to coincide with the timing of events in both of Paul's Thessalonian letters.

Another epiphany came through intense examination of the Greek words used in First Thessalonians 4:17. The results of this research indicate that the rapture is technically the transformation of the body, not the relocation of the body. The meeting/gathering known as the "catching up" will occur only after the body has been prepared to meet the Lord by putting on immortality. The proposed logical system, and its basis in the Old Testament, will be discussed in the latter chapters of this book. These discoveries take the discussion of the rapture beyond talking about what Paul is not saying; and provide a reasonable interpretation of what the Thessalonian letters are stating about the Lord's second coming.

In fact, there is another, more obvious, reason why Paul would use two different terms for the rapture. The Old and New Testaments have sometimes spoken about future events using different voices concerning the same prophetic events. The Old Testament generally spoke to God's people on the national level in terms of the sins of the nation and the redemption of Israel. The New Testament gospels and epistles primarily address the forgiveness of personal sin and the future redemption of the human body. Within the New Testament, Peter and Paul referred metaphorically to the temple and its pillars, the building and its stones, and the body and its members. Whether God was speaking to the plurality or to the individual, He was speaking about the same events.

The resurrection and the rapture of First Thessalonians 4:17 describe the resurrection and transformation of the individual members of the body of Christ. Paul used the word "rapture" instead of "gathering" because he was drawing attention to the transformation process of the individual body in order to comfort the bereaved. Paul used the broader term "gathering" in his second letter because he was warning the greater assembly about a coming time of deception that would be international in scope.

Because both authors came out of the same Jesus Movement denomination, each has been fully trained in Pre-Tribulation Rapture Doctrine. Likewise, both authors recognize that they must speak the truth in love and with compassion; realizing that neither author had anything but the best intentions as they supported their previous Pre-Tribulation position. The reader may wonder; "Then what makes the authors certain they have arrived at the best understanding of Scripture?" Their confidence comes from the fact that the Pre-Tribulation doctrine is based on little more than sporadic inferences to a Pre-Tribulation rapture (thus the need for college training in order to properly teach it). Whereas, the doctrine of the gathering on the Day of the Lord is based on the overwhelming consensus of Bible prophecy.

Doug and Chris want to be the first to acknowledge that we cannot *"show you a better way"* (1 Cor. 13) unless *Reclaiming the Rapture* challenges the Pre-Tribulation Doctrine in a spirit of love. God is Love, and it is not the authors' intention to be unkind to those who currently believe in a Pre-Tribulation rapture. It is the Pre-Tribulation theological system that is contrary to the Old Testament prophecies of the gathering. The biblical doctrine of the gathering synchronizes the Second Coming and with the entire Commonwealth of Israel. The Pre-Tribulation concept of the gathering is a gathering removed from the Church in time, and isolating from the Church in scope. Despite this flaw in Pre-Tribulation rapture theology, the authors do acknowledge that Dispensational theology is far less anti-Semitic than the Church's historical attitude toward the Jews.

Whole chapters of this book are devoted to letting the Bible speak for itself. In fact, the Bible is quoted extensively throughout the book in order to let the Scriptures interpret the Scriptures. Thus, the authors' conclusions find their primary support from the loving God of the Bible rather than from their personal opinions.

It will be necessary, nonetheless, to unwind or deprogram what has been impressed upon the minds of Protestant Christianity by seminaries, novels, movies, and digital imagery. Again, these corrections are not meant to discourage the Pre-Tribulation reader. They should, rather, be taken as the confessions of two former Pre-Tribbers, who were so caught up in the Pre-Tribulation program that they failed to investigate verses that were presented to them as proof-texts. The authors, like our readers, are growing in their knowledge of God.

The signs and wonders that will be part of the Day of the Lord involve the dimensional dynamics of heaven colliding with the physical world. Three of the chapters are devoted to understanding the Bible's detailed description of the Second Coming, the veil between heaven and earth, and the transformation of the body.

Three chapters are included as vignettes to help the reader visualize these events as though they were living through them. These vignettes are excerpts from Doug Hamp's book, *The Millennium Chronicles*[1]. The leading characters in these vignettes are easily identified, but they will also be formally introduced at the beginning of each scene.

All Scripture is profitable... A keen awareness of the significance of end time events should result from the topical presentations of Scriptures included in this study. These verses communicate the saving gospel, and the awesome power of God to fulfill everything that He has promised. No matter what the reader concludes about the purpose and timing of the rapture, the study of God's Word is certain to impart the knowledge of God - the knowledge of His authority and of His holiness.

> So shall My word be that goes forth from My mouth;
> It shall not return to Me void,
> But it shall accomplish what I please,
> And it shall prosper in the thing for which I sent it.
> —Isa. 55:11

CHAPTER ONE
"Where's the Beef?" and "Where's the Verse?"
- Doug Hamp

"Where's the Beef?"

That question framed a very successful marketing campaign for Wendy's Hamburgers™ when they asserted that the other burger places were all bun but no burger. When it comes to theology and eschatology, we must ask not, "where's the beef?" but rather, "where's the verse?" Having a doctrine with no supporting verses is like having a hamburger with no beef – it's just wrong. Strangely, however, one of the most popular doctrines does just that – it has an entire theology without an actual verse supporting it. The Pre-Tribulation rapture is a doctrine with no verse; and this is not just our opinion but readily admitted by the most salient Pre-Tribulation authors.

Hal Lindsey, author of the best-selling book *The Late Great Planet Earth*, and one of the world's best known advocates of a Pre-Tribulation rapture, candidly admits in his book *The Rapture*, "Pre-Tribulationism is based largely on arguments from inference and silence."[2] He then follows up that admission by confessing that he cannot "point to any single verse that clearly says the rapture will occur before... the tribulation."[3] This naturally begs the question, if it is based largely on arguments from inference and silence, and there isn't a verse pointing to the timing of a Pre-Tribulation rapture, then how does he know when it will occur?

Tim LaHaye, author of the phenomenally successful *Left Behind* series, which sold over 60 million copies, makes similar confessions as Hal Lindsey. LaHaye reveals in his book, *No Fear of the Storm: Why Christians Will Escape All the Tribulation* (this book was later republished as *Rapture Under Attack*):

"One objection to the Pre-Tribulation Rapture is that not one passage of Scripture teaches the two aspects of His Second Coming separated by the Tribulation. This is true. But then, no one passage teaches a post-trib or mid-trib Rapture, either."[4] LaHaye reveals more saying:

"WHERE'S THE BEEF?" AND "WHERE'S THE VERSE?"

"No single verse specifically states, 'Christ will come before the Tribulation.' On the other hand, no single passage teaches He will not come before the Tribulation, or that He will come in the middle or at the end of the Tribulation. Any such explicit declaration would end the debate immediately."[5]

Lindsey and LaHaye are by no means two lone wolves who are exposing the big secret of Pretribulationalism, namely that it is a doctrine with no substantiating verse. David Reagan with *Lamb and Lion Ministries* likewise confesses that the timing of the rapture is inferred, not stated, in his article entitled "The Mystery of the Rapture":

"The Bible never specifically defines the timing of the Rapture by tying it to any other event like the re-establishment of Israel or the rebuilding of the Temple. Even its proximity to the Tribulation is inferred rather than definitely stated. That's because the Rapture is an imminent event that could occur at any moment."[6]

This admission of not having a single verse seems to actually be something that Pre-Tribulation authors tout proudly rather than burying because of embarrassment. One Pre-Tribulation website, *bible-truth.org*, has outlined exactly where the Pre-Tribulation rapture is not in, what they call, "The Mystery of the Rapture."

1. "The Rapture of the Body of Christ is **not** found in the Old Testament for the obvious reason that the institution of the local church was not revealed until the New Testament. The Old Testament deals with God working with the nation of Israel."
2. "The Rapture is also **not** found in the Gospels, and again the reason being, the Gospels primarily deal with Israel and not the churches."
3. "The catching up of Christians is a different resurrection (the Rapture), than that of Restored Israel, which was a mystery **not** revealed to the Jews in the Old Testament."
4. "God used the Apostle Paul to explain how it is that believers in the church age have a different relationship with Christ and also a different resurrection."[7] [emphasis mine]

We will examine all of their points later in our study and demonstrate all of their points to be false; as God does clearly speak of the rapture, or better known as the gathering, throughout the entire Bible. Nevertheless, how can all of these teachers justify teaching a Pre-Tribulation rapture when they freely admit that it is nowhere to be found in the Bible? According to the author of *Beginningandend.com*, in an article, "Believers Escape God's Wrath: Biblical Foreshadows of the Rapture," they do so by claiming that the rapture is a type and shadow in the Bible.

Shadows

"By looking at Old Testament types and shadows, God's method of saving His people before judgment becomes apparent and foreshadows timing of the rapture of the church in the prophetic timeline."[8] However, if you have ever stood in the shade of a tree, then you know that the shade is only there because there is a real tree. Take away the tree, and the shadow goes away. I have stood in the shadow of the Eifel Tower only by virtue of the tower being there to block the sun. If there were no Eifel Tower, there would be no shadow. This seems obvious, yet it appears to have been overlooked somehow. The conclusion is simple; if there is no verse indicating that the rapture will happen before the tribulation then it is not a biblical doctrine – it is, unfortunately, make believe.

Look, a Distraction!

Acknowledging this massive deficiency, the Pre-Tribulation teaching has had to look for an ally; which they find in the doctrine of the trinity. They point out that there is no single verse which teaches the trinity, and yet we believe that; therefore, we are not required to demand a verse in defense of the Pre-Tribulation rapture. Yet this is nothing more than a clever diversion to distract Bible students from wanting to see the proof of the Pre-Tribulation doctrine. In his book, *The End*, Dr. Mark Hitchcock, predictably (and probably unwittingly) employs this well used and effective defense:

"WHERE'S THE BEEF?" AND "WHERE'S THE VERSE?"

"While no single verse says Jesus is coming to rapture His saints before the seven-year Tribulation, there are clear statements that He is coming to deliver His people from the coming wrath. Many biblical doctrines, such as the Trinity, the inerrancy of Scripture, and the dual nature of Christ, are NOT SPELLED CLEARLY IN ONE VERSE."[9] (emphasis mine)

This distraction is very effective because most Christians believe in the tri-unity of the Godhead. They believe in the inerrancy of Scripture. And also believe that Jesus was fully God and fully man. Such comparisons are used to imply that doubting the doctrine of the Pre-Tribulation rapture is tantamount to doubting these other foundational doctrines. The conversation effectively shifts from discussing the absence of evidence for the Pre-Tribulation rapture to whether or not the doubter is orthodox in his or her beliefs.

This is in fact a false dichotomy, since there are actual verses which *do* teach the triune nature of God. When Jesus commissioned his disciples to go out to make disciples, He said to baptize in the name of the Father, Son, and Holy Spirit.

Go therefore and make disciples of all the nations, baptizing them in the name of the Father and of the Son and of the Holy Spirit... Matt. 28:19

The triune nature of God is not even something uniquely Christian. The ancient Israelites long understood there to be something peculiar about the nature of God. They clearly knew about the Holy Spirit from Genesis 1:2, where the Spirit was hovering over the face of the deep. The Prophet Isaiah recorded God saying:

"Come near to Me, [God is the subject] hear this: I [God is the subject] have not spoken in secret from the beginning; from the time that it was, I [God is the subject] was there. And now the Lord GOD [God is the subject – so who is this?] and His Spirit [i.e. Holy Spirit] have sent Me." Isa. 48:16

The above verse is a powerful example of the triunity of God before the writing of the New Testament. Thus in at least two places we have direct evidence of triune nature of God spelled out in a single verse. Pre-Tribbers make the case that the word "trinity" is not in the Bible; but that fact is simply not the issue.

Whether we find the word "Pre-Tribulation rapture" in the Bible or not is beside the point. The book of *Zohar*, an ancient Jewish writing, underscores the ancient concept of the triunity found in Scripture. They speak of "three in one", and *"hameshulleshet"* (threefold), which is the very basis of the tri-unity or "Trinitarian" doctrine.

"The Ancient Holy One is revealed (found) with three Heads, which are united in One, and that Head is threefold exalted. The Ancient Holy One is described as being Three; it is because the other Lights (i.e., two Lights) emanating from Him are included in the Three. Yet the Ancient One is described as being two (Dan. 7:13). The Ancient One includes these two (i.e. the two are found in Him). He is the Crown of all that is exalted; the Chief of the chief, so exalted, that He cannot be known to perfection. Thus the other Lights (Shining Ones) are two complete ones, yet is the Ancient Holy One described and complete as One, and He is One, positively One; thus are the other Lights united and glorified in One; because they are One."[10]

Taking the time to explain the trinity is exactly what the Pre-Tribulation distraction is all about. The easier, and adequate, answer would be to simply stay on target. Nevertheless we have taken the time to demonstrate that it is not reasonable to say we shouldn't demand to see a Pre-Tribulation timing verse simply because there is no verse with the word "trinity". We have clearly seen that there is sufficient (and powerful) evidence of the trinity in both the Hebrew Bible and New Testament, as well as ancient Jewish extra-biblical sources.

The Intimidating List

Getting back to the true issue of the timing of the Pre-Tribulation rapture, let's now consider the verses that they do give in support of the doctrine. On the one hand, we are told that there isn't a single verse which describes it, and then we are told that there are verses all over the place which describe it. We refer to this as "the intimidating list," so called because when someone flashes the list at you, it looks impressive. It can be intimidating to doubt the rapture when there are just so many verses.

1. John 14:1-3
2. Romans 8:19
3. 1 Corinthians 1:7-8
4. 1 Corinthians 15:51-53
5. 1 Corinthians 16:22
6. Philippians 3:20-21
7. Philippians 4:5
8. Colossians 3:4
9. 1 Thessalonians 1:10
10. 1 Thessalonians 2:19
11. 1 Thessalonians 4:13-18
12. 1 Thessalonians 5:9
13. 1 Thessalonians 5:23
14. 2 Thessalonians 2:1, 3
15. 1 Timothy 6:14
16. 2 Timothy 4:1, 8
17. Titus 2:13
18. Hebrews 9:28
19. James 5:7-9
20. 1 Peter 1:7,
21. 1 Peter 1:13
22. 1 Peter 5:4
23. 1 John 2:28—3:2
24. Jude 21
25. Revelation 2:15
26. Revelation 3:10

"Twenty-six places in the New Testament that speak of the Pre-Tribulation rapture!" That is intimidating; and it works. The average person is happy with the impressive list and it settles the matter. However, once we take a closer look at the verses, we begin to see a different picture. Despite the claim, not even one of the verses gives the timing of the Pre-Tribulation rapture. Not even one!

Let's take a look at these verses and see for ourselves if their claim, that these verses teach the Pre-Tribulation rapture, holds water.

Let not your hearts be troubled. Believe in God; believe also in me. In my Father's house are many rooms. If it were not so, would I have told you that I go to prepare a place for you? And if I go and prepare a place for you, I will come again and will take you to myself, that where I am you may be also. John 14:1-3

Just where is Jesus saying that He will come to catch believers up before the tribulation? Jesus said He was going away, and He would come back and collect His followers. It is true that this passage teaches Jesus will come back for His own. However, Jesus simply did not give any indication whether taking His followers to Himself would be a pre, mid, or post tribulation event.

The next passages on the intimidating list are Romans 8:1 and 8:19. Paul speaks of no condemnation, and the revealing of the sons of God, but he says nothing about rapture or the timing of rapture.

There is therefore now no condemnation for those who are in Christ Jesus...For the creation waits with eager longing for the revealing of the sons of God. Rom. 8:1, 19

Likewise, in the next passage, First Corinthians 1:7-8, Paul mentions the revealing of Jesus, but nothing about the timing of the rapture.

...so that you are not lacking in any gift, as you wait for the revealing of our Lord Jesus Christ, who will sustain you to the end, guiltless in the day of our Lord Jesus Christ. 1 Cor. 1:7-8

Next on the list is First Corinthians 15:51-53. Paul discusses the transformation of our bodies at the resurrection, which is undoubtedly linked to the rapture, yet Paul does not give any indication when this will occur in relation to the Great Tribulation. He gives no hint in this passage of a Pre-, Mid-, or Post-Tribulation rapture. His language of the resurrection of the dead is straightforward, but he is silent on the timing of the rapture.

Behold! I tell you a mystery. We shall not all sleep, but we shall all be changed, in a moment, in the twinkling of an eye, at the last trumpet. For the trumpet will sound, and the dead will be raised imperishable, and we shall be changed. For this perishable body must put on the imperishable, and this mortal body must put on immortality. 1 Cor. 15:51-53

First Corinthians 16:22 is a plea for Jesus to return, but it is once again silent on the timing of the rapture.

If anyone has no love for the Lord, let him be accursed. Our Lord, come!

We have now examined five passages on the list and yet we haven't seen anything remotely indicating a gathering, catching up (rapture) happening *before* the tribulation. So far, their intimidating list is yielding no results. Where is the timing of the Pre-Tribulation rapture in any of the verses examined so far? It is conspicuously absent. Somehow this exercise is beginning to feel like the shell game where the onlooker is tricked by fast moving shells and a fast-talking dealer.

The two verses listed from the book of Philippians likewise contain no timing references to the rapture. In the first one, Philippians 3:20-21, Paul speaks of heaven and resurrection but nothing about the rapture:

But our citizenship is in heaven, and from it we await a Savior, the Lord Jesus Christ, who will transform our lowly body to be like his glorious body, by the power that enables him even to subject all things to himself. Phil. 3:20-21

Philippians 4:5 says nothing about either the rapture or the resurrection but is merely an exhortation that Jesus is "at hand."

Let your reasonableness be known to everyone. The Lord is at hand. Phil. 4:5

The passage on the list from Colossians is similar to Philippians 4:5 in that Paul is exhorting believers to live right since we will be like Jesus when he returns. No timing is even remotely given concerning the rapture.

If then you have been raised with Christ, seek the things that are above, where Christ is, seated at the right hand of God. Col. 3:4 When Christ who is your life appears, then you also will appear with him in glory. Col. 3:1

Paul's two letters to the Thessalonians contain Paul's most definitive statements on the resurrection and the rapture or gathering, and these also appear on the list. Both First Thessalonians 1:10 and 5:9 speak of how we will be delivered from the "wrath to come." The "wrath to come" is almost certainly related to either the tribulation or the second coming.

...and to wait for his Son from heaven, whom he raised from the dead, Jesus who delivers us from the wrath to come. 1 Thess. 1:10

For God has not destined us for wrath, but to obtain salvation through our Lord Jesus Christ. 1 Thess. 5:9

Most Pre-Tribulation teachers maintain that the "wrath to come" is simply another name for the Great Tribulation period. However, when we compare Paul's statements with John's vision in the Book of Revelation, and passages in Isaiah, we see that the wrath to come is specifically identified as the day of Jesus' return. We will deal with the day of the Lord exhaustively in another chapter. For now, notice how the two texts below both have the following elements:
1. Mountains and hills are radically moving out of their places.
2. People going into the caves and holes.
3. Proud and powerful people are humbled.
4. They are both about God's "day".

These conditions are present on the day when God alone is exalted. The Antichrist will be blaspheming those in heaven for the latter half of the seven years of the tribulation; which means that God alone is not being exalted during that time. Likewise in Revelation, John records that the kings of the earth will admit they cannot stand because of the great day of His wrath. The parallel parts of the verses below are in bold to show that they are speaking of the same event.

Then the sky receded as a scroll when it is rolled up, and every mountain and island was moved out of its place. And the kings of the earth...said to the **mountains** and **rocks**, Fall on us, and hide us from the face of him that sitteth on the throne, and from the wrath of the Lamb. For the great **day of his wrath** is come; and who shall be able to stand? Rev. 6:14, 16, 17

Enter into the **rock,** and hide in the dust, from the terror of the LORD and the glory of His majesty.

The lofty looks of man shall be humbled, the haughtiness of men shall be bowed down, and the LORD alone shall be exalted in that day. Isa. 2:10-11

For the **day** of the LORD of hosts shall come upon everything proud and lofty, upon everything lifted up– And it shall be brought low– Isa. 2:12

Upon all the cedars of Lebanon that are high and lifted up, And upon all the oaks of Bashan; Isa. 2:13

Upon all the high **mountains**, And upon all the hills that are lifted up; Isa. 2:14

Upon every high tower, And upon every fortified wall; Isa. 2:15

They shall go into the holes of the rocks, And into the caves of the earth, from the terror of the LORD and the glory of His majesty, when He arises to shake the earth mightily. Isa. 2:19

Therefore, once again the supposed evidence does not support the claim made by the Pre-Tribulation teachers that the Thessalonian letters point to a Pre-Tribulation rapture. The only way that First Thessalonians One and Five could be talking about a Pre-Tribulation rapture is if the wrath to come is synonymous with the tribulation itself. Even if our interpretation were wrong, the text does not imply a timing feature; it is, once again, inferred by Pre-Tribulation teachers.

The next passage on their list is, likewise, completely devoid of anything to do with the timing of the rapture. Paul is sharing a little bit of history, but is completely silent on the tribulation, resurrection, or the rapture.

For this reason we also thank God without ceasing, because when you received the word of God which you heard from us... For you also suffered the same things from your own countrymen, just as they did from the Judeans, who killed both the Lord Jesus and their own prophets... forbidding us to speak to the Gentiles that they may be saved...; but wrath has come upon them to the uttermost. 1 Thess. 2:13-16.

Therefore we wanted to come to you…but Satan hindered us. *1 Thess. 2:18 (truncated for space)*

The classic passage for the Pre-Tribulation rapture is Paul's statement to the Thessalonians about the resurrection. We agree that this is a very clear passage about the resurrection and rapture but a time marker for the pre-trib rapture is absent. In this passage, First Thessalonians 4:13-18, Paul wants to encourage the Thessalonians that their loved ones who have already died have not missed the resurrection. There appears to have been some teaching going around that the resurrection had already happened in conjunction with the resurrection of Jesus when *graves were opened; and many bodies of the saints who had fallen asleep were raised,* Matt. 27:52. Therefore, Paul exhorts his readers:

But I do not want you to be ignorant, brethren, concerning those who have fallen asleep, lest you sorrow as others who have no hope. 1 Thess. 4:13

It must be noted that the comfort he is bringing them is about the resurrection, and not the rapture, per se. The rapture is simply an add-on to the resurrection – it isn't the main event. This is logical because for all those who have been martyred throughout the centuries, the thought of coming back to life would have brought them peace – and not whether some future group would be caught up to heaven. Notice, however, how Paul speaks of Jesus coming throughout this passage – it is speaking of the second coming and not a secret coming - a secret coming revealed only to believers.

For if we believe that Jesus died and rose again, even so God will bring with Him those who sleep in Jesus. (1 Thess. 4:14) For this we say to you by the word of the Lord, that we who are alive and remain until the coming of the Lord will by no means precede those who are asleep. (1 Thess. 4:15)

For the Lord Himself will descend from heaven with a shout, with the voice of an archangel, and with the trumpet of God. And the dead in Christ will rise first. (1 Thess. 4:16)

Then we who are alive and remain shall be caught up together with them in the clouds to meet the Lord in the air. And thus we shall always be with the Lord. (1 Thess. 4:17)

For you yourselves are fully aware that the day of the Lord will come like a thief in the night. (1 Thess. 5:2)

Now may the God of peace himself sanctify you completely, and may your whole spirit and soul and body be kept blameless at the coming of our Lord Jesus Christ. *(1 Thess. 5:23)*

AGAIN...NO MENTION OF THE RAPTURE

Now, brethren, concerning the coming of our Lord Jesus Christ and our gathering together to Him, we ask you, not to be soon shaken in mind or troubled, either by spirit or by word or by letter, as if from us, as though the day of Christ had come. Let no one deceive you by any means; for **that Day will not come** unless the falling away comes first, and the man of sin is revealed, the son of perdition. 2 Thess. 2:1-3

THE DAY OF THE LORD WILL NOT COME UNTIL THE MAN OF SIN IS REVEALED.

Those who have believing masters must not be disrespectful on the ground that they are brothers... Teach and urge these things. 1 Tim. 6:2

to keep the commandment unstained and free from reproach until the appearing of our Lord Jesus Christ, 1 Tim. 6:14

I charge you in the presence of God and of Christ Jesus, who is to judge of the living and the dead, and by his appearing and his kingdom: 2 Tim 4:1

Henceforth there is laid up for me the crown of righteousness, which the Lord, the righteous judge, will award to me on that Day, and not only to me but also to all who have loved his appearing. 2 Tim. 4:8

Waiting for our blessed hope, the appearing of the glory of our great God and Savior Jesus Christ. Titus 2:13

Not one of these verses say the Lord's appearing will happen before the tribulation???

Come now, you rich, weep and howl for the miseries that are coming upon you. Jas. 5:1

So that the tested genuineness of your faith—more precious than gold that perishes though it is tested by fire—may be found to result in praise and glory and honor at the revelation of Jesus Christ. 1 Peter 1:7

Therefore, preparing your minds for action, and being sober-minded, set your hope fully on the grace that will be brought to you at the revelation of Jesus Christ. 1 Pet. 1:13

When the chief Shepherd appears, you will receive the unfading crown of glory. 1 Pet. 5:4

THE REVELATION OF JESUS IS LITERALLY THE UNVEILING OF JESUS, A.K.A. THE SECOND COMING

Timing?

28 …abide in him, so that when he appears we may have confidence and not shrink from him in shame at his coming. 29 If you know that he is righteous, you may be sure that everyone who practices righteousness has been born of him. 3:1 See what kind of love the Father has given to us, that we should be called children of God; and so we are. The reason why the world does not know us is that it did not know him. 3:2 Beloved, we are God's children now, and what we will be has not yet appeared; but we know that when he appears we shall be like him, because we shall see him as he is. 1 John 2:28-3:2

Where is the Pre-Tribulation Rapture?

So Christ, having been offered once to bear the sins of many, will appear a SECOND TIME, not to deal with sin but to save those who are eagerly waiting for him. Heb. 9:28 (emphasis added)

THIS IS TALKING ABOUT THE SECOND COMING!

Be patient, therefore, brothers, until the coming of the Lord….8 You also, be patient. Establish your hearts, for the coming of the Lord is at hand. 9 Do not grumble…the Judge is standing at the door. Jas. 5:7-9

Keep yourselves in the love of God, waiting for the mercy of our Lord Jesus Christ that leads to eternal life. Jude 1:21

So also you have some who hold the teaching of the Nicolaitans. Rev. 2:15

Because you have kept my word about patient endurance, I will keep you from the hour of trial that is coming on the whole world, to try those who dwell on the earth. Rev. 3:10

AN HOUR OF TEMPTATION - NOT A SEVEN YEAR TRIBULATION

Did you see any Pre-Tribulation timing verses? Mystery solved: look for the resurrection and the "gathering".

The Bible is very clear about the timing of the resurrection and gathering; and they are specifically given to Israel, not to the "church," apart from Israel.

CHAPTER TWO
Coming Like a Thief in the Night
- Doug Hamp

As a boy I remember an evening when our church showed the movie *A Thief in the Night*[11]. I remember the opening scene of the woman running to the bathroom looking for her husband, only to discover the electric razor running and abandoned in the sink – her husband obviously raptured, all the while the radio explained the disappearance of perhaps millions of people around the world.

The basis of the movie was derived from First Thessalonians Chapter Five where, *the Day of the Lord comes as a **thief in the night**. 1 Thess. 5:2* The opening scene made a lasting impression on me, and millions of other Americans, that the rapture will come unexpectedly and without warning, just like a thief in the night!

It is commonly argued that "the thief in the night" must refer to the rapture and cannot refer to the second coming because that would be obvious, as people could simply read in their Bible. Dr. Dwight J. Pentecost, a professor at Dallas Theological Seminary, writes in his book *Things to Come*:

"If the Day of the Lord did not begin until the second advent, since that event is preceded by signs, the Day of the Lord could not come as a "thief in the night," **unexpected**, and **unheralded**, as it is said it will come in First Thessalonians 5:2. The only way this could break unexpectedly upon the world is to have it begin immediately after the rapture of the church."

The supposed problem is resolved in the rest of the First Thessalonians Five passage. Unfortunately, many people stop reading at verse two and do not continue to see to whom Jesus will come as a thief; **He is coming 'as a thief' to those not expecting him, that is, to those in darkness!** The language is clear that "they", the ones in darkness, are the ones to whom sudden destruction will come; and "you," the brethren, are sons of light, not darkness. The day of the Lord will not be as a thief to the brethren. This means it could not refer to the rapture itself, but rather to the day Jesus comes back.

For when **they** say, "Peace and safety!" then **sudden** destruction comes upon them…and they shall not escape. 1 Thess. 5:3 **But you,** brethren, are **not** in **darkness, so that this Day should overtake you as a thief.** 1 Thess. 5:4 You are all sons of light and sons of the day. We are not of the night, nor of darkness. 1 Thess. 5:5 (emphasis added)

Jesus used this expression Himself in the example of Him coming as a thief is in relation to the unprepared homeowner, who does not know the time that the thief would come and let his house be broken into; for *if the homeowner had known at what time the **thief** were coming, he would have watched and would not have let his house be broken into. Luke 12:39* (See also Matt. 24:43.) The timing of a thief is a complete surprise to people **who are in darkness**, who are sleeping and not paying attention.

The people who are not paying attention are the non-believers which Jesus exemplifies in His exhortation to the church of Sardis, the dead church, whose names are ready to be blotted out of the book of life (Rev. 3:5). Because they were considered dead and were therefore not counted as sons of light, Jesus' coming would be to them as a thief because they were not alert. He admonished them that they must repent, for if they would not, and were ***not alert**, I will come **like a thief**, and you won't know the time when I will come to you.* Rev. 3:3 ISV Again, we see that his coming **will be as a thief**, and it will be at a time that they do not expect; and when He comes, sudden destruction will come upon them (1Thess. 5:3). We must consider that the phrase "thief in the night" appears not to apply to the event known as the rapture, but applies to the actual second coming of Jesus, that is, the day that He returns.

As further evidence of this, we turn to Revelation 16:14 where Satan, the Antichrist, and the False Prophet open their mouths and something like frogs come out to go to deceive the whole world to bring them together for the battle of the great day of God at the place called Armageddon. The timing, therefore, is toward the end of the time of Jacob's trouble (the second half of the seven year period filled with intense suffering never experienced before on earth). The nations are getting ready for their final attack against Jerusalem, the battle known as Armageddon (see Chapter 16). It is here in the text, sandwiched between verses 14 and 16, that Jesus strongly admonished the armies of the world by saying He was coming as a thief.

They are demonic spirits that perform signs. They go to the kings of the whole earth and gather them for the war of the great Day of God Almighty.

"See, **I am coming like a thief**. How blessed is the person who remains alert and keeps his clothes on! He won't have to go naked and let others see his shame." The spirits gathered the kings to the place that is called Armageddon in Hebrew. Rev. 16:14-16 ISV

It is no accident that Jesus' admonition is placed there. He has graciously warned the rebels one last time of what will happen at His return; and anyone who does not have a garment of Yeshuáh on at that point will be in a world of hurt. They will suffer - exposed to His glory forever - because they will have to go naked so that others will see their shame.

The fact that Jesus directs the exhortation to those gathering together for the day of battle demonstrates that the Day of the Lord coming as a thief in the night can only be a reference to the second coming of Jesus, which is the very day that He returns to planet earth in a blaze of glory and flames of fire. The basic thesis of the movie, *A Thief in the Night,* has incorrectly applied the phrase to the rapture. The day coming like a thief is coming to those who are not anticipating the Lord's return. Coming like a thief means it is sudden and is a big surprise!

All the nations of the world will be in utter shock and dumbfounded by Jesus coming because they arrogantly and boastfully gather themselves together against Jerusalem in order to lay it waste. The following verses demonstrate how all of the nations will be coming against Jerusalem in order to destroy it; and hence, when Jesus comes back they will be sorely surprised.

- *I will make **Jerusalem** a heavy weight; so everyone who burdens themselves with it will be crushed, even though **all of the nations** of the earth gather themselves against it.* Zech. 12:3 ISV

- *Let the **nations** be awakened and come to the **Valley of Jehoshaphat**; because I will sit to judge all the surrounding nations. Put in the **sickle**, because the **harvest is ripe**.   Come* and go down, because the **winepress is full**. *The wine vats are overflowing, because their evil is great!* Joel 3:12-13 ISV

- *Now many* **nations** *have gathered against you, saying, 'Let her be defiled,' and 'Let's look down on* **Zion**.*'* Micah 4:11 ISV

They fully anticipate that they will be victorious in their battle efforts, just as Pharaoh imagined he would be when he mustered his army against Israel by the Red Sea. Imagine the incredible surprise he felt as the walls of water came crashing over him. So too will the nations of the earth be utterly shocked when the heavens roll back and there stands Jesus. Habakkuk prophesied about Jesus' return; *He stood up and shook the land; with his stare he* <u>startled</u> *the* **nations**. Hab. 3:6 ISV The nations will be startled because they won't be expecting Him, which only serves to prove that His second coming is like a thief in the night.

The book of Zephaniah also records how the day of God's wrath will bring a sudden end to the nations which will come as a terrible surprise.

...in the **Day of the Lord's wrath**; but the entire land will be consumed by the **fire of his jealousy**, for he will bring the inhabitants of the land to a <u>sudden</u> end...the **Day of the Lord's wrath** [which] <u>surprises</u> you. Zeph. 1:18; 2:2 ISV

The Thief in the Night in Second Peter

The element of the surprise is confirmed in Second Peter. This is perhaps the most significant passage concerning the day of the Lord. Because the heavens pass away in the passage, Dr. Pentecost and others argue that the Day of the Lord must include the Millennium because they understand the heavens to pass away afterward. However, our study of Second Peter 3:10 will prove that the heavens pass away the day that Jesus returns.

First of all, we need to consider the context of the chapter. Peter is discussing the return of Jesus and answering the mockery of the skeptics who ridicule; *What happened to the Messiah's promise to return? Ever since our ancestors died, everything continues as it did from the beginning of creation.* 2 Pet. 3:4 ISV

Peter then reminds his readers that the mockers *deliberately ignore the fact that long ago the heavens existed and the earth was formed by God's word out of water and with water, by which the world at that time was deluged with water and destroyed.* 2 Pet. 3:5-6 ISV The judgment of God is absolutely certain, Peter concludes, because just as the world was destroyed by water, a future judgment will destroy it by fire. *Now by that same word, the present heavens and earth have been reserved for fire and are being kept for the day when ungodly people will be judged and destroyed.* 2 Pet. 3:7 ISV

Concerning Jesus' apparent tardiness, Peter says that in the Lord's economy a day is like a thousand years and vice versa. His delay is due to His patience and desire that all should come to repentance. However, just like the unsuspecting people in Noah's day who, according to Jesus, *were unaware of what was happening until the flood came and swept all of them away; that's how it will be when the Son of Man comes.* Matt. 24:39 ISV

Peter obviously took his cues from Jesus and so he tells his readers that just as people were caught off guard on the very day the flood waters came and swept them away, so too the very day Jesus returns will be a surprise. It will come like a thief.

But the Day of the Lord will come like a thief. On that day [en he ἐν ᾗ] the heavens will disappear with a roaring sound, the elements will be destroyed by fire, and the earth and everything done on it will be exposed. 2 Pet. 3:10 ISV

Peter is not telling his readers anything new; he is simply reiterating either what is in the Hebrew Scriptures (his Bible back then) or, in this case, what Jesus said directly: *Watch therefore, for **you know** neither the day nor the hour <u>in which</u> the Son of Man is coming.* Matt. 25:13

Jesus ties the known day and hour specifically to when ***Heaven and earth will pass away****... Matt. 24:35* It is the day that the heavens and earth pass away that will be completely unannounced and unheralded. The event will be a big surprise to everyone – even to the angels. *But of that **day and hour no one knows**, not even the angels of heaven, but My Father only.* Matt. 24:36

The day in question is not referring to a pre-tribulation event (such as the rapture) but specifically to the day that Jesus returns, which aligns perfectly with Peter's reference to the heavens and earth passing away on the Day of the Lord. Peter then follows up his exposition of the Day of the Lord with a similar exhortation to watch or look because that is the day when (in which) the heavens will be set ablaze and the elements of the earth dissolved.

Since everything will be destroyed in this way, think of the kind of holy and godly people you ought to be as you **look** forward to and hasten the **coming of the day of God, when the heavens will be set ablaze** and dissolved and the elements will melt with fire. 2 Pet. 3:11, 12 ISV

He closes his exhortation with the hope that we have that once Messiah comes, He will set up a new era including a new heavens and new earth. *But in keeping with his promise, we are looking forward to new heavens and a new earth, where* **righteousness** *is at home.* 2 Pet. 3:13 ISV His reference to righteousness dwelling in the new age appears to be a reference to Isaiah 11 where Messiah Jesus will rule over a new creation; in which even the animals will be in perfect harmony with mankind.

But with **righteousness** He will judge the needy, and decide with equity for earth's poor. He will strike the earth with the rod of His mouth, and the wicked will be killed with the breath of his lips. **Righteousness** will be the sash around His loins, and faithfulness the belt around his waist. The wolf will live with the lamb; the leopard will lie down with the young goat. The calf and the lion will graze together, and a little child will lead them. At that time, as to the root of Jesse, who will be standing as a banner for the peoples, the nations will rally to Him, and His resting place is glorious. Isa. 11:4-6, 10 ISV

Peter was looking forward to the new heavens and earth, specifically mentioned in Isaiah 65:17, as well as the general abundance of righteousness described in Isaiah 11 and other passages. There will be an obvious need for new heavens because the (current) heavens and earth will pass away at Jesus coming, which Jesus, Peter, Isaiah (Isa. 34:4) and others have said. The next question, however, is what exactly does it mean that the heavens will pass away?

According to Peter, the surprising and unexpected day Jesus comes back ("the Day of the Lord **will come like a thief**") is when the heavens will pass away ("on that day [*en he* ἐν ἡ] the heavens will disappear with a roaring sound,"). It is also the day that the creation will begin to melt like wax and all of man's works will be destroyed by fire ("the elements will be destroyed by fire"), and the earth and everything done on it will be exposed (2 Pet. 3:10 ISV).

This verse clearly shows the unexpectedness of the day in which end-of-the-world events will take place! The heavens will pass away, the elements (*stoixia* στοιχεῖα), the base materials of the world, will dissolve, and the works of men will be exposed to God.

Here we discover that in (or on) the Day of the Lord, which comes like a thief, the heavens will pass away and the earth will be destroyed by fire. We must not miss that it is on that very day (not a seven year period and not one thousand years); on that very day that the heavens will disappear.

But the Day of the Lord **will come like a thief**. <u>**On that**</u> day [en he ἐν ἡ] the heavens will disappear with a roaring sound, the elements will be destroyed by fire... 2 Pet. 3:10 ISV

The evidence is overwhelming that the Day of the Lord is the day that Jesus comes back; and is not referring to a pre-tribulational event, regardless of what we believe about the timing of the rapture itself. In the next chapter we will take another look at Second Peter Three to help us understand the events of that day more clearly.

CHAPTER THREE
The Day of the Lord is the Second Coming
- Doug Hamp

But the day of the Lord will come as a thief in the night, in which the heavens will pass away with a great noise, and the elements will melt with fervent heat; both the earth and the works that are in it will be burned up. 2 Pet. 3:10

According to both Peter and Paul, the day of the Lord, is an event that will come as a big surprise, like a thief in the night. Paul says that it comes like a thief not to those who are of the light but to those in darkness. The Day of the Lord is the very day that Jesus returns. It is on that day the heavens and the earth are going to pass away. Nevertheless, the day of the Lord is often interpreted as being a longer period of time. Arnold Fruchtenbaum, in his book, *The Footsteps of the Messiah*, defines it as the seventieth week of Daniel. He states:

"In the Old Testament, the most common name for the Great Tribulation is the Day of Jehovah or the Day of the Lord...it is always and without exception a reference to the Tribulation period."[12]

Dr. Dwight Pentecost believes that the day of the Lord "will include all the events of the millennial age, with the final revolt of Satan."[13] These are the two most common opinions of dispensational premillenialists. (Premillennialism is the doctrinal position that Jesus will return before the Millennium.) We will see that the day of the Lord is in fact the day that Jesus returns; the second coming.

Scripture tells us that the Day of the Lord will be the day that Jesus' feet will stand on the Mount of Olives in Jerusalem, when He comes to fight for His people Israel.

Behold, **the day of the LORD is coming**... For I will **gather all the nations to battle against Jerusalem; Then the LORD will go forth** And fight against those nations, As He fights in the day of battle. And **in that day** His feet will stand on the Mount of Olives, which faces Jerusalem on the east. Zech. 14:1, 3, 4

THE DAY OF THE LORD IS THE SECOND COMING

Notice that it will be a day in which God will gather all of the nations to battle against Jerusalem, in the valley of Jehoshaphat, which is in fact the place where the battle of Armageddon will occur – something we will explore in Chapter Sixteen. We read that **in that day** the feet of Jesus (the LORD) will touch the Mount of Olives so that it splits. However, before that dark and climactic day, Scripture describes the buildup to war before that day.

Events Before the Day of the Lord

The book of Joel tells us of God's gathering and calling together the nations for the battle of Armageddon (in the valley of Jehoshaphat). Joel 2:1 tells us that the day has not yet arrived – only that it is close, signified by the Hebrew word *karov*; *for the **day of the LORD is coming**, for it is **at hand*** (קָרוֹב *karov* – literally "close").

The buildup to that day will include the opening of the Abyss in Revelation Nine, which will darken the sun and sky due to thick smoke and soot.

And He opened the bottomless pit, and **smoke** arose out of the pit like the **smoke of a great furnace**. So the **sun** and the **air** were **darkened** because of the **smoke** of the pit. Rev. 9:2

The book of Joel confirms that the darkening of the sun and moon into blood will come before the day of the Lord.

And I will show wonders in the heavens and in the earth: **Blood** and **fire** and **pillars of smoke**. The **sun** shall be turned into **darkness**, and the **moon** into **blood**, <u>**before**</u> the coming of the great and awesome **day of the LORD**. Joel 2:30, 31

Several passages confirm the conditions and the timing of the sun and sky being darkened before the day of the Lord.

- *Woe to you who desire the **day of the LORD**! For what good is the day of the LORD to you? It will be **darkness**, and **not light**. Is not the **day of the LORD darkness**, and not light? Is it not **very dark**, with no brightness in it?* Amos 5:18, 20
- *Wail, for the day of the **LORD is at hand**!* [קָרוֹב *karov* – literally "close"] *It will come as destruction from the Almighty.* Isa. 13:6

- *For the day is **near**, even the **day of the LORD** is near [קָרוֹב karov* – literally "close"]; *it will be a day of **clouds**, the time of the Gentiles.* Ezek. 30:3
- *...there was a great earthquake; and the **sun** became **black** as **sackcloth** of hair, and the **moon** became like **blood**.* Rev. 6:12

The darkening of the sun, and the moon turning to blood, will be due to the ash-filled sky. The connection between the great darkness and the color of celestial bodies will be discussed in a later chapter. While eclipses may act as harbingers of events coming, the continual discoloration of the sun and moon, and complete blocking of the stars will be due to the smoke from the Abyss. The opening of the Abyss in Revelation 9 happens at the midpoint, or three and a half year mark, of the seven year treaty which Israel will sign.

What follows in Joel is the declaration of God's intentions to gather the nations to the valley of Jehoshaphat (also known as the Kidron valley) in Jerusalem.

I will also gather all nations, and bring them down to the **Valley of Jehoshaphat**; And I will enter into judgment with them there on account of **My people, My heritage Israel**, Whom they have scattered among the nations; They have also divided up My land. Joel 3:2

God challenges the nations to come to battle; if they don't have a weapon, He encourages them to obtain one because they will need it on the day that He comes to fight against them.

Proclaim this among the nations: "Prepare for war! Wake up the mighty men, let all the men of war draw near, let them come up. Beat your plowshares into swords and your pruning hooks into spears; let the weak say, 'I am strong.' " Assemble and **come, all you nations,** and gather together all around. Cause Your mighty ones to go down there, O LORD. "Let the nations be wakened, and come up to the Valley of Jehoshaphat; For there I will sit to judge all the surrounding nations. **Put in the sickle**, for the harvest is ripe. Come, go down; for the winepress is full, the vats overflow– For their wickedness is great." Multitudes, multitudes in the valley of decision! For the **day of the LORD is near** in the valley of decision. Joel 3:9-14

Verses 9-13 describe the buildup for war which will be the precursor to the actual day of the Lord, which has still not yet come. In verse 14 we read that the day is **near**, but is **not yet**. The actual event, the very day of the Lord is ever so close but not yet because that day is the day that Jesus' feet will touch the Mount of Olives; when He comes to do battle with His enemies who have attempted to destroy Israel, the apple of His eye.

The day of the Lord will bring tremendous destruction to the inhabitants of the earth but not to Israel, for it is the day that Jesus comes to defend them; it is the day of His ***vengeance**, the year of recompense for the cause of **Zion**.* Isa. 34:8 The time of Jacob's trouble is the second 3 ½ year period of the seven year *treaty of many.* Dan. 9:27. This will be an incredible time of suffering for the Jewish people, to which both Daniel and Jesus attest. (Dan. 12:1; Matt. 24:21, 22) The day of the Lord, by contrast, is the day that the Lord returns to deal with the Antichrist, and all of the nations that are attempting to completely eradicate Israel. It is the great day of Israel's salvation rather than her destruction!

Elijah

Another proof demonstrating that the day of the Lord is not referring to the seven year treaty, or even the time of Jacob's trouble, is found in Malachi 4:5 where God says He *will send you Elijah the prophet **before** the coming of the great and dreadful **day of the LORD**.*

If the entire seven year period were also called the day of the Lord; and if, as many believe including myself, that Elijah will be one of the two witnesses mentioned in Revelation 11 (who apparently come at the beginning of the seven year treaty) then the two witnesses would need to arrive before that period of seven years (the Tribulation). However, because the day of the Lord is the very day that Jesus returns, there is no problem reconciling Elijah coming before that day.

Everything will be humbled on the Day of the Lord. According to Isaiah, *The LORD alone will be exalted in that day.* Isa. 2:17 We see in Revelation 16 that Satan, the Antichrist, and the False Prophet, open their mouths and deceptive spirits come forth to gather the nations *for the war of the great Day of God Almighty.* Rev. 16:14 ISV

Clearly, the inhabitants of the earth are still acting haughtily and thinking that they can actually wage a war to destroy Israel.

> The haughty looks of mankind will be brought low, the lofty pride of human beings will be humbled, and the Lord alone will be exalted at that time. Isa. 2:11
> For the Lord of the Heavenly Armies has reserved a time to oppose all who are proud and haughty, and the self-exalting— they will be humbled. Isa. 2:12
> He will take his stand against all the cedars of Lebanon, against the proud and self-exalting; and against all the oaks of Bashan; Isa. 2:13
> against all the high mountains, and against all the lofty hills; Isa. 2:14
> against every high tower, and against every fortified wall; Isa. 2:15
> Humanity's haughtiness will be humbled, male arrogance will be brought low, and the Lord alone will be exalted in that day. Isa. 2:17
> They will enter caverns in the rocks and holes in the ground, to escape the presence of the terror of the Lord, to escape the splendor of his majesty, when he arises to terrify the earth. Isa. 2:19 ISV

We discover in Isaiah Two that only on the day that the Lord arises to terrify the earth will the haughtiness of man be brought low, and not before. In fact, during the time of Jacob's trouble, the Antichrist will be speaking all kinds of blasphemies and arrogant boasts against those who dwell in heaven and against God (Dan. 7:8, 11, 25)

> It had eyes like those of a human being and a **mouth that boasted with audacious claims.** Dan. 7:8

> I continued watching because of **the audacious words** that the horn was speaking. I kept observing until the animal was killed and its body destroyed and given over to burning fire. Dan. 7:11.

He'll speak out against the Most High and wear down the saints of the Highest One. He'll attempt to alter times and laws, and they'll be given into his control for a time, times, and half a time. Dan. 7:25

Daniel 7:11 demonstrates that the Antichrist will be speaking haughtily up until the very end. Only when he is routed at the coming of Jesus, and his body is given over to the burning flame (which is the same as the lake of fire in Revelation 19:20) will he be silenced.

Thus there is no way to substantiate the claim that the day of the Lord is the entire period of the seven year treaty or even of the time of Jacob's trouble. The haughtiness of man, including the Antichrist, will only be silenced on the day that Jesus comes back. In fact, we know exactly what the men of the earth are going to do and say. They will scamper into the caves and into clefts of the rocks when Jesus comes back. They will be overwhelmed with fear and will say to the mountains and rocks:

Fall on us and hide us from the face of the one who sits on the throne and from the wrath of the lamb. Rev. 6:16 ISV For **the great day of their wrath has come**, and who is able to endure it? Rev. 6:17 ISV

CHAPTER FOUR
The Return of Jesus - Vignette from *The Millennium Chronicles*
- Doug Hamp

This vignette finds Therion (the Beast), Oracle (the False Prophet), and the chief commander of the armies of the nations (forces of Antichrist) rejoicing over their supposed victory over the remnant of Israel (represented as Ben, Kristiana and others). But victory is snatched from them by the triumphant return of Jesus.

"We have located them!" Oracle said to Therion, gleefully surveying the smoke rising from the rubble of toppled buildings and burning houses throughout the City of Jerusalem. "They are all assembled in the valley of Jehoshaphat and are almost standing on top of each other. They are hemmed in by slopes in front and in back and they have no place to go. The land has closed them in; they are trapped!"

"Exterminate the vermin," Therion commanded coldly, looking out contentedly over the valley. "Everything is going according to our plan. Two-thirds of the Hebrews in this land have died and now only this small remnant survives and soon they will be no more!

"Oracle," he said callously, "kill them slowly so that Adonai hears every one of their screams. We shall give meaning to that valley. The valley of Jehoshaphat, also known as Arema-ge-don; henceforth, it shall be known as the place of Adonai's judgment, that is, the place where we judged him and found him wanting!"

Kristiana took hold of Ben's hand. He could feel her shaking with fear. He too felt the fearful anticipation overwhelm him. He realized his unexpected companion was bringing him comfort on his journey.

The chief commander of the armies of the nations noted his orders received from Oracle. His face was slowly recovering from the foul sores which had originated near the place where the virus containing the Mark of Therion first began changing his DNA.

The mingling of his DNA with Therion's had given him strength greater than a horse, perhaps even more than two or three horses. He felt the vigor and power inside of him which he loved. He had overcome the frailties of his natural-born body, and now he understood that the seething power of Lucifer was his to the core. The soldiers of these armies were not like in previous wars; these were hybrids because they had taken the mark of Therion, which placed his seed into them, in the name of evolution and progress. Having mingled themselves with him they were now recast in his image. They had gained greater intelligence than the weak humans. He eyed both Therion and Oracle, thinking of how perhaps someday, he might take their place. All in its proper time, he thought. He finally responded to the command Oracle had given him, "Yes sir, with pleasure!"

"Today is the day we wipe the Hebrews off the map once and for all!" Therion said confidently with the armies of the entire planet standing behind him ready to attack Jerusalem. There were millions and millions that stood with him that could also fight against Yeshua's returning army if need be. Additionally, Therion commanded the two hundred million horsemen that came out of the Abyss.

The solar flare which had scorched part of the earth some time ago had made most of the conventional, high-tech weapons of the day inoperable, therefore they had converted every conceivable instrument into some kind of weapon; plowshares had been beaten into swords, and pruning hooks into spears and horses now served as their transportation!

With all the might of the world and the kingdom of Lucifer gathered with him at his disposal, Therion was eager to desecrate and destroy what he believed was the last remnant of the Hebrews so that he and his forces could set their eye upon Jerusalem. Lucifer was incensed against the Hebrews because their existence was a direct threat to his kingdom. Once it was no more, Adonai would never be able to establish his kingdom on the earth.

"You are beaten, Yeshua!" Therion boasted, gazing beyond the veil toward the upper City of Jerusalem, raising his hands and then flicking them back as if daring Adonai to respond. "Our struggle, our 'holy war' with you ends here and ends today! Our siege against your beloved lower City of Jerusalem has prevailed and it has fallen into our hands. Our soldiers, who took my mark containing my father's image, have ravished the women of this city! We have taken half of the residents of this city hostage and are leading them into exile where they shall take my mark or lose their heads. Your people, your elect, your heritage is now mine! You have failed to protect them. You failed to keep your word! Can't you hear the nations mocking you, saying 'where is their King?'" he said again, shaking his hands toward Adonai. "Look, all of the nations of the earth are assembled against your chosen City and we have defiled her! This City shall become a trash heap and the bodies of your elect shall be its refuse!"

"You have accomplished nothing by pouring out your life-force to save these people. My father was right to revolt against your foolish idea of the mighty serving the weak. You surrendered yourself for the world and now the whole world is following me! They realize that my father is worthy of reverence because he is strong and now they revere me! Can you not hear them saying, 'who is like Therion' and 'who is able to make war with him?' You should have accepted my father's offer of all the kingdoms of the world when you had the chance. Look, he has given me his power, his throne, and great authority. I have all authority over every tribe, tongue, and nation and all who dwell on the earth worship me. Even your beloved elect, the Hebrews, are in my hand and I am overcoming them completely and shattering their power. I am doing as I please and there is none who can withstand me.

Who can make war against me? I have destroyed the weak and the mighty alike and soon even your people, the Hebrews, shall be no more! I defy you, O Ancient One! Your authority is broken and you are a liar! Now the world shall know the truth about you and all who are with you. You are weak and cowardly. Your sacrifice has amounted to nothing and is completely undone. The name of Adonai is a rubble heap and any who would run to it will be destroyed! Yeshua does not keep his promises; your word is a sham, bogus, phony!" Therion raged. "All who trust in you are put to shame."

"You have allowed your people to be hemmed in on every side. They are now trapped like birds in a cage with my forces ready to decimate them. We shall do what the ancient king of Egypt was not able to do!" He turned to Oracle, "This is our moment of great victory. Send in the hybrids to tear them limb from limb and let their blood splatter on every side."

****

Caleb decided to address the alarmed faces in front of him which had courageously crowded into the valley over the past hour: "My people, inhabitants of Jerusalem, surely our *Yeshuáh* is coming; behold, his reward is with him and his work before him. We will trust, and will not be afraid for Yeshua is our strength and our song, and will be our *Yeshuáh*."

"*Hoshanna! Barukh haba beshem Adonai!*" they again chanted with their voices swelling with expectation and desire. "Please save us! Come Yeshua! Come, O great King, you are our only hope. We trust in no one else, only in you. We are waiting for you and we will be glad and rejoice in you, *Yeshuatenu!*"

Just then the wind picked up, laced with a freshness none of them had smelled in years. They all heard the words like a whisper on the wind, like they had heard in the shelter: "See, I have inscribed you on the palms of my hands. Your sons shall make haste; your destroyers and those who laid you waste shall go away from you. Don't you know? I am the eternal King, the Creator. I do not grow tired or weary; and my understanding cannot be fathomed." Caleb watched as a blue butterfly drifted past him again. He looked over at his father who saw it too, who looked back at him and smiled. "Can a woman forget her nursing child," Yeshua said, overwhelmed that the Hebrews had finally called upon him, "and not have compassion?" "Surely they may forget, yet I will not forget them," he said leaning over, blowing the words gently through the veil to his people. "See, I have inscribed you on the palms of my hands. Your walls are continually before me. Your sons shall make haste; your destroyers and those who laid you waste shall go away from you. Don't you know? I am the eternal King, the Creator of the ends of the earth. I do not grow tired or weary; and my understanding cannot be fathomed."

Yeshua was wearing many golden crowns; his face was like the sun. He was holding a sickle in his hand as the one who would administer justice and wage war with righteousness, his head and hair were white as wool or even snow, his eyes were like flames of fire, and his feet were like red-hot glowing metal. His perfect justice was like a breastplate on his chest and his ability to rescue and save his people was like a helmet on his head; his zeal to avenge his people was like a garment which covered him.

"I am proclaiming the year of Adonai's favor, and the day of vengeance to comfort all who mourn in Jerusalem!" Yeshua thundered powerfully from upper Jerusalem to the earth so that the sky and the earth quaked.

Therion, Oracle, and Lucifer looked up to the sky after hearing the peals of thunder and considered what they might mean.

"I will have compassion on my people, the Hebrews," Yeshua proclaimed passionately as the sound of their cries and petitions mixed with the words *"Hoshanna! Barukh haba beshem Adonai"* rose up to his throne like incense. Those were words that he had been waiting to hear from the leadership of the Hebrews. He had vowed to them: "you will not see my face again until you say, 'blessed is he who comes in the name of Adonai,'" and now after two-thousand years they were earnestly seeking him. Finally, they saw with great clarity their need for the one who had come to his own, yet his own had not received him.

"I will give them a beautiful headdress instead of ashes, the oil of gladness instead of mourning, the garment of praise instead of a faint spirit; that they may be called oaks of righteousness, the planting of Adonai, that he may be glorified. They shall build up the ancient ruins; they shall raise up the former devastations of many generations. Look my people, you will be fully satisfied. I will never again make you an object of mockery among the nations.

"I am displeased that there is no justice," Yeshua said as fiery-lightning surged from his sides. "I am appalled that there is no one to intervene."

"Great King, you are a refuge to your people, a stronghold to the Hebrews," someone shouted out, answering the audacious claims of Therion to those around him.

"I am the one who has gathered them and the armies of the world into the valley of Jehoshaphat, for there I will judge them for harming my people, for scattering my inheritance among the nations, and for dividing up my land. They cast lots to decide which of my people would be their slaves and abused the little ones for their pleasures. I will bring them back again from all the places to which they were sold, and I will pay the nations back for all they have done. I will strike Therion from the house of the wicked, by laying his neck bare."

"Lucifer, his son Therion, and Oracle do not grasp my thoughts," Yeshua declared, "nor do they understand my counsel; for I am gathering them like sheaves to the threshing floor because the time has come for the Hebrews to take possession of the kingdom. I have made Jerusalem a trap and now I shall go and spring the trap!" Yeshua said in a mighty and thunderous voice, even as Therion was boasting in his apparently unstoppable victory. "Look, I am making Jerusalem an unstable cup toward all of its surrounding armies as they lay siege against Judah and Jerusalem. I am making Jerusalem a heavy weight; so everyone who burdens themselves with it will be crushed, even though all of the nations of the earth have gathered themselves against it. I am about to strike every horse with panic and every rider with insanity. I will keep my eyes on the house of Judah, but I will blind every horse of the invading armies."

"Swing your sickle, and gather the harvest," an Angel said in a loud voice coming out of the temple of Adonai, "for the hour has come to gather it, because the harvest of the earth is fully ripe."

"Bring down your warriors, Yeshua!" the prophet Joel suddenly called out. "Rush forth with the sickle, for the harvest is ripe! Go, stomp the grapes, for the winepress is full! The vats overflow. Indeed, their wickedness is great! Crowds, great crowds are in the valley of threshing, the valley of Jehoshaphat, Armageddon!"

"Michael," Yeshua said, "when you hear the trumpet blast, you will go out and gather my elect from the four winds, from one end of heaven to another."

"The rest of you," Yeshua commanded the mighty Angels following him among the vast army, "Go and gather the weeds first and tie them in bundles for burning, but bring the wheat into my barn."

Gabriel smiled, understanding exactly what Yeshua referred to. In fact, he had longed for this day when they would finally be authorized to go in every direction to first gather out of his kingdom all things that offend and those who practice lawlessness. He peered through the veil to the earth noting the location of several of Lucifer's army of Watchers as well as the rulers of the earth and all who had taken the mark and those that were attempting to destroy the Hebrews.

Their vast numbers, he considered, were of no consequence, for they were like a drop in a bucket, and were reckoned as dust on the scales before Yeshua, the mighty! All the nations were as nothing before him, they were reckoned by him as nothing and chaos.

"The end of the age has come for the world to be harvested in judgment!" Yeshua proclaimed and then stood up from his Father's throne and walked over to his majestic pure-white war-horse. An astoundingly sharp, two-edged sword could be seen coming out of his mouth. It was something like an intensified particle-wave beam of light.

"Go forth, great King, with your great army!" Enoch, the seventh from Adam, encouraged him. "Execute judgment on all; convict all who are wicked for all of the wickedness they have committed and of all the harsh things which the wicked have spoken against you."

"Nations far and wide, get ready for war!" Gabriel taunted. "Call out your best warriors! Let all your fighting men advance for the attack!" The cry for help of the Hebrews was the key to establishing Yeshua's kingdom and he would not rest until he had vanquished all their enemies and established Jerusalem as a praise throughout the earth and the Hebrews as the head of nations and no longer the tail.

"The day of my vengeance has finally come," Yeshua bellowed, "The day to bring in the acceptable year of Adonai. Now, my glory shall be revealed, and all the Adamites will see it at once."

"Oh great King," Isaiah exclaimed, "rend the heavens and go down and may the mountains quake at your presence! Repay your enemies according to their action: anger to your enemies, retribution to your foes; to the coastlands render their due!" Isaiah was eager to see Yeshua defend the Hebrews; every one of her allies had forsaken her. "Go with strength, and may your arm rule for you."

Ben and Kristiana watched in amazement as an Angel threw the contents of his bowl across the sky.

"It is done!" someone in a loud voice shouted from the throne in the temple.

"The kingdoms of this world," others resonated in loud voices, "have become the kingdoms of Adonai and of Yeshua, and Adonai shall reign forever and ever! The nations were angry, and your wrath has come. Now is the time that the dead should be judged and that you should reward your servants the prophets, the saints, and those who fear your name, unimportant and important and for you to destroy those who have destroyed the earth."

Suddenly the temple of Adonai began opening, exposing the ark of his covenant. Lightning and thundering booms emanated out of the place.

All eyes were on Yeshua.

"I am coming quickly," he said with a voice like the sound of many waters. He was silent for a moment and then ferociously roared out like a raging lion, shaking the throne itself. "I have heard you, my beloved, and I am coming!"

The armies of Yeshua began taking their positions on their side of the veil ready for battle.

The scene turned white. "Ben and Kristiana," Antipas startled Ben, who had been immersed in the scene, "to understand the removal of the veil, you must first know why the veil was created. So long as it was between the two domains, there could never be complete and open communication between Adonai and the Adamites. It happened just after the degeneration of the earth, which took place after the assassination."

Yeshua sat on his horse behind the veil ready to advance; behind him were millions and millions of riders plus horses and chariots of fire.

"After six millennia," John said to Isaiah, who was on his horse next to him, "Yeshua is finally revealing himself to the world with his mighty Angels in blazing flames of fire, which will inflict vengeance on those who do not know Adonai and on those who have not obeyed his good news. They will needlessly suffer the punishment of eternal destruction by virtue of exposure to his presence and from the glory of his might."

"The world has no idea of what is coming!" Isaiah confirmed. "He is coming in fire with his chariots like a tornado, to render his anger in fury, and his rebuke with flames of fire!"

Yeshua opened his mouth and a beam of light pierced through the veil creating a shock-wave blasting the inhabitants on the other side. A deafening boom immediately thundered throughout the world.

Therion and Oracle were knocked to the ground from the blast. They lay flat on their backs and turned pale with fear as they witnessed the laser-like shaft of light, brighter than the midday sun, piercing through a point in the dark, ash-filled sky. They covered their ears to guard them from the horrific, ear-piercing roar that was created as the sky began rolling up like a scroll from the point where the particle-beam sword from Yeshua's mouth struck it.

The veil which had cloaked the other domain from the earth was dissolving, like a dark filter becoming transparent. Therion, Oracle, and their army watched as dark, thick clouds began rolling out and flames of fire and raging bolts of lightning blazed brilliantly through the clouds, lighting the world. They then saw Yeshua step into the domain of the Adamites. The veil which had so long separated the domain of Adonai and that of the Adamites, was gone and finally all could see Yeshua.

He stood there for several moments surveying the earth, which had suffered incredible destruction during the time of the Hebrews' trouble and had become practically uninhabitable. All the seas and rivers had turned to blood and everything in the seas had died: all the fish, the coral, the whales, dolphins, starfish, shellfish, even the plankton were dead.

Therion, Oracle, and all the kings of the earth, and their armies which had declared war against Yeshua by gathering to destroy the Hebrews watched as smoke poured out of Yeshua's nostrils and a consuming fire from his mouth. Their hearts skipped a beat as they fixed their eyes on the champion towering over them and the armies of heaven coming behind him. Everyone on the entire planet saw his brighter-than-the-sun radiance and the powerful beams of light coming out from his hands, and the sharp sword protruding out of his mouth. They all lamented at seeing the sign of Yeshua coming on the clouds of heaven with power and great glory.

When the people of Egypt, just south of Jerusalem looked up, their hearts failed seeing Yeshua leading his army on a swift cloud over their heads.

In a flash like lightning, Yeshua circled the earth in an east-west direction. The earth began to groan violently as Yeshua and his army passed overhead. Like a great furnace his fiery-lightning presence began to set the mountains and hills ablaze. The continents quaked and waves of the oceans surged violently upward as Yeshua's army passed over, and they were exposed to his power. The degenerate planet reacted violently being finally exposed to the brilliance and blazing power of the King because the veil had been removed.

Hills collapsed and fire broke out burning to the deepest part of the Abyss, consuming the earth and its produce and igniting the foundations of the mountains.

Ben and Kristiana watched in awe as the removal of the veil left the earth exposed to the glorious fire of Yeshua so that even the dirt was melting with fervent heat, and the earth and everything on it began to burn. The heavens declared his righteousness so that all the nations would see his glory.

"It appears in the Chronicles," Ben said to Kristiana, "that only the cloud surrounding Yeshua shielded the earth and the inhabitants from the full impact of his consuming fire and lightning."

"I think you are right," Kristiana answered. "Do you suppose," she asked while witnessing the flash floods on the earth's surface, "he was displeased with the rivers or was his anger directed against the watercourses or against the sea when he came back with his chariots of deliverance?"

"I don't know," Ben admitted. "But clearly pestilence went before him and disease followed behind him." They both watched as all over the earth people were wailing and lamenting as fear flooded over them.

"For so long," Kristiana realized, "they had foolishly said in their hearts that there was no King, no Creator. Now, for the first time since the Fall, the Adamites could see directly into the other realm beyond the veil and they realized that death would soon be upon them." The Chronicles focused on Yeshua again, who, with a nod gave the command to Gabriel and the other commanders of his army; each knew their mission: to gather all the things that offend out of Yeshua's kingdom. "Who among us can live with the consuming fire?" Therion's chief commander asked. "Who among us can live with everlasting flames?"

"The great day of Yeshua's wrath has come, and who is able to endure it?" many around the world struggled to say being short of breath and barely able to vocalize their words as fear gripped them tenaciously. All who were able traveled as fast as they could to their underground bunkers and even entire cities they had built for themselves in the caves and among the rocks in the mountains. They shut the reinforced nuclear-blast doors of their secret underground command posts around the world.

They imagined that, under the cover of the mountains and rocks, they could hide themselves from the face of the one who sat on the throne and from the wrath of Yeshua.

"At last," Isaiah said to John as they rode their horses among Yeshua's army, "their lofty looks are humbled. Their haughtiness is bowed down, and the King alone shall be exalted this day. Everything proud and lofty, all of the high towers of the Adamites, every fortified wall, and every ship shall be brought to ruin today."

"They wanted to be gods," John responded, "by taking the mark of Therion and transforming their DNA and they wanted to lift themselves up to the highest place. But all they can do now is go into the holes of the rocks, and into the caves of the earth, from the terror of the great King and the glory of his majesty, now that he has arisen to shake the earth mightily."

In just a few moments they circled the earth and arrived back where they started; they flew east to west over Teman-Jordan, the area of Bozrah, where the other Hebrews who had heeded Yeshua's warning had fled when they saw the destructive abomination set up by Oracle, and were being protected from the awful time of trouble. Yeshua's eyes were fixed on rescuing those who had recently called upon Him in the Lower Jerusalem.

CHAPTER FIVE
Unwinding Common Pre-Trib Assumptions
- Chris Steinle

Who Is Returning from Heaven with Jesus?

The Pre-Tribulation rapture doctrine teaches that the Church must already be in heaven (by way of the pre-trib rapture) prior to the Second Coming, so that the Church can return to the earth with Jesus. The Book of Jude is usually quoted because many English translations say that the Lord will come with His "saints."

Now Enoch, the seventh from Adam, prophesied about these men also, saying, "Behold, the Lord comes with **ten thousands of His saints (hagiais**[14] **myriasin**[15]**)**, to execute judgment on all, to convict all who are ungodly among them of all their ungodly deeds which they have committed in an ungodly way, and of all the harsh things which ungodly sinners have spoken against Him." Jude 14, 15

The Greek word translated above for "saints" is the Greek word, *hagias*, which can be translated either as "holy ones," or "saints." But "holy ones" can also refer to the holy angels. So how can we know whether the Church or an army of angels will come from heaven with Jesus?

Matthew 25:31 gives us clarification about the holy ones who are coming with Jesus. Christ Himself stated that these "holy ones" are holy angels.

When the Son of Man comes in His glory, and all the **holy angels (hagiais**[16] **oi aggelloi**[17]**)** with Him, then He will sit on the throne of His glory.

Verse 32 also places this Second Coming ahead of the same time of judgment described in Jude 15.

All the nations will be gathered before Him, and He will separate them one from another, as a shepherd divides his sheep from the goats. Matt. 25:32

So Matthew's description of Christ's return identifies these "holy ones" as the holy angels. But even if some people should be included with the army of angels that are coming with Jesus, these could be any of the millions of Christians who have died over the ages before Christ's return because, to be absent from the body is to be present with the Lord.

The Church has had nearly 2000 years to add souls to the spiritual realm. Based on a 70 year generation, 97% of all the "saints" who have lived up until now are already residing in heaven with Jesus. Therefore, there is no requirement that any of the people who might be coming with Jesus and the angels should have ever experienced the rapture. The rapture is simply not necessary to get more Christians into heaven in advance of His second coming.

Paul's Epistles to the Thessalonians contain the verses most often quoted as the basis for the theory of a Pre-Tribulation rapture. Amazingly though, the Thessalonian letters not only place the First Thessalonians Four rapture at Christ's second coming; but Second Thessalonians prepares the Church for persecutions and tribulations, and goes on to state expressly that "mighty angels", rather than saints, will be accompanying Christ back to earth.

We are bound to thank God always for you, brethren, as it is fitting, because your faith grows exceedingly, and the love of every one of you all abounds toward each other, so that we ourselves boast of you among the churches of God for your patience and faith in all your persecutions and tribulations that you endure, which is manifest evidence of the righteous judgment of God, that you may be counted worthy of the kingdom of God, for which you also suffer; since it is a righteous thing with God to repay with tribulation those who trouble you, and to give you who are troubled rest with us when the Lord Jesus is revealed from heaven with His **mighty angels (angelon[18] dynameos[19])**, in flaming fire taking vengeance on those who do not know God, and on those who do not obey the gospel of our Lord Jesus Christ. These shall be punished with everlasting destruction from the presence of the Lord and from the glory of His power, when He comes, in that Day, to be glorified in His saints and to be admired among all those who believe, because our testimony among you was believed. 2 Thess. 1:3-10

From the verses above we can see plainly that the holy ones coming from heaven with Jesus will be angels. The verse most often used to support the notion that people are coming back with Jesus is Revelation 19:14; *And the **armies in heaven**, clothed in fine linen, white and clean, followed Him on white horses.*

Pre-Tribulation advocates would say that the mention of clean white clothing must be referring to the bride. But does this mention of fine linen override all of the other verses above? And what about the first part of Verse 14? The **Lord of Hosts (Sabaoth)** refers throughout the Old Testament to the **armies of heaven** - the angels; once again confirming that the ones coming from heaven are angels, not people. The resurrected dead and those left alive at Jesus' return will meet the Lord in the air, they just won't be coming from heaven. They will be coming from earth to meet Jesus in the air. Where they go from there will be discussed later in the book.

What about the Church of Philadelphia?

Revelation 3:7-13 is Jesus' letter to the Church at Philadelphia. The Pre-Tribulation teachers claim that God is promising, in these verses, to take the Church out of the world just before the Great Tribulation. The verse of particular interest is Verse Ten.

Because you have kept My command to persevere, I also will keep you from the hour of trial which shall come upon the whole world, to test those who dwell on the earth. Rev. 3:10

The argument is that "kept from" actually means "taken out of." The underlying assumption is that the Philadelphians, or a similar type of church, will be "taken out" of the world before the "hour of trial." The best way to test this theory is to examine the original Greek words; and then to ask the question, "Has St. John ever used these same Greek words meaning, "to take" and "to keep," in his other writings?"

***Ares*[20]** (should take). This is the root word "to take" or "to lift." (If reading the digital version click on the words to go directly to Strong's for examples of usage.)

***Tereso*[21]** (will keep). This is the future tense of "to keep." *Tereso* is the word John used in the verse above. In fact, he used it twice in this one verse. This word implies; maintenance of, safety, or care. The changes in prefixes and suffixes below only indicate tense and usage in the Greek. Now look again at Revelation 3:10.

"Because you have kept (*eteresa*[22]) My command to persevere, I also will keep (*tereso*[23]) you from the hour of trial which shall come upon the whole world, to test those who dwell on the earth."

You see that John is using the same root word in both instances. The epsilon prefix on the first mention of "kept" merely puts it in the past tense, indicating that the Philadelphian Church had already kept His command to persevere. Should the verse be interpreted, "Because you have "taken out" My command?" Of course not!

Now let's look at how John used these words, "kept" and "taken," in his gospel. In Chapter 17 of John, we find Jesus' prayer to the Father. Here John used this word for safekeeping - profoundly contrasting the idea of being "lifted out of trouble" with the promise of being "kept safe through trials."

I do not pray that You should **take (ares**[24]**)** them out of the world, but that You should **keep (terese**[25]**)** them from the evil one. John 17:15

Now in the same way, Jesus spoke to the Church of Philadelphia. He promised to keep them in the midst of their trial, just as they had kept His command to persevere. Jesus was merely reciprocating their obedience "to keep" His command to persevere, with the promise of keeping the Philadelphia Church in return. He was not submitting the dissimilar promise of "taking them out" of harm's way. This is a simple apples-to-apples reward for the Philadelphians' own perseverance.

Likewise, keeping the Apostles from the evil one did not mean "taking them out" of the world, but "keeping them" from being overcome by the evil one; even though, they would still remain in the world to accomplish Christ's purpose (the purpose for which He was sending them into the world in the first place). Christ was sent into the world, and was not taken out of the world until He had accomplished his death and resurrection. Why would God remove His Church from the world (into which it was likewise sent) until such time as it had also accomplished its purpose? Didn't Jesus clearly state that His followers (servants) would not be treated better than their Master?

If further proof of Revelation 3:10's failure to support the Pre-Tribulation theory is needed, we only have to consider the order in which these "types" of churches appear in Revelation; and how they are expected to emerge over history (by those who choose to extrapolate the seven church-types into the future). The Laodicean Church is the type expected to exist at the end of the age, **not** the Philadelphian type. Why didn't Jesus give the Laodicean Church an opportunity to escape from the hour of trial, if they were the type of church that would exist in the final days of the age?

Will Christians Experience God's Wrath?

There is therefore now no condemnation to those who are in Christ Jesus. Rom. 8:1

Who shall separate us from the love of Christ? Shall tribulation, or distress, or persecution, or famine, or nakedness, or peril, or sword? As it is written:

"For Your sake we are killed all day long;
We are accounted as sheep for the slaughter."
Yet in all these things we are more than conquerors through
Him who loved us. Rom. 8:35-37

Christians cannot come under God's wrath; but they will be required to endure a time of slaughter - a season of tribulation on the earth. Paul quoted the Old Testament reference above in Romans Chapter Eight specifically speaking to the Church about going through tribulation. Throughout the Book of Daniel the saints are being persecuted and slain by wicked rulers; and by the Beast who will "devour the whole earth." If it were not possible for God's people to experience an hour of trial that involves all the inhabitants of the world, then how could the Jews experience such a time? (Making the Pre-Tribulation assumption that Daniel pertains only to the Jews.)

Would Christians who were saved during the Great Tribulation be under God's grace (favor), and under God's wrath, at the same time? Would the "elect" (supposed by Pre-Tribulation proponents to refer to the 144,000) experience favor and wrath at the same time? Furthermore, there would be no reason for preaching the eternal gospel during that time - for the same reason. Grace simply means, "God's favor." Is it possible to be one of God's favored, and to be out of God's favor, at the same time?

Christians "have passed from judgment into life" because of their obedience to the gospel. And up until the *redemption of the body* their salvation is spiritual, just as Christ's kingdom was not of this world. This great salvation cannot be jeopardized by being in the wrong place at the wrong time. Therefore the entire argument against the Church's existence on the earth during the time of God's wrath is either irrelevant, or it must be applied equally to all of God's people (Jews included). If Christ is for us, He cannot at the same time be against us. This is a kingdom principle.

The Book of Revelation does talk about a time when God's people will be sealed for protection. One of the difficulties in discussing the tribulation is that the Pre-Tribulation system typically groups everything in Revelation into the time of the Wrath of God. As Doug will bring out in the following chapters, God's people will enter some type of hiding place during the time of God's indignation. Will God warn His people to take cover, but to know that His anger is not being directed toward them? Will the saints be glorified and become impervious to physical harm? Or will they be taken to an isolated area that will not be affected? These are some of the possible interpretations we will discuss throughout the book.

The Mystical *Meta Tauta*

Pre-Tribulation rapture teachers say that *"after these things,"* (Gr. *meta tauta*) signifies that the Church has just been raptured at the beginning of Revelation Chapter Four. This conclusion is based on the premise that the previous chapters had been speaking about "the Church"; and therefore, *meta tauta* must mean that the conversation about the Church has ended - for the next 19 chapters of Revelation.

Pre-Tribulation presumes that the letters to the seven churches weren't exclusively written to the seven churches to which the letters were addressed; but that they were intended to provide a template for the problems that would successively plague the Church-at-large over a theoretical "Church Age".

Pre-Tribulation advocates place great significance upon John's use of the words *Meta Tauta,* as if these Greek words contain some kind of encrypted meaning pointing directly to the rapture of the Church. The drill goes something like this: "When you read *meta tauta,* think rapture. See it? It's so obvious that John was indicating the rapture when he chose to use these special words. John meant, "After the things of the Church." See it now?

In his work diagramming the four views of Revelation, Steve Gregg makes this observation. *"It should be remembered that when John says, 'After these things I saw ...' (as he frequently does), he is giving us the sequence in which he saw the visions—not necessarily implying anything about the chronological order in which the visions would find fulfillment in events."*[26] In fact, "after these things" is such a common phrase to John that he uses these exact words, *meta tauta,* **13 times** in his Biblical writings.

Chapter Seven of Revelation opens with the words, *after these things.* The wrath of God had just come upon the earth at the end of Chapter Six. Does *meta tauta* mean in this instance that Revelation has no more to say about the wrath of God after Chapter Six?

Look at what has just taken place before the words, *meta tauta,* in Revelation 7:9. The 144,000 have just been sealed. Does *meta tauta* mean that the Jews are not to be found in the remainder of Revelation - *"after these things?"*

Chapters 17 and 18 of Revelation both reveal the details of Mystery Babylon. Yet right in the middle, at the beginning of Chapter 18, John wrote, *meta tauta*; "After these things." All three of these examples from the Book of Revelation demonstrate two truths about *meta tauta.* First, "after these things" does not signify a completion of whatever was being discussed before the "things" that follow the phrase, *meta tauta.* Secondly, *meta tauta,* at the beginning of Revelation Chapter Four does not mean, "rapture". But the need by Pre-Tribulation proponents to resort to finding special meaning in such a common phrase does mean something.

CHAPTER SIX
The Unmysterious Timing of the Rapture
- Doug Hamp

The timing of the rapture (the gathering) is not a mystery. Scripture repeatedly says in plain and simple language that it will occur *immediately after the tribulation of those days...He will send out his angels to gather His elect.* Matt. 24:29-31 The prophets, Jesus, and the disciples plainly tell us the timing; we need not look to shadows and types in Scripture nor to the Jewish wedding feast, nor any other complex reasoning in order to deduce it - it will happen after the tribulation of those days. The goal of this chapter is to show the overwhelming amount of Scripture which plainly speaks of the timing of the resurrection, rapture, and return of the Lord.

The terms "rapture" and "gathering" will be used interchangeably since "rapture" is used only once to describe this event; the more common term is "gathering". Paul uses this term interchangeably with rapture in Second Thess. 2:1, *Now, brethren, concerning the **coming of our Lord Jesus Christ** and our **gathering** together to Him...*

It is my belief that many cannot see this (including myself formerly) because they believe that God started a new and different program with "the Church," and that He put His promises to Israel on hold until the time of the last seven years of this age. However, from Genesis 12 to the last page of Revelation the story is all about the descendants (both physical and spiritual) of Abraham, Isaac, and Jacob. Consequently, the resurrection and rapture directly pertain to Israel. God will graciously include the Gentiles in these events because, as Paul stated;

You, once Gentiles...were without Christ, being aliens from the commonwealth of Israel and strangers from the covenants of promise...Now, therefore, you are no longer strangers and foreigners, but fellow citizens with the saints and members of the household of God. Eph. 2:12, 13, 15, 16 19.

This means that the Gentiles should be fellow heirs, of the same body, and partakers of His promise in Christ through the gospel. Eph. 3:6. This is true because there is neither Greek nor Jew, circumcised nor uncircumcised, barbarian, Scythian, slave nor free, but Christ is all and in all. Col. 3:11

The bottom line is, the gathering/rapture will include all who have the testimony of Jesus Christ (Rev. 12:17) whether they are Jewish or Gentile.

The missing link in understanding the rapture is, in my opinion, the restoration of the two houses of Judah and Israel. There are dozens of verses which speak specifically about the two houses, yet somehow the fact that the prophets mentioned these houses by name has been overlooked by popular theologians.

The ability to recognize the plethora of Bible verses about the resurrection and rapture requires a basic understanding of who will be resurrected, raptured, and gathered. A full discussion of the scattering of Israel, and the identity of the God fearing people who would become the Gentile church, is beyond the scope of this book. Suffice it to say that there is a household of God (according to Paul's definition above) of which the Gentiles have become fellow citizens. The Gathering will be the time when Jesus will gather all of His people who have been scattered.

It is my hope that this book will bring clarity and show how straightforward the passages concerning this event are. There was a time I could not see what I am now teaching. It was not until I demanded to see the actual verses for the timing of the Pre-Tribulation rapture that I found there were none. And no one else could find any verses either. Once I was willing to reconsider the rapture paradigm, I discovered that despite this fact, there are many people who maintain that it will come before the time of Jacob's trouble; and yet they cannot give even one verse to prove their timing.

Consider, for example, the popular Pre-Tribulation defender Mark Hitchcock. Hitchcock correctly states in his book, *The End*, that there is no verse! "While **no single verse** says Jesus is coming to rapture his saints before the seven-year Tribulation, there are clear statements that He is coming to deliver His people from the coming wrath."[27] (emphasis mine)

The reality is that God plainly revealed the timing of the resurrection and the gathering (rapture) through the prophets Isaiah, Daniel, and others.

Isaiah 26:19-21 Resurrection/Rapture/Second Coming

Let's start with the earliest, and perhaps the clearest, passage we have. Isaiah 26:19-21 contains the resurrection, rapture, and return of the Lord. This passage will serve as our standard by which all other prophetic passages will be measured. (Key words are highlighted to make the comparison with other passages easier.)

> Your dead shall live;
> Together with my dead body they shall arise.
> Awake and sing, you who dwell in dust;
> For your dew is like the dew of herbs,
> And the earth shall cast out the dead.
> Come, my people, enter your chambers,
> And shut your doors behind you;
> Hide yourself, as it were, for a little moment,
> Until the indignation [זַעַם za'am] is past.
> For behold, the LORD comes out of His place
> To punish the inhabitants of the earth for their iniquity;
> The earth will also disclose her blood,
> And will no more cover her slain. Isa. 26:19-21

The phrase "Your dead shall live" is the resurrection, plain and simple. Those sleeping in the dust, God says, will awake and sing. The prophet Daniel was also promised (Dan. 12:2) that he would *arise to his inheritance at the end of the days.* Dan. 12:13 Likewise, Martha confessed that her brother Lazarus would rise on the last day (John 11:24).

The resurrection is also pegged after the time of trouble when Michael "shall stand up".

> At that time **Michael** shall **stand** up, the great prince who stands watch over the sons of your people; And there shall be a **time of trouble**, such as never was since there was a nation, Even to that time. And at that time your people shall be delivered,

Every one who is found written in the book. And many of those who **sleep** in the **dust** of the earth shall **awake**, some to everlasting life, some to shame and everlasting contempt. Dan. 12:1, 2

This time of trouble is apparently a reference to a conflict between the angel Michael and Satan in Revelation 12.

And war broke out in heaven: **Michael** and his angels **fought** with the **dragon**; and the dragon and his angels fought, but they did not prevail, nor was a place found for them in heaven any longer. So the great dragon was cast out, that serpent of old, called the Devil and Satan, who deceives the whole world; he was cast to the earth, and his angels were cast out with him. Rev. 12:7-9

The conflict between Michael and Satan is 3 ½ years before the return of Jesus. According to Revelation 12:14, Satan will attempt to destroy the Woman (Israel) but she will be protected for a time, times, and half a time, or 3 ½ years. This time of protection concurs with Daniel 12:1 which says, *and at that time your people shall be delivered*. The resurrection then **follows** the time of great trial; it does **not precede** it, as taught by the Pre-Tribulation rapture doctrine.

The Rapture (Gathering and Hiding Away)

The resurrection is then followed by God inviting His people to enter their chambers, shut the doors and hide for a bit until His indignation is past. Just as the apostle Paul said that *the dead in Christ will rise first. Then we who are alive and remain shall be caught up...*1 Thess. 4:16-17. Why does God invite them to enter into chambers and hide? He tells them to do so because He is coming "out of His place to punish inhabitants of the earth"! Thus according to Isaiah, the resurrection will occur, followed by the rapture (gathering and hiding away) which is necessary because God Himself is coming out of his place with great indignation.

In Isaiah 13:4-5 we read that the nations are gathered in the mountains and that *"the LORD of hosts musters the army for battle. They come from a far country, from the end of heaven– The LORD and His weapons of **indignation** [זַעַם za'am], to destroy the whole land.* The indignation spoken of is the same word used in Isaiah 26 – this is the day of the Lord, also known as the second coming of Jesus.

On that day people will *wail, for the day of the LORD is at hand! It will come as destruction from the Almighty*. Isa. 13:6 As a result of His coming, *all hands will be limp; every man's heart will melt. And they will be afraid. Pangs and sorrows will take hold of them; they will be in pain as a woman in childbirth; they will be amazed at one another; their faces will be like flames*. Isa. 13:7-8 Jesus said that all the nations will wail at his return (Matt. 24:30). Both Isaiah and John mention that they will run into the caves of the rocks and call on them to fall on them and hide them from the face of God, which we will discuss in more detail later.

This **indignation** [זַעַם *za'am*] is the reason that God calls His people to enter into their chambers and hide for a moment until it is passed. As we read in Isaiah 13:9, *the day of the LORD comes, cruel, with both wrath and fierce anger, to lay the land desolate; And He will destroy its sinners from it." It will also be that the "stars of heaven and their constellations will not give their light; the sun will be darkened in its going forth, and the moon will not cause its light to shine,"* Isa. 13:10 in that day when He returns.

Jesus reiterated all of these details while adding just a bit of His own flair; everything Jesus (and later the disciples) said about the resurrection, rapture, and return had already been mentioned in the Scriptures (the *Tanakh*[28]). It is important to understand that they were not adding new doctrines; they were simply reiterating (and sometimes elaborating on) what God had already revealed previously. If there were any questions in anyone's mind as to when the rapture would happen, Jesus stated plainly that it will come after the tribulation. He was drawing upon the words of Isaiah.

Immediately **after** the tribulation of those days the sun will be darkened, and the moon will not give its light; the stars will fall from heaven, and the powers of the heavens will be shaken. Then the sign of the Son of Man will appear in heaven, and then all the **tribes** of the earth will **mourn**, and they will see the Son of Man **coming** on the clouds of heaven with power and great glory. Matt. 24:29, 30

As mentioned before, the reason **they will mourn** is because the **Day of the Lord** has come. In Chapter 2, Isaiah describes the time of tribulation that is coming upon the whole earth in the "latter days" (Isa. 2:2) because God Himself was coming to shake the earth.

God revealed to Isaiah that people would *Enter into the **rock**, and hide in the dust, from the terror of the LORD and the glory of His majesty.* The message is reiterated in verses 19 and 21 to demonstrate its certainty; and the timing is given precisely when men will go into hiding:

They shall go into the **holes** of the **rocks**, and into the **caves** of the earth, from the terror of the LORD and the glory of His majesty, **when** He **arises** to **shake** the **earth** mightily. Isa. 2:19, 21

We then have another witness from the book of Revelation which is exactly parallel to Isaiah's: *And the kings of the earth, the great men, the rich men, the commanders, the mighty men, every slave and every free man, hid themselves in the **caves** and in the **rocks** of the mountains.* Rev. 6:15

The kings, great men, etc. then serve as eye witnesses as to why they seek refuge in the caves; *because the great day of God's wrath has come...and [they] said to the mountains and rocks, "Fall on us and **hide** us from the face of Him who sits on the throne and from the wrath of the Lamb! For the **great** day of His **wrath** has come, and who is able to stand?"* Rev. 6:16, 17

Isaiah 2 provides the key to understanding that the day of the Lord is the day that Jesus comes, because the blasphemies will cease: *The lofty looks of man shall be humbled, the haughtiness of men shall be bowed down, And the LORD alone shall be exalted in that day, Isa. 2:11* God revealed in both Daniel 7:25 and Revelation 13:5, 6 that the Beast (Antichrist) would be given 3 ½ years, or 42 months, to blaspheme those in heaven.

And he was given a mouth speaking great things and blasphemies, and he was given authority to continue for **forty-two months**. Then he opened his mouth in **blasphemy** against God, to **blaspheme** His name, His tabernacle, and those who dwell in heaven. Rev. 13:5-6

Since the Antichrist will blaspheme God in heaven for the last 42 months at the end of the age, then the day of the Lord **cannot** begin until **after** that time, since God so clearly revealed:

For the **day** of the LORD of hosts shall come **upon everything proud and lofty**, upon everything lifted up– and it **shall be brought low**– upon all the cedars of Lebanon that are high and lifted up, and upon all the oaks of Bashan; upon all the high mountains, and upon all the hills that are lifted up; upon every high tower, and upon every fortified wall; upon all the ships of Tarshish, and upon all the beautiful sloops. The **loftiness of man shall be bowed down**, and the **haughtiness of men** shall be brought low; the LORD alone will be exalted in that day, but the idols He shall utterly abolish. Isa. 2:12-18

The Beast will exalt himself for 42 months and his loftiness will be brought low in the day of the Lord; which means that the Day of the Lord only begins *when He arises to shake the earth mightily.* Isa. 2:19, 21

Isaiah 24 describes in gruesome detail what the destruction will look like when *the LORD makes the earth empty and makes it waste, distorts its surface and scatters abroad its inhabitants.* Isa. 24:1 It will be a time when *the land shall be entirely emptied and utterly plundered.* Isa. 24:3 God declares that *the earth mourns and fades away, the world languishes and fades away.* Isa. 24:4 An important time marker is given: *the **haughty** people of the earth languish.* Isa. 24:4 The haughtiness of men will be brought low in this chapter as in Chapter Two. This judgment will come about because the *"earth is also defiled under its inhabitants, because they have transgressed the laws, changed the ordinance, broken the everlasting covenant.* Isa. 24:5 Instead of the blasphemies that the Beast had been hurling up to God and those in heaven, *fear and the pit and the snare are upon you, O inhabitant of the earth. Isa. 24:17*

We know this time is precisely parallel to Revelation 6:15-17 because we are told that the *windows from on high are open, and the foundations of the earth are shaken.* Isa. 24:18 John saw in Revelation 6 that the heavens would recede like a scroll (Rev. 6:14, see also Isa. 34:4.) The heavens will open up on the day that Jesus is revealed from heaven in fire (2 Thess. 1:7, 8) to judge the inhabitants of the earth.

...when the Lord Jesus is **revealed** from heaven with His mighty angels, in **flaming fire** taking **vengeance** on those who do not know God, and on those who do not obey the gospel of our Lord Jesus Christ. 2 Thess. 1:7, 8

This is parallel to Isaiah:

For behold, the LORD will come with **fire** and with His chariots, like a whirlwind, to render His **anger** with fury, and His **rebuke** with **flames** of **fire**. For by fire and by His sword the LORD will judge all flesh; and the slain of the LORD shall be many. Isa. 66:15,16

Jesus' unveiling (revelation) from heaven is the time when the heavens will recede like a scroll. When that happens the entire earth will be startled completely and the mountains and hills will be scattered and bowed down (Hab. 3:6) because God will come from Teman (Hab. 3:3) and He will have "rays *flashing* from His hand," where "His power *was* hidden." (Hab. 3:4)

Accordingly, when this moment comes, the earth will be "violently broken," and "split open," and "shaken exceedingly" (Isa. 24:19). Furthermore,

The earth shall reel to and fro like a drunkard, and shall totter like a hut; its transgression shall be heavy upon it, and it will fall, and not rise again. Isa. 24:20

The day that this happens is the day that God will judge both the fallen angels on high and also the kings and the mighty men on the earth, which John also saw in Revelation 6.

It shall come to pass in that **day** that the LORD will **punish** on high the host of exalted ones, and on the **earth** the **kings** of the earth. Isa. 24:21

We are now ready to compare the rapture from our three sources: Isaiah 26, Matthew 24, and First Thessalonians Four. We discovered in Isaiah 26 that the people are told to enter their chambers until the indignation is past, which is the very day that Jesus returns. Jesus said that at His coming He would *send his angels with a great sound of a trumpet, and they will gather together His elect from the four winds, from one end of heaven to the other.* Matt. 24:31.

The verses listed in the next chapter follow the pattern shown in Isaiah 26:19-26, with the resurrection followed by the hiding away because Jesus is coming to judge. The verses are listed in order of relevance rather than the order in which they appear in the Bible. As stated earlier in the chapter, God's promise to reunite the House of Israel with the House of Judah is the key to understanding the importance of the Gathering (the united kingdom had split into two nations).

CHAPTER SEVEN
Unmysterious Rapture Timing Verses
- Doug Hamp

In contrast to the Bible's lack of verses supporting a secret Pre-Tribulation rapture, there are so many verses confirming the timing of the Second Coming rapture/gathering that they will be presented below in groups. Verses that prove that there will be a resurrection and rapture are listed first. Then, verses establishing the order of events are grouped to show: that the resurrection will happen before the rapture/gathering; the resurrection will happen at the end (last trumpet); and the resurrection, rapture, and gathering will happen at the time of judgment/indignation.

Verses Affirming the Resurrection

Isa. 26:19 Your dead shall live...Awake **and sing**, you who dwell in dust...

Dan. 12:2 And many of those who **sleep** in the **dust** of the earth shall **awake**...

Psa. 17:15 As for me, I will see Your face in righteousness; I shall be satisfied when I awake in Your likeness.

Isa. 25:8 He will swallow up death forever, and the Lord GOD will wipe away tears from all faces; the rebuke of His people He will take away from all the earth; for the LORD has spoken.

Job 19:25-27 For I know that my Redeemer lives, and He shall stand at last on the earth; and after my skin is destroyed, this I know, that in my flesh I shall see God, whom I shall see for myself, and my eyes shall behold, and not another. How my heart yearns within me!

Psa. 49:14, 15 Like sheep they are laid in the grave; death shall feed on them; the upright shall have dominion over them in the morning; and their beauty shall be consumed in the grave, far from their dwelling. But God will redeem my soul from the power of the grave, for He shall receive me. Selah.

Job 14:12 So man lies down and does not rise. Till the heavens are no more, they will not awake nor be roused from their sleep. [Rev. 6:14 Then the sky receded as a scroll...]

Phil. 3:11, 20, 21 If, by any means, I may attain to the resurrection from the dead...for our citizenship is in heaven, from which we also eagerly wait for the Savior, the Lord Jesus Christ, who will transform our lowly body that it may be conformed to His glorious body, according to the working by which He is able even to subdue all things to Himself.

Acts 24:15 I have hope in God, which they themselves also accept, that there will be a resurrection of the dead, both of the just and the unjust.

Titus 2:13 looking for the blessed hope and glorious appearing of our great God and Savior Jesus Christ,

Acts 23:6 But when Paul perceived that one part were Sadducees and the other Pharisees, he cried out in the council, "Men and brethren, I am a Pharisee, the son of a Pharisee; concerning the hope and resurrection of the dead I am being judged!"

Luke 14:14 And you will be blessed, because they cannot repay you; for you shall be repaid at the resurrection of the just.

Luke 20:34, 35 Jesus answered and said to them, "The sons of this age marry and are given in marriage. But those who are counted worthy to attain that age, and the resurrection from the dead, neither marry nor are given in marriage."

Rapture/Gathering Verses

The terms "rapture" and "gathering" will be used interchangeably since "rapture" is used only once to describe this event. The more common term is "gathering". Paul uses this term interchangeably with rapture in **Second Thess. 2:1** *Now, brethren, concerning the **coming of our Lord Jesus Christ** and our **gathering** together to Him...*

Isa. 11:12, 13 He will set up a banner for the nations, and will assemble the outcasts of Israel, and gather together the dispersed of Judah from the four corners of the earth...Ephraim shall not envy Judah, And Judah shall not harass Ephraim.

Deut. 30:3-6 That the LORD your God will bring you back from captivity, and have compassion on you, and gather you again from all the nations where the LORD your God has scattered you. If any of you are driven out to the farthest parts under heaven, from there the LORD your God will gather you, and from there He will bring you. Then the LORD your God will bring you to the land which your fathers possessed, and you shall possess it. He will prosper you and multiply you more than your fathers. And the LORD your God will circumcise your heart and the heart of your descendants, to love the LORD your God with all your heart and with all your soul, that you may live.

Ezek. 11:16-20 Therefore say, "Thus says the Lord GOD: 'Although I have cast them far off among the Gentiles, and although I have scattered them among the countries, yet I shall be a little sanctuary for them in the countries where they have gone.'" Therefore say, "Thus says the Lord GOD: 'I will gather you from the peoples, assemble you from the countries where you have been scattered, and I will give you the land of Israel. And they will go there, and they will take away all its detestable things and all its abominations from there. Then I will give them one heart, and I will put a new spirit within them, and take the stony heart out of their flesh, and give them a heart of flesh, that they may walk in My statutes and keep My judgments and do them; and they shall be My people, and I will be their God.'"

Ezek. 36:24-28 "For I will take you from among the nations, gather you out of all countries, and bring you into your own land. Then I will sprinkle clean water on you, and you shall be clean; I will cleanse you from all your filthiness and from all your idols. I will give you a new heart and put a new spirit within you; I will take the heart of stone out of your flesh and give you a heart of flesh. I will put My Spirit within you and cause you to walk in My statutes, and you will keep My judgments and do them. Then you shall dwell in the land that I gave to your fathers; you shall be My people, and I will be your God."

Ezek. 28:25, 26 "Thus says the Lord GOD: 'When I have gathered the house of Israel [there were two houses: Judah and Israel] from the peoples among whom they are scattered, and am hallowed in them in the sight of the Gentiles, then they will dwell in their own land which I gave to My servant Jacob. And they will dwell safely there, build houses, and plant vineyards (see Isa. 65:21); yes, they will dwell securely, when I execute judgments on all those around them who despise them. Then they shall know that I am the LORD their God.'"

Isa. 49:5, 6 And now the LORD says, "Who formed Me from the womb to be His Servant, to bring Jacob back to Him [referring to Jesus], so that Israel is gathered to Him" (For I shall be glorious in the eyes of the LORD, and My God shall be My strength), Indeed He says, "It is too small a thing that You should be My Servant to raise up the tribes of Jacob, and to restore the preserved ones of Israel; I will also give You as a light to the Gentiles, that You should be My salvation to the ends of the earth."

Isa. 54:7 For a mere moment I have forsaken you, But with great mercies I will gather you.

Isa. 56:8 The Lord GOD, who gathers the outcasts of Israel, says, "Yet I will gather to him others besides those who are gathered to him."

Jer. 23:3-6 "But I will gather the remnant of My flock out of all countries where I have driven them, and bring them back to their folds; and they shall be fruitful and increase. I will set up shepherds over them who will feed them; and they shall fear no more, nor be dismayed, nor shall they be lacking," says the LORD. "Behold, the days are coming," says the LORD, "That I will raise to David a Branch of righteousness; a King shall reign and prosper, and execute judgment and righteousness in the earth. In His days Judah will be saved, and Israel will dwell safely; Now this is His name by which He will be called: THE LORD OUR RIGHTEOUSNESS."

Jer. 31:1, 8-12, 33 "At the same time," says the LORD, "I will be the God of all the families of Israel, and they shall be My people." "Behold, I will bring them from the north country, and gather them from the ends of the earth, among them the blind and the lame, the woman with child and the one who labors with child, together; a great throng shall return there. They shall come with weeping, and with supplications I will lead them. I will cause them to walk by the rivers of waters, in a straight way in which they shall not stumble; for I am a Father to Israel, and Ephraim is My firstborn." Hear the word of the LORD, O nations, and declare it in the isles afar off, and say, 'He who scattered Israel will gather him, and keep him as a shepherd does his flock.' for the LORD has redeemed Jacob, and ransomed him from the hand of one stronger than he. Therefore they shall come and sing in the height of Zion, streaming to the goodness of the LORD– for wheat and new wine and oil, for the young of the flock and the herd; their souls shall be like a well-watered garden, and they shall sorrow no more at all..." "But this is the covenant that I will make with the house of Israel after those days, says the LORD: I will put My law in their minds, and write it on their hearts; and I will be their God, and they shall be My people."

Jer. 32:37-40 "Behold, I will gather them out of all countries where I have driven them in My anger, in My fury, and in great wrath; I will bring them back to this place, and I will cause them to dwell safely. They shall be My people, and I will be their God; then I will give them one heart and one way, that they may fear Me forever, for the good of them and their children after them. And I will make an everlasting covenant with them, that I will not turn away from doing them good; but I will put My fear in their hearts so that they will not depart from Me."

Ezek. 20:34 "I will bring you out from the peoples and gather you out of the countries where you are scattered, with a mighty hand, with an outstretched arm, and with fury poured out. And I will bring you into the wilderness of the peoples, and there I will plead My case with you face to face. Just as I pleaded My case with your fathers in the wilderness of the land of Egypt, so I will plead My case with you," says the Lord GOD.

Ezek. 20:41, 42 I will accept you as a sweet aroma when I bring you out from the peoples and gather you out of the countries where you have been scattered; and I will be hallowed in you before the Gentiles. Then you shall know that I am the LORD, when I bring you into the land of Israel, into the country for which I raised My hand in an oath to give to your fathers.

Ezek. 28:25, 26 Thus says the Lord GOD: "When I have gathered the house of Israel from the peoples among whom they are scattered, and am hallowed in them in the sight of the Gentiles, then they will dwell in their own land which I gave to My servant Jacob. And they will dwell safely there, build houses, and plant vineyards [see Isaiah 65:21]; yes, they will dwell securely, when I execute judgments on all those around them who despise them. Then they shall know that I am the LORD their God."

Ezek. 34:11-13, 16, 17, 23-25, 30 For thus says the Lord GOD: "Indeed I Myself will search for My sheep and seek them out. As a shepherd seeks out his flock on the day he is among his scattered sheep, so will I seek out My sheep and deliver them from all the places where they were scattered on a cloudy and dark day. And I will bring them out from the peoples and gather them from the countries, and will bring them to their own land; I will feed them on the mountains of Israel, in the valleys and in all the inhabited places of the country. I will seek what was lost and bring back what was driven away, bind up the broken and strengthen what was sick; but I will destroy the fat and the strong, and feed them in judgment." "And as for you, O My flock, thus says the Lord GOD: 'Behold, I shall judge between sheep and sheep, between rams and goats [see Matt. 25:32].'" "I will establish one shepherd over them, and he shall feed them–My servant David. He shall feed them and be their shepherd." "And I, the LORD, will be their God, and My servant David a prince among them; I, the LORD, have spoken. I will make a covenant of peace with them, and cause wild beasts to cease from the land; and they will dwell safely in the wilderness and sleep in the woods." "Thus they shall know that I, the LORD their God, am with them, and they, the house of Israel, are My people," says the Lord GOD.

Ezek. 37:19-28 ...say to them, "Thus says the Lord GOD: 'Surely I will take the stick of Joseph, which is in the hand of Ephraim, and the tribes of Israel, his companions; and I will join them with it, with the stick of Judah, and make them one stick, and they will be one in My hand. And the sticks on which you write will be in your hand before their eyes.'" "Then say to them, 'Thus says the Lord GOD: "Surely I will take the children of Israel from among the nations, wherever they have gone, and will gather them from every side and bring them into their own land; and I will make them one nation in the land, on the mountains of Israel; and one king shall be king over them all; they shall no longer be two nations, nor shall they ever be divided into two kingdoms again. They shall not defile themselves anymore with their idols, nor with their detestable things, nor with any of their transgressions; but I will deliver them from all their dwelling places in which they have sinned, and will cleanse them. Then they shall be My people, and I will be their God. David My servant shall be king over them, and they shall all have one shepherd; they shall also walk in My judgments and observe My statutes, and do them. Then they shall dwell in the land that I have given to Jacob My servant, where your fathers dwelt; and they shall dwell there, they, their children, and their children's children, forever; and My servant David shall be their prince forever. Moreover I will make a covenant of peace with them, and it shall be an everlasting covenant with them; I will establish them and multiply them, and I will set My sanctuary in their midst forevermore. My tabernacle also shall be with them; indeed I will be their God, and they shall be My people. The nations also will know that I, the LORD, sanctify Israel, when My sanctuary is in their midst forevermore.'"

Ezek. 39:25-29 Therefore thus says the Lord GOD: "Now I will bring back the captives of Jacob, and have mercy on the whole house of Israel; and I will be jealous for My holy name – after they have borne their shame, and all their unfaithfulness in which they were unfaithful to Me, when they dwelt safely in their own land and no one made them afraid. When I have brought them back from the peoples and gathered them out of their enemies' lands, and I am hallowed in them in the sight of many nations, then they shall know that I am the LORD their God, who sent them into captivity among the nations, but also brought them back to their land, and left none of them captive any longer. And I will not hide My face from them anymore; for I shall have poured out My Spirit on the house of Israel," says the Lord GOD.

Hos. 1:11 Then the children of Judah and the children of Israel shall be gathered together, and appoint for themselves one head; and they shall come up out of the land, for great will be the day of Jezreel!

Joel 3:1 For behold, in those days and at that time, when I bring back the captives of Judah and Jerusalem.

Mic. 2:12 I will surely assemble all of you, O Jacob, I will surely gather the remnant of Israel; I will put them together like sheep of the fold, like a flock in the midst of their pasture; they shall make a loud noise because of so many people.

Zeph. 3:19, 20 "Behold, at that time I will deal with all who afflict you; I will save the lame, And gather those who were driven out; I will appoint them for praise and fame In every land where they were put to shame. At that time I will bring you back, Even at the time I gather you; For I will give you fame and praise Among all the peoples of the earth, When I return your captives before your eyes," Says the LORD.

Zech. 10:6-10 I will strengthen the house of Judah, and I will save the house of Joseph. I will bring them back, because I have mercy on them. They shall be as though I had not cast them aside; for I am the LORD their God, and I will hear them. Those of Ephraim shall be like a mighty man, and their heart shall rejoice as if with wine. Yes, their children shall see it and be glad; their heart shall rejoice in the LORD. I will whistle for them and gather them, for I will redeem them; and they shall increase as they once increased. I will sow them among the peoples, and they shall remember Me in far countries; they shall live, together with their children, and they shall return. I will also bring them back from the land of Egypt, and gather them from Assyria. I will bring them into the land of Gilead and Lebanon, until no more room is found for them.

Matt. 13:30, 38-43, 47-49 Let both grow together until the harvest, and at the time of harvest I will say to the reapers, "First gather together the tares and bind them in bundles to burn them, but gather the wheat into my barn."

The field is the world, the good seeds are the sons of the kingdom, but the tares are the sons of the wicked one. The enemy who sowed them is the devil, the harvest is the end of the age, and the reapers are the angels. Therefore as the tares are gathered and burned in the fire, so it will be at the end of this age. The Son of Man will send out His angels, and they will gather out of His kingdom all things that offend, and those who practice lawlessness, and will cast them into the furnace of fire. There will be wailing and gnashing of teeth. Then the righteous will shine forth as the sun in the kingdom of their Father. He who has ears to hear, let him hear!

Again, the kingdom of heaven is like a dragnet that was cast into the sea and gathered some of every kind, which, when it was full, they drew to shore; and they sat down and gathered the good into vessels, but threw the bad away. So it will be at the end of the age. The angels will come forth, separate the wicked from among the just.

Matt. 25:32 All the nations will be gathered before Him, and He will separate them one from another, as a shepherd divides his sheep from the goats.

Mark 13:27 And then He will send His angels, and gather together His elect from the four winds, from the farthest part of earth to the farthest part of heaven.

Luke 3:17 His winnowing fan is in His hand, and He will thoroughly clean out His threshing floor, and gather the wheat into His barn; but the chaff He will burn with unquenchable fire.

Second Thess. 2:1 Now, brethren, concerning the coming of our Lord Jesus Christ and our gathering together to Him...

Jer. 30:3, 4 "For behold, the days are coming," says the LORD, "that I will bring back from captivity My people Israel and Judah," says the LORD. "And I will cause them to return to the land that I gave to their fathers, and they shall possess it." Now these are the words that the LORD spoke concerning Israel and Judah.

Jer. 30:6-11 "Ask now, and see, whether a man is ever in labor with child? So why do I see every man with his hands on his loins like a woman in labor, and all faces turned pale? Alas! For that day is great, so that none is like it; and it is the time of Jacob's trouble, but he shall be saved out of it." "For it shall come to pass in that day," says the LORD of hosts, "that I will break his yoke from your neck, and will burst your bonds; foreigners shall no more enslave them. But they shall serve the LORD their God, and David their king, whom I will raise up for them. Therefore do not fear, O My servant Jacob," says the LORD, "nor be dismayed, O Israel; for behold, I will save you from afar, and your seed from the land of their captivity. Jacob shall return, have rest and be quiet, and no one shall make him afraid." "For I am with you," says the LORD, "to save you; though I make a full end of all nations where I have scattered you, yet I will not make a complete end of you. But I will correct you in justice, and will not let you go altogether unpunished."

Jer. 30:18-24 Thus says the LORD: "Behold, I will bring back the captivity of Jacob's tents, and have mercy on his dwelling places; the city shall be built upon its own mound, and the palace shall remain according to its own plan. Then out of them shall proceed thanksgiving and the voice of those who make merry; I will multiply them, and they shall not diminish; I will also glorify them, and they shall not be small. Their children also shall be as before, and their congregation shall be established before Me; and I will punish all who oppress them. Their nobles shall be from among them, and their governor shall come from their midst; then I will cause him to draw near, and he shall approach Me; for who is this who pledged his heart to approach Me?' says the LORD. You shall be My people, and I will be your God. Behold, the whirlwind of the LORD Goes forth with fury, a continuing whirlwind; it will fall violently on the head of the wicked. The fierce anger of the LORD will not return until He has done it, and until He has performed the intents of His heart. In the latter days you will consider it. But I will bring back Israel to his home, and he shall feed on Carmel and Bashan; his soul shall be satisfied on Mount Ephraim and Gilead. In those days and in that time," says the LORD, "The iniquity of Israel shall be sought, but there shall be none; and the sins of Judah, but they shall not be found; for I will pardon those whom I preserve."

Resurrection/Gathering at Christ's Coming

First Thess. 4:15, 16 For this we say to you by the word of the Lord, that we who are alive and remain until the coming of the Lord will by no means precede those who are asleep. For the Lord Himself will descend from heaven with a shout, with the voice of an archangel, and with the trumpet of God. And the dead in Christ will rise first.

Matt. 24:30, 31 And they will see the Son of Man coming on the clouds of heaven with power and great glory. And He will send His angels with a great sound of a trumpet, and they will gather together His elect from the four winds, from one end of heaven to the other.

Psa. 50:3-5 Our God shall come, and shall not keep silent; a fire shall devour before Him, and it shall be very tempestuous all around Him. He shall call to the heavens from above, and to the earth, that He may judge His people: "Gather My saints [elect] together to Me, Those who have made a covenant with Me by sacrifice."

Resurrection Before the Rapture/Gathering

Ezek. 37:12-14 "Therefore prophesy and say to them, 'Thus says the Lord GOD: "Behold, O My people, I will open your graves and cause you to come up from your graves, and bring you into the land of Israel. Then you shall know that I am the LORD, when I have opened your graves, O My people, and brought you up from your graves. I will put My Spirit in you, and you shall live, and I will place you in your own land. Then you shall know that I, the LORD, have spoken it and performed it," says the LORD.'"

Resurrection/Gathering at Last Trumpet/End of Days

Matt. 24:30, 31 Son of Man coming on the clouds of heaven with power and great glory. And He will send His angels with a great sound of a trumpet,* and they will gather together His elect from the four winds, from one end of heaven to the other. *(Rev. 1:10 I heard behind me a loud voice, as of a trumpet, I am the Alpha and Omega…)

Dan. 12:13 But you, go your way till the end; for you shall rest, and will arise to your inheritance at the end of the days.

John 11:24 Martha said to Him, "I know that he will rise again in the resurrection at the last day."

John 6:39 This is the will of the Father who sent Me, that of all He has given Me I should lose nothing, but should raise it up at the last day.

First Cor. 15:52 …in a moment, in the twinkling of an eye, at the last trumpet. For the trumpet will sound, and the dead will be raised incorruptible, and we shall be changed.

First Thess. 4:16, 17 For the Lord Himself will descend from heaven with a shout, with the voice of an archangel, and with the trumpet of God. And the dead in Christ will rise first. Then we who are alive and remain shall be caught up together with them in the clouds to meet the Lord in the air…

Isa. 27:12, 13 And it shall come to pass in that day that the LORD will thresh, from the channel of the River to the Brook of Egypt; and you will be gathered one by one, O you children of Israel. So it shall be in that day: the great trumpet will be blown; they will come, who are about to perish in the land of Assyria, and they who are outcasts in the land of Egypt, and shall worship the LORD in the holy mount at Jerusalem.

Resurrection and Indignation/Judgment on the Nations

John 5:25, 27 Most assuredly, I say to you, the hour is coming, and now is, when the dead will hear the voice of the Son of God; and those who hear will live... and has given Him authority to execute judgment also, because He is the Son of Man.

Isa. 26:20, 21 Come, my people, enter your chambers, And shut your doors behind you; Hide yourself, as it were, for a little moment, Until the indignation is past. For behold, the LORD comes out of His place to punish the inhabitants of the earth for their iniquity...

Isa. 24:21 It shall come to pass in that day that the LORD will punish on high the host of exalted ones, And on the earth the kings of the earth.

Isa. 2:19 They shall go into the holes of the rocks, and into the caves of the earth, from the terror of the LORD and the glory of His majesty, when He arises to shake the earth mightily.

Isa. 13:2-13 Lift up a banner [see Isa. 11:12] on the high mountain, raise your voice to them; wave your hand, that they may enter the gates of the nobles. I have commanded My sanctified ones [e.g. Jude 1:14 "Behold, the Lord comes with ten thousands of His saints,"] I have also called My mighty ones for My anger– those who rejoice in My exaltation. The noise of a multitude in the mountains, like that of many people! A tumultuous noise of the kingdoms of nations gathered together! The LORD of hosts musters the army for battle. They come from a far country, from the end of heaven– the LORD and His weapons of indignation, to destroy the whole land. Wail, for the day of the LORD is at hand! It will come as destruction from the Almighty. Therefore all hands will be limp, every man's heart will melt, and they will be afraid. Pangs and sorrows will take hold of them; they will be in pain as a woman in childbirth; they will be amazed at one another; their faces will be like flames. Behold, the day of the LORD comes, cruel, with both wrath and fierce anger, to lay the land desolate; and He will destroy its sinners from it. For the stars of heaven and their constellations will not give their light; the sun will be darkened in its going forth, and the moon will not cause its light to shine. I will punish the world for its evil, and the wicked for their iniquity; I will halt the arrogance of the proud, and will lay low the haughtiness of the terrible. I will make a mortal more rare than fine gold, a man more than the golden wedge of Ophir. Therefore I will shake the heavens, and the earth will move out of her place, in the wrath of the LORD of hosts and in the day of His fierce anger.

Isa. 66:15, 16 For behold, the LORD will come with fire and with His chariots, like a whirlwind, to render His anger with fury, and His rebuke with flames of fire. For by fire and by His sword The LORD will judge all flesh; and the slain of the LORD shall be many.

Matt. 24:29, 30 Immediately after the tribulation of those days the sun will be darkened, and the moon will not give its light; the stars will fall from heaven, and the powers of the heavens will be shaken. Then the sign of the Son of Man will appear in heaven, and then all the tribes of the earth will mourn, and they will see the Son of Man coming on the clouds of heaven with power and great glory.

Second Thess. 1:7, 8 When the Lord Jesus is revealed from heaven with His mighty angels, in flaming fire taking vengeance on those who do not know God, and on those who do not obey the gospel of our Lord Jesus Christ.

Rev. 6:15-17 And the kings of the earth, the great men, the rich men, the commanders, the mighty men, every slave and every free man, hid themselves in the caves and in the rocks of the mountains, and said to the mountains and rocks, "Fall on us and hide us from the face of Him who sits on the throne and from the wrath of the Lamb! For the great day of His wrath has come, and who is able to stand?"

Psa. 18:7-13 Then the earth shook and trembled; the foundations of the hills also quaked and were shaken, because He was angry. Smoke went up from His nostrils, and devouring fire from His mouth; coals were kindled by it. He bowed the heavens also, and came down with darkness under His feet. And He rode upon a cherub, and flew; He flew upon the wings of the wind. He made darkness His secret place; His canopy around Him was dark waters and thick clouds of the skies. From the brightness before Him, His thick clouds passed with hailstones and coals of fire. The LORD thundered from heaven, and the Most High uttered His voice, hailstones and coals of fire.

Psa. 18:14-22 He sent out His arrows and scattered the foe, lightnings in abundance, and He vanquished them. Then the channels of the sea were seen, the foundations of the world were uncovered At Your rebuke, O LORD, at the blast of the breath of Your nostrils. He sent from above, He took me; He drew me out of many waters. He delivered me from my strong enemy, from those who hated me, for they were too strong for me. They confronted me in the day of my calamity, but the LORD was my support. He also brought me out into a broad place; He delivered me because He delighted in me. The LORD rewarded me according to my righteousness; According to the cleanness of my hands He has recompensed me. For I have kept the ways of the LORD, and have not wickedly departed from my God. For all His judgments were before me, and I did not put away His statutes from me.

Rev. 16:13-21 And I saw three unclean spirits like frogs coming out of the mouth of the dragon, out of the mouth of the beast, and out of the mouth of the false prophet. For they are spirits of demons, performing signs, which go out to the kings of the earth and of the whole world, to gather them to the battle of that great day of God Almighty. "Behold, I am coming as a thief. Blessed is he who watches, and keeps his garments, lest he walk naked and they see his shame." And they gathered them together to the place called in Hebrew, Armageddon. Then the seventh angel poured out his bowl into the air, and a loud voice came out of the temple of heaven, from the throne, saying, "It is done!" And there were noises and thunderings and lightnings; and there was a great earthquake, such a mighty and great earthquake as had not occurred since men were on the earth. Now the great city was divided into three parts, and the cities of the nations fell. And great Babylon was remembered before God, to give her the cup of the wine of the fierceness of His wrath. Then every island fled away, and the mountains were not found. And great hail from heaven fell upon men, each hailstone about the weight of a talent. Men blasphemed God because of the plague of the hail, since that plague was exceedingly great.

Rev. 19:17-21 Then I saw an angel standing in the sun; and he cried with a loud voice, saying to all the birds that fly in the midst of heaven, "Come and gather together for the supper of the great God, that you may eat the flesh of kings, the flesh of captains, the flesh of mighty men, the flesh of horses and of those who sit on them, and the flesh of all people, free and slave, both small and great."

And I saw the beast, the kings of the earth, and their armies, gathered together to make war against Him who sat on the horse and against His army. Then the beast was captured, and with him the false prophet who worked signs in his presence, by which he deceived those who received the mark of the beast and those who worshiped his image. These two were cast alive into the lake of fire burning with brimstone. And the rest were killed with the sword which proceeded from the mouth of Him who sat on the horse. And all the birds were filled with their flesh.

Jer. 4:20-31 Destruction upon destruction is cried, for the whole land is plundered. Suddenly my tents are plundered, and my curtains in a moment. How long will I see the standard, and hear the sound of the trumpet? "For My people are foolish, they have not known Me. They are silly children, and they have no understanding. They are wise to do evil, But to do good they have no knowledge." I beheld the earth, and indeed it was without form, and void; and the heavens, they had no light. I beheld the mountains, and indeed they trembled, and all the hills moved back and forth. I beheld, and indeed there was no man, and all the birds of the heavens had fled. I beheld, and indeed the fruitful land was a wilderness, and all its cities were broken down at the presence of the LORD, By His fierce anger.

For thus says the LORD: "The whole land shall be desolate; yet I will not make a full end. For this shall the earth mourn, and the heavens above be black, because I have spoken. I have purposed and will not relent, nor will I turn back from it. The whole city shall flee from the noise of the horsemen and bowmen. They shall go into thickets and climb up on the rocks. Every city shall be forsaken, and not a man shall dwell in it. And when you are plundered, what will you do? Though you clothe yourself with crimson, though you adorn yourself with ornaments of gold, though you enlarge your eyes with paint, In vain you will make yourself fair; your lovers will despise you; they will seek your life. For I have heard a voice as of a woman in labor, The anguish as of her who brings forth her first child, The voice of the daughter of Zion bewailing herself; She spreads her hands, saying, 'Woe is me now, for my soul is weary Because of murderers!'"

Jer. 50:21-23 "Go up against the land of Merathaim, against it, and against the inhabitants of Pekod. Waste and utterly destroy them," says the LORD, "and do according to all that I have commanded you. A sound of battle is in the land, and of great destruction. How the hammer of the whole earth has been cut apart and broken! How Babylon has become a desolation among the nations! I have laid a snare for you."

In Conclusion

We have seen the actual rapture verses and multiple witnesses. There is no mystery verse needed. We have seen that the resurrection will occur, followed by a gathering and hiding away of those who are in Christ - from the House of Israel and the House of Judah - to be protected from Jesus' fiery wrath when he returns. The event known as the rapture clearly happens after the tribulation of those days. There is no Pre-Tribulation rapture. The Pre-Tribulation rapture doctrine has distorted the many verses that speak clearly of the Lord's return.

CHAPTER EIGHT
First Century Expectations of the End of the Age
- Chris Steinle

The Hope of the Pharisees

What were the end time events anticipated by the God fearing people in the time of Christ? Ancient Hebrew studies scholar Emil Schürer noted eleven elements of Jewish eschatology from the Second Temple Period through the Apostolic Age. These elements are listed below in roughly the order in which they occur in the pseudepigraphical books of this time period - especially the *Fourth Book of Ezra*[29], the *Apocalypse of Baruch*[30], and the *Assumption of Moses*[31].

1. The last tribulation and perplexity.
2. Elijah as the forerunner.
3. The appearing of the Messiah.
4. The last attack of the hostile powers.
5. Destruction of the hostile powers.
6. Renovation of Jerusalem.
7. Gathering of the dispersed.
8. The kingdom of glory in Palestine.
9. Renovation of the world.
10. The general resurrection.
11. The last judgment - Eternal salvation and condemnation.

It is important to note, especially in studying the rapture (which is not mentioned above), that a *resurrection of the righteous*, or *resurrection of the just*, was expected to occur around the time of the *gathering of the dispersed.*[32]

All of these events could be said to represent the pieces of the great end time puzzle. The goal for students of eschatology is to assemble these events so that the overall picture agrees with Bible prophecy. Most students of biblical eschatology agree that the resurrection is the first event anticipated after the time of tribulation. The Apostle Paul states very clearly that the rapture will not precede the resurrection of *those who have fallen asleep.*

Pre-Tribulation proponents often assert the imminence of Christ's return as a primary reason why a recognizable Great Tribulation could not precede the Second Coming. But up until the twentieth century an imminent return could not work in the Pre-Tribulation model either. The Jewish presence (or control) of Jerusalem was a logical prerequisite within the Pre-Tribulation rapture doctrine. These Pre-Tribulation doctrinal assumptions being:

1. The end time events contained in Revelation occur after the rapture; and,
2. The end time events described in Revelation occur within a seven-year time span; and,
3. The Antichrist will enter the Temple 3 1/2 years after the rapture.

Therefore, the Jews must have either taken control of the Temple Mount or be so close to gaining control of Jerusalem that the rapture might commence at any moment.

According to this typical Pre-Tribulation interpretation of Revelation, the rapture was not imminent between the years 70 AD and 1800 AD. The rapture could not have happened during that time because the Jews did not control the land of Israel. Thus, a Temple could not have been built during that time. Furthermore, the procurement of the Temple real estate, planning, and construction of the Temple, are still unlikely to be accomplished within a 3 1/2 year period - making an imminent rapture unrealistic until such time as the Temple project is nearly or actually under construction.

But finally, in the early 1800s, at the hope of the formation of a Jewish nation, some Christians began to expect an imminent return of the Lord prior to the time of tribulation. This may sound strange, but up until that point in time, the Church *strongly* rejected the idea that Jesus would return before the tribulation. Consider the following quote from John Calvin's *Commentary of the Second Epistle to the Thessalonians*.

Begin quote - "On the other hand, those false prophets whom Paul expenses, while they ought to have kept men's minds in suspense, bid them feel assured of his speedy advent, that they might not be wearied out with the irksomeness of delay." "Let no man deceive you." That they may not groundlessly promise themselves the arrival in so short a time of the joyful day of redemption, he presents to them a melancholy prediction as to the future scattering of the Church. This discourse entirely corresponds with that which Christ held in the presence of his disciples, when they had asked him respecting the end of the world. For he exhorts them to prepare themselves for enduring hard conflicts, (Matt. 24:6) and after he has discoursed of the most grievous and previously unheard of calamities, by which the earth was to be reduced almost to a desert, he adds, that the "end is not yet", but that "these things are the beginnings of sorrows". In the same way, Paul declares that believers must exercise warfare for a long period, before gaining a triumph."[33] - end quote

Few references occur in the writings of the Church Fathers to a Pre-Tribulation rapture. In fact, the idea was always quickly dropped. And a Pre-Tribulation rapture never became a source of debate among church leaders, never surfaced in any of the great councils, nor did it make its way into any creed or statement of faith - prior to the late 20th century. The reason why these infrequent references to a Pre-Tribulation rapture were often quickly contradicted by the Fathers themselves is that the *imminence of the tribulation* was recognized as an essential element of the Second Coming.

There is a good case to be made that the first resurrection is not *the general resurrection* of the dead which will immediately precede that *last judgment* - the Great White Throne Judgment. Paul specifically mentions the glorification of those left alive who are in Christ. Only those will be transformed, together with the resurrected dead. It would then stand to reason that only the just would likewise be raised in this resurrection at Christ's Second Coming. The reality of a first and second resurrection is verified by Revelation Chapter 20. The second death will have no power over those who have been glorified immediately after the first resurrection.

Because the scope of this book only covers the time up until the onset of the Millennium, it is this first resurrection (presumably the resurrection of the just) which we will discuss in some detail. We will also build the case throughout this study that the meeting in the air at the time of the rapture is the *gathering of the dispersed*.

Furthermore, we will submit that the *kingdom of glory in Palestine* and the *Renovation of the world* also take place at this same time and are not separated by a gap in time. Nor do they involve two separate groups of people, except that some have been resurrected and some will have remained alive until the time of the rapture. The authors believe the Bible supports the conclusion that these remaining events will transpire in the same Day of the Lord.

Christ's First Coming marked the beginning of the Messianic Age, prompting the Apostles to expect the supernatural appearing of the eighth event on the list above, *the kingdom of glory in Palestine*. Jesus gave the parable of the Minas *because He was near Jerusalem and because they thought the kingdom of God would appear immediately*. Just prior to Christ's ascension the Disciples asked, *"Lord, are you at this time going to restore the kingdom to Israel?"* The Jews of the first century didn't foresee the events of the last days unfolding in a long, drawn out manner. These unfulfilled pieces of the Messianic puzzle were not only presumed to be supernatural and apocalyptic; they were also expected to appear suddenly, quickly. The authors will demonstrate that the Bible calls for a number of these end time events to occur/appear on a literal Day of the Lord – the Day of the Lord's Second Coming.

Saul, who was called Paul, was a Pharisee before he was a Christian.

But this I confess to you, that according to the Way which they call a sect, so I worship the God of my fathers, believing all things which are written in the Law and in the Prophets. I have hope in God, (which they themselves also accept), that there will be a resurrection of the dead, both of the just and the unjust. Acts 24:14, 15

On more than one occasion, Paul defended himself against the Jewish authorities by stating his hope in the resurrection of the dead.

But perceiving that one group were Sadducees and the other Pharisees, Paul began crying out in the Council, "Brethren, I am a Pharisee, a son of Pharisees; I am on trial for the hope and resurrection of the dead!" As he said this, there occurred a dissension between the Pharisees and Sadducees, and the assembly was divided. For the Sadducees say that there is no resurrection, nor an angel, nor a spirit, but the Pharisees acknowledge them all. Acts 23:6-8

In both of these passages above, Paul stated that the hope of the Pharisees was their hope in the resurrection of the dead. But what did the Pharisees expect the resurrection to entail? Can we know when the resurrection would occur and who would be involved? In fact, the Sadducees' position died out and became more or less irrelevant after the destruction of the Temple in 70 A.D. Today's Judaism is predominantly based on the Pharisaic view and has been passed down in the writings of the rabbis. From these writings, and by the teaching of leading rabbis of today, we can understand the concepts of the Pharisees in the time of Christ.

These Jewish sources teach that the purpose of the resurrection is to provide a setting for man to be judged for sins committed in his mortal state. This belief springs from the opinion that the body and soul cannot be adequately judged independently and, therefore, must be reunited; which requires the resurrection of the body.[34]

Of note:
- A resurrection straight into the World of Souls without providing a time on the earth was not expected, and would not accomplish the intended purpose of a second season of mortality according to the rabbis.
- The resurrection of the body, only to leave the earth immediately thereafter, likewise, would not provide the time of bodily judgment anticipated by the rabbis.
- To the contrary, the resurrection prophesied by Paul is immediately followed by the change to immortality – into the image of Christ's glorified body, which is immutable and therefore could not be punished according to the rabbis' expectations.

Chapter 10 of Sanhedrin, *Mishnah* One, reads, "All Israel will have a portion in the world to come, for it says, "Your people, all of them righteous, shall possess the land for ever; They are the shoot that I planted, my handiwork in which I glory" (Isaiah 60:21).[35] *Mishna* 2,2a even goes so far as to say that, "He who maintains that resurrection is not a biblical doctrine…[will] have no portion in the world to come."[36]

Traditional Judaism continues to refer to the afterlife as the World to Come (Olam HaBa).

FIRST CENTURY EXPECTATIONS OF THE END OF THE AGE

The Afterlife in Modern Jewish Thought

For the sake of understanding the hope of first century Pharisees and how it compares to the Christian hope, it is helpful to know what is taught by today's Jewish rabbis.

Using the terms generally employed by the Modern Jewish community: When a person dies it takes some time for the soul to disengage from their mortal body. The soul might hover in close proximity to their dead body for days as it (re)adjusts to its spiritual (disembodied) state. As time goes by the soul feels more accustomed to the spiritual state and ventures evermore heavenward. (This appears to be contradiction because the soul is also supposed to be in Gehenna during this time. See below) The bereaved are encouraged to pray for their beloved departed to adjust quickly to the new environment.

In the meantime, the departed soul remembers what life was like in the World of Souls before it was united with a body. Souls are thought to exist before birth because they contain the essence of God, and therefore must be immortal like God.

Simultaneously with the soul's departure, the soul is thought to be bound for a time in Gehenna - a kind of holding tank for departed souls. Not the Christian idea of Hell, but a type of purgatory where the soul is purged of its mortal inclinations. It is said that most souls only require twelve months to be purified and then go on to Gan Eden, some kind of non-physical paradise (Garden of Eden).

The bereaved are encouraged to pray for the souls of the departed, for a quick cleansing from the soul's defilement while on earth. These prayers are to end after eleven months because it would be shameful to assume that any soul was so wicked as to require more than eleven months in Gehenna. Particularly evil souls, who indulged in especially vile sins while on earth, remain stuck in Gehenna. This is thought to concern only the worst of souls who refused to repent or who were disqualified from Gan Eden by expressly transgressing a few conditions established by the rabbis.

Since the belief in the immortality of the soul opens the door to reincarnation, some rabbis teach that people might be made to come back into this world to correct misbehavior or omissions from their previous life. For instance, if someone needed to overcome a particular sin; or, if they had not been given the opportunity to be challenged in a certain area of life (e.g. someone died too young to prove themselves.)

At some time in the future, known only to God, the dead are required to rejoin their bodies at the resurrection of the dead. As stated above, this is only for the purpose of judgment. The soul would never choose to leave its spiritual state because it is perfectly happy in Gan Eden. After the resurrection, the soul will leave the body and spend eternity in the World of Souls.

It can be seen at once that these Jewish beliefs about life after death share components of Dualism and Catholicism. The former undoubtedly affected first century Jewish thought in the time of Christ and beyond. The Dualistic aspect of the late Second Temple era will be discussed later in chapters.

If Modern Judaism was indeed formulated before the time of the Talmudic writings, then Catholicism's adoption of purgatory was yet subsequent to the Pharisaic notion of Gehenna. The fact that the Book to the Hebrews specifically uses the Jewish term, *World to Come*, adds credence that these notions about the afterlife were indeed present at the time of Christ. *For He has not put the <u>world to come</u>, of which we speak, in subjection to angels. Heb. 2:5.*

But as an Apostle, Paul was given the mind of Christ to understand the true wisdom of God. The Pauline epistles contain several passages correcting and refuting Gnostic and Pharisaical thought. Below are just a few of Paul's arguments against his former Pharisaic position.

- *The spiritual is not first, but the natural* – in opposition to the notion of the pre-existence of the soul.
- *We will not be found naked but further clothed* – in opposition to an ethereal or nebulous spiritual existence (disembodied spirits, or World of Souls).[37]
- *To be absent from the body is to present with the Lord* – in opposition to spending a season in Gehenna before entering into Gan Eden.

As we will see when studying Paul's philosophy about the spiritual realm, he believed that spiritual bodies and a glorified earth would both possess some enduring form. Whereas, the notion of the World of Souls seems quite similar to the Eastern Mystical idea of elevated consciousness - a spiritual realm *without form and void*. Paul, indeed believed along with Pharisees in the hope of the resurrection, but rejected any such ethereal concept of a bodiless soul existing only in the mind of God, with no dimensional definition.

The hope of a ransom from sin was realized when Jesus laid down his life for the sins of the world. This hope has already been realized in the forgiveness of sins, the deliverance from judgment, and Christ's righteousness imputed to those who believe. But there is another hope which has not yet been realized, the hope of glory. This unrealized hope in a future transformation into the glorious state of existence is part of the knowledge of our salvation.

For we were saved in this hope, but hope that is seen is not hope; for why does one still hope for what he sees? But if we hope for what we do not see, we eagerly wait for it with perseverance. Rom. 8:24, 25

Surely God's people should understand what they are hoping for in order to eagerly wait for this future glorification. The Apostles each acknowledged that our position and fellowship with Christ is already established. These are realized blessings and part of the grace which we have already received. In this sense, Christians are already partakers of *every spiritual blessing in Christ.* Nevertheless we don't yet see ourselves, or the world, fully conformed to the image of Christ or creation restored. It is an unscriptural and sad position to deny that the earth will be restored as the Bible states. It is tantamount to denying the resurrection because they are both correlated with Christ's appearing.

Furthermore, Paul spends a great deal of time detailing the resurrection, the rapture, and the restoration of all things. Paul is the fountainhead of apostolic knowledge of the coming glorification, giving the most detailed account of the glorification process in his first letter to the Corinthians. *Reclaiming the Rapture* examines most of the fifteenth chapter, along with commentary exploring Paul's discourse on the resurrection and transformation of the body.

Paul wrote most prolifically about our justification by faith and Christ's imputed life and righteousness. But he was also very excited about the Second Coming and the restoration. This restoration consisted of the redemption of the physical body, the redemption of the body of Christ, that is, the Commonwealth of Israel, and the restoration of all things.

The best way to study these supernatural events is to follow the flow of thought within Paul's longest discourse on the subject of the dimensional transformation. This study begins below, laying the foundation for the Bible's own multidimensional adventure; which, along with Christ's appearing should be the object of every Christian's hope.

In keeping with his upbringing as a PK (Pharisee's kid) Paul rebuked those who denied a future resurrection in Chapter 15 of his first letter to the Corinthians.

Christian Belief in the Resurrection

The opening verses of First Corinthians Chapter 15 constitute a certification of Christ's resurrection. The verses that follow firmly establish that believing in God's ability to perform a bodily resurrection is essential to Christian doctrine; that in fact, the dead do rise; and that, in fact, Jesus was raised in a glorified body.

Now if Christ is preached that He has been raised from the dead, how do some among you say that there is no resurrection of the dead? But if there is no resurrection of the dead, then Christ is not risen. And if Christ is not risen, then our preaching is empty and your faith is also empty. Yes, and we are found false witnesses of God, because we have testified of God that He raised up Christ, whom He did not raise up—if in fact the dead do not rise. For if the dead do not rise, then Christ is not risen. And if Christ is not risen, your faith is futile; you are still in your sins! Then also those who have fallen asleep in Christ have perished. If in this life only we have hope in Christ, we are of all men the most pitiable.

15:20 But now Christ has been raised from the dead, the first fruits of those who are asleep.

Paul begins his change of focus from Jesus' resurrection to the *resurrection of the dead* by making a distinction between the two. This is necessary from a technical standpoint in order to prove that Christ's resurrection did not fully satisfy what Paul is about to designate *"the last enemy"* - death. Even though Christ had risen, the last enemy has still not been defeated with regard to *"those who are asleep."* Thus, the need to make the distinction that this last enemy remains undefeated, even after Christ's own resurrection. Verses 21 through 23 meticulously differentiate these two resurrections. This distinction is initially made by calling Christ's resurrection the *"first fruits"* and classifying it separately from the resurrection of the rest of the dead - *"those who are asleep"* in the language of Second Thessalonians Chapter Four.

15:21 For since by a man came death, by a man also came the resurrection of the dead.

Paul points out that Christ has been given the power and honor of being the initiator of the *resurrection of the dead*. Jesus said, *"Because I live, you shall live also."* Jesus also declared in John Chapter Five;

"Most assuredly, I say to you, the hour is coming, and now is, when the dead will hear the voice of the Son of God; and those who hear will live. For as the Father has life in Himself, so He has granted the Son to have life in Himself and has given Him authority to execute judgment also, because He is the Son of Man. Do not marvel at this; for the hour is coming in which all who are in the graves will hear His voice and come forth—those who have done good, to the resurrection of life, and those who have done evil, to the resurrection of condemnation." John 5:25-29

15:22 For as in Adam all die, so also in Christ all will be made alive.

The fuller development of Paul's thought on this subject is found in Romans 5:23-29.

"Therefore, just as through one man sin entered the world, and death through sin, and thus death spread to all men, because all sinned—

(For until the law sin was in the world, but sin is not imputed when there is no law. Nevertheless death reigned from Adam to Moses, even over those who had not sinned according to the likeness of the transgression of Adam, who is a type of Him who was to come. But the free gift is not like the offense. For if by the one man's offense many died, much more the grace of God and the gift by the grace of the one Man, Jesus Christ, abounded to many. And the gift is not like that which came through the one who sinned. For the judgment which came from one offense resulted in condemnation, but the free gift which came from many offenses resulted in justification. For if by the one man's offense death reigned through the one, much more those who receive abundance of grace and of the gift of righteousness will reign in life through the One, Jesus Christ.) Therefore, as through one man's offense judgment came to all men, resulting in condemnation, even so through one Man's righteous act the free gift came to all men, resulting in justification of life. For as by one man's disobedience many were made sinners, so also by one Man's obedience many will be made righteous."

15:23 But each in his own order: Christ the first fruits, after that those who are Christ's at His coming,

Paul adds a further distinction by placing these two resurrections in sequence; "first" - and then "after." Notice Paul's use of the term *"first fruits"* rather than referring to the "first resurrection" and "second resurrection." Paul is careful not to call Christ's resurrection the first resurrection because, technically, the first resurrection *is* the *resurrection of the dead* which occurs in First Thessalonians. (Recall from study of first century expectation above that this first resurrection was expected to be the resurrection of God's people - the just.) The second resurrection (Revelation 20:5) is what was designated by Schürer (above) to be the *general resurrection* before the *last judgment*.

It is also important to note that Paul's *order* only consists of two categories; Christ, and those who are Christ's at His coming. This would infer that the resurrection of many seen in Jerusalem at the time of the crucifixion was not considered to be one of the two major resurrections which are the subject of Old Testament prophecy.

They were not raised from the dead at His coming, but at His crucifixion. This point is made in response to those who would use this passage as proof of multiple resurrections beyond the two specifically mentioned.

Praise be to the God and Father of our Lord Jesus Christ! In his great mercy he has given us new birth into a living hope through the resurrection of Jesus Christ from the dead, and into an inheritance that can never perish, spoil or fade. This inheritance is kept in heaven for you, who through faith are shielded by God's power until the coming of the salvation that is ready to be revealed in the last time.   1 Peter 1:3-5

That coming salvation is that same future salvation that Paul said we eagerly await. We were saved in the hope of the restoration of all things.

CHAPTER NINE
Revelation is Thematic - Not Chronological
- Doug Hamp

Part of the challenge of understanding the day of the Lord and its timing is due to a tendency to interpret the book of Revelation chronologically rather than thematically. Though there is some chronology in the book, it is primarily laid out thematically. What that means is that rather than view the seals, trumpets and bowls as chronological events that come one after the other in future time, they represent the order in which the future judgments were communicated to John. John was shown in a series of visions events that "were, are, and will be". The order they are placed in the book is the order that they were communicated to him and not necessarily the order in which they will actually play out in the world.

Imagine John being given a tour of a television control room. Before him there are dozens of screens. All the scenes of a particular show are being shot at the same time. For the sake of illustration, let's imagine that the show has five distinct scenes. Each scene has separate cameras and cameraman to capture it. John merely sees the video feed. Each scene is complex and requires varying camera angles to appreciate the complexity. Some cameras are placed above the set to get a wide angle – top-down approach. Other cameras are zoomed in on the faces of the main characters. Finally, other cameras are constantly panning to give the greater comprehension.

The book of Revelation is essentially laid out in such a fashion. There are a certain number of events that take place, but with several different camera angles we, the readers, can get several perspectives.

All the Mountains and Islands Flee Away

As evidence of these different camera angles, we turn to Revelation 16:20: ***Every island*** *vanished, and the* ***mountains*** *could no longer be found.* Rev. 16:20 ISV

REVELATION IS THEMATIC – NOT CHRONOLOGICAL

Imagine the kind of destruction that planet earth is going to experience when every island and every mountain vanish and disappear! When even just one earthquake happens on one part of the earth, there is incredible damage to buildings and great loss of life. The 9.0 earthquake that happened in the spring of 2011 in Japan caused phenomenal damage (mostly from the tsunami that followed). What will happen when every island and mountain is moved from its place? This is clearly an extinction level event that is coming upon the planet – that is to say, it will not be repeated. The mini-apocalypse in Isaiah 24 describes how earth will be completely rocked to such an extent that it will "fall and not rise again."

The earth is **utterly shattered**, the earth is split apart, the earth is **violently shaken**. The earth **reels** to and fro like a drunkard; it **sways** like a hut; its transgression lies so heavy upon it, that it **falls, never to rise again**. Isa. 24:19, 20 ISV

Given the absolute finality of the parallel language of these two passages we must conclude that they are referring to the same event. The earthquake spoken of in Isaiah is so massive that the earth is down for the count, "never to rise again." We must conclude that the Isaiah 24 event is the same as the Revelation 16 event where *there was a great earthquake, such a mighty and great earthquake as had not occurred since men were on the earth. Rev. 16:18* Certainly all of the islands and all of the mountains disappearing would qualify for that event.

However, Revelation 6 also says, ***every mountain and island was moved from its place.*** Rev. 6:14 ISV How could it be that every mountain and island can be moved **twice**? If we think that they can, then we are not truly considering the enormity of such an event. Imagine all of the mountains crumbling around your home! If you live on an island, imagine it falling into the ocean! Once that happens, then it cannot happen again. Therefore we see how Revelation 16:20, which is at the end of the tribulation, is the same event as Revelation 6:14.

The word "every" in the case of 'every island and mountain' precludes the event from happening twice. The fact that it says "every" means that once it happens there will be no repeat. Therefore, Revelation 6:14, Revelation 16:20 and Isaiah 24 are the same event.

There are, in fact, many passages that speak of the complete and utter shaking of the mountains in a way that will only happen once.
- *For the day of the LORD of hosts Shall come upon everything proud and lofty, Upon **everything lifted up**– And it shall be brought low– against **all the high mountains**, and against **all the lofty hills**; Isa. 2:12-14 ISV*
- ***He stood up** and **shook** the land; with his stare he startled the nations. The **age-old mountains were shattered,** and the ancient **hilltops bowed** down. His ways are eternal. Hab. 3:6 ISV*
- ***Mountains melt** like wax in the Lord's presence— in the presence of the Lord of all the earth. Psa. 97:5 ISV*
- *I looked at the **mountains**; they were **quaking**, and **all the hills** moved **back** and **forth**. I looked, and no people were there. All the birds of the sky had gone. Jer. 4:24, 25 ISV*
- ***Every island** vanished, and the **mountains** could no longer be found. Rev. 16:20 ISV*

Therefore, Revelation 6:14 is identical to the many descriptions of the ultimate shaking that will take place on planet earth - which will happen in the day that Jesus startles the nations. If we hope to take Revelation 6:14 even remotely literally, as we ought to, then it is impossible that the timing of the passage should be placed anywhere but at the day Jesus comes back - at the very end.

According to the passage, everyone on earth understands that their end has come. The rich, poor, powerful, and slaves – everyone who is on the earth will recognize it, and they call it the day of the Lord – as revealed by the Lord to John.

Then the kings of the earth, the important people, the generals, the rich, the powerful, and all the slaves and free people concealed themselves in caves and among the rocks in the mountains. They told the mountains and rocks, "Fall on us and hide us from the face of the one who sits on the throne and from the wrath of the lamb. For the great day of their wrath has come, and who is able to endure it?" Rev. 6:15-17 ISV

Keep in mind that in Revelation 16 the same people are marching against Jerusalem ostentatiously, attempting to make war against Jesus (Rev. 16:14).

REVELATION IS THEMATIC – NOT CHRONOLOGICAL

For they are spirits of demons, performing signs, which go out to the kings of the earth and of the whole world, to gather them to the battle of that great day of God Almighty. Rev. 16:14

They undoubtedly do not understand what they are truly getting into in Revelation 16. However, in Revelation 6, reality quickly becomes apparent – so much so that they go running into the caves, for the rocks to fall on them, and readily admit, *"For **the great day of their wrath has come**, and who is able to endure it?"* Rev. 6:15-17 ISV

Are we to believe that the mighty men of the earth are throwing in the towel in Revelation Six and fully admit that the day of Jesus' wrath has come, but in chapter 16 they think that they can actually defeat him? The simple answer is that the book of Revelation is thematically arranged so that the chronology of events is not in conflict with the order in which these events occur in the book.

Commentator Thomas Constable has suggested that Revelation 6 is simply hyperbole, in other words, exaggeration. He suggests that the men on the earth *supposed* the end of the world to have come though it really hadn't.

"Evidently the sky will **appear** to split and roll back in two opposite directions (cf. Isa. 34:4). The universe will **seem** to be coming apart. Apparently the opening of the sky will give earth-dwellers a glimpse into the throne-room of heaven (v. 16). Probably the earthquake (v. 12) will cause mountains and islands to rise and fall (cf. Nah. 1:6). The reaction of every category of humanity all over the world is amazing. It indicates that people's perception of God and the Lamb in heaven will be far more terrifying to them than the physical consequences of this judgment. Literal interpretation does not rule out the **use of hyperbole**, which appears at this point. If all the mountains moved out of their places, there would be no places for people to seek to hide. This "great day of their wrath" is the Tribulation, Daniel's seventieth week (cf. Jer. 30:7; Dan. 12:1; Joel 2:2; Matt. 24:21). These people will not turn to God in repentance but from Him in terror (cf. Isa. 2:19, 21; Hos. 10:8; Luke 23:30). By the end of the sixth seal judgment, they will know that what they are experiencing is the outpouring of His wrath. This is the first part of the judgment phase of the day of the Lord (cf. Joel 2:11, 30-31; Isa. 2:10-11, 19-21; 13:8-13; 26:17-19; 34:4, 8; 66:7-9; Jer. 30:6-8; Ezek. 32:7-8; Hos. 10:8; Mic. 4:9-10; Matt. 24:8; 1 Thess. 5:3)."[38] (emphasis mine)

Though Thomas Constable is an excellent commentator, his predisposition to interpreting the book of Revelation chronologically rather than thematically has not allowed him to see the parallels as we have studied. To suggest that hyperbole is being used is complete speculation. John faithfully recorded what the men in the Tribulation will say and do. If they say that it is the day of the Lord, who are we to disagree? If the sky has rolled up, who are we to suggest that it just appears so? If all of the mountains and islands move out of their place, who are we to say it only seems so?

Zephaniah One and Two underscore the conclusion that Revelation 6:14-17, the day of the Lord, is the Second Advent itself; when there will be a great sacrifice of kings and mighty men, when the nations have gathered together and the whole land shall be devoured by fire very suddenly.

It will come about during the Lord's sacrifice that I'll punish the officials, the royal descendants, and all who wear foreign clothing. The **great Day of the Lord** approaches— How it comes, hurrying faster and faster! The sound of the **Day of the Lord** there includes the bitter cry of the mighty soldier. That day will be filled with wrath, a day of trouble and tribulation; a day of desolation and devastation, a **day of doom and gloom**, a day of clouds and shadows…. a day of trumpet and battle cry against fortified cities and **watch towers**. And I'll bring so much distress to people that they will walk around like the blind. Because they have sinned against the Lord, **their blood will be poured out like dust** and their intestines will spill out like manure. Neither their silver nor their gold will deliver them in the **Day of the Lord's** wrath; but the **entire land will be consumed by the fire of his jealousy**, for he will bring the inhabitants of the land to a **sudden** end. **Gather together!** Yes, indeed, gather together, you shameless nation! Before the decree is carried out, before the day flies away like chaff, before the fierce anger of the Lord visits you, before the **Day of the Lord's** wrath surprises you seek the Lord, all you humble people of the land, who do what he commands. Seek righteousness! Seek humility! Maybe you will be **protected in the Day of the Lord's anger**. Zeph. 1:8, 14-18, 2:1-3 ISV.

Angels are Stars

Further demonstration of the book of Revelation being thematically arranged is found in the events of Satan being cast out of heaven in Revelation 12. The dragon taking stars with its tail is the same as the dragon and his angels being cast to the earth.

- *A huge red dragon... its tail swept away one-third of the **stars** in the sky and knocked them down to the **earth**.* Rev.12: 3, ISV
- *The **huge dragon was hurled down**. That ancient serpent, called the Devil and Satan, the deceiver of the whole world, was hurled down to the **earth**, **along with its angels**.* Rev.12: 7-9 ISV

There is no question that there are many symbols in the book of Revelation. However, once we have the key to unlock them, the interpretation follows incredibly literally. The term "stars" is actually a fairly common reference to angels in Scripture. Though we don't know exactly why they are referred to as such, we could speculate it is because they are literally shining, as when the angels shone down on the shepherds to announce the birth of Jesus. Nevertheless, the internal of use of stars in the book of Revelation firmly establishes that "stars" is a reference to angels.

*The **secret meaning** of the seven **stars** that you saw in my right hand and the seven gold lamp stands is this: the **seven stars** are the messengers [angeloi ἄγγελοι] of the seven churches, and the seven lamp stands are the seven churches.* Rev.1:20 ISV

That meaning is further underscored in the book of Job where the sons of God (*benei ha'elohim*) are also called stars. *While the morning stars sang together and all the divine beings shouted joyfully?* Job 38:7 ISV

With the secret meaning revealed to us, we can properly understand the rest of the references to stars as actually being angels in the book of Revelation. In Revelation 9:1 we read of a ***star* that *had fallen* to earth from the sky.** Rev.9:1 ISV

This star cannot simply be a meteorite or asteroid that has fallen to the earth because in the second part of the verse we read that the star *was given the key to the shaft of the bottomless pit.* Rev.9:1 ISV

Unless an asteroid can be given a key, then it must be a reference to an angel. Just a few verses earlier we hear of a great star burning like a torch that falls upon the earth. The star even has a name – Wormwood.

A huge **star** blazing like a torch fell from heaven. It fell on one-third of the rivers and on the springs of water. The name of the **star** is Wormwood... Rev.8:10, 11 ISV

The star in question, or Wormwood by name, is the same star that "had fallen" in Revelation 9:1 which was given the key to the Abyss. We notice that it was a great star and not just a common star – in Revelation 12 the dragon threw his **stars** to the earth and in verse nine it is the dragon, Satan, and his **angels**. Essentially, we have two different camera angles recorded for us. In Chapter 12 the camera angle is from above watching as Satan and his angels fall to the earth. We could almost imagine Michael or one of the angels getting out his camera to film the event. In Chapter Eight the camera angle is on the planet surface with the inhabitants of the earth watching as Satan falls to the earth. To them he looks like *a huge star blazing like a torch fell from heaven.* Rev.8:10 ISV They are the same event but from different vantage points.

The casting out of Satan's angels (stars) in Chapter 12 is referenced in Chapter Six and also in Isaiah 34:

- *The **stars** in the sky fell to the earth like a **fig tree drops** its fruit when it is shaken by a strong wind.* Rev.6:13 ISV
- *And all the **host of heaven** [צְבָא הַשָּׁמַיִם] shall be dissolved, and the heavens shall be rolled together as a scroll: and all **their host** shall fall down, as the leaf falleth off from the vine, and as a **falling fig from the fig tree**.* Isa. 34:4

The stars falling to the ground like figs in Revelation are referred to as the host of heaven falling down in Isaiah. We see that many other places in Scripture the term *tzevah hashamaim* is talking about the armies of heaven. The following scene from First Kings demonstrates the literal meaning this term:

...I saw the Lord, sitting on his throne, and the entire **Heavenly Army** [צְבָא הַשָּׁמַיִם] was standing around him on his right hand and on his left hand. "The Lord asked, 'Who will tempt King Ahab of Israel to attack Ramoth-gilead, so that he will die there?'

And one was saying one thing and one was saying another. But then a **spirit** approached, stood in front of the Lord, and said, 'I will entice him.' "And the Lord asked him, 'How?' "'I will go,' he announced, 'and I will be a deceiving spirit in the mouth of all of his prophets!' So the Lord said, 'You're just the one to deceive him. You will be successful. Go and do it.'" 1 Kings 22:19-22 ISV

Though the phrase "host of heaven / heavenly army" does not always refer to the angelic army, there are many examples that demonstrate that the phrase is commonly referring to angels. In Jeremiah 19 the hosts of heaven are equated with "gods".

...because of all the houses upon whose roofs they have burned incense unto all the **host of heaven** [צְבָא הַשָּׁמַיִם]**, and have poured out drink offerings unto other gods.** Jer. 19:13 KJV

Those "gods," "host of heaven" or "fallen angels" are also referred to as the armies of exalted ones in the heavens in Isaiah 24 which happens at "that time" - a reference to the day of the Lord.

And it will come about at that time, the Lord will punish the **armies** tzevah [צְבָא] of the **exalted ones in the heavens** [הַשָּׁמַיִם], and the rulers of the earth on earth. Isa. 24:21 ISV

Paul writing to the Ephesians makes reference to the reality of the cosmic powers (κοσμοκράτορας *cosmokratoras*). Those cosmic powers, which are all around us, are part of the spiritual forces which are in the heavenly realm, which is a reference to angels and not to balls of gas in outer space.

For our struggle is not against human opponents, but against rulers, authorities, **cosmic powers** in the darkness around us, and evil spiritual forces in the **heavenly realm.** Eph. 6:12 ISV

Now we are prepared to understand what Jesus meant when He said that *the **powers of heaven** will be shaken loose.* Matt. 24:29 ISV He was not referring to the sun, moon, and stars going away. Rather He was referring to the end of the kingdom of Satan.

"For The Great Day Of His Wrath Has Come, And Who Is Able To Stand?" (Rev. 6:17)	And there were loud voices in heaven, saying, "The kingdoms of this world have become [*the kingdoms*] of our Lord and of His Christ, and He shall reign forever and ever!" (Rev. 11:15) (Rev. 11:17) The nations were angry, and Your wrath has come, And the time of the dead, that they should be judged, And that You should reward Your servants the prophets and the saints, And those who fear Your name, small and great, And should destroy those who destroy the earth." (Rev. 11:18)	...They go to the kings of the whole earth and gather them for the war of the great Day of God Almighty. (Rev. 16:14) "See, I am coming like a thief. How blessed is the person who remains alert and keeps his clothes on! He won't have to go naked and let others see his shame." (Rev. 16:15) [day of the Lord = thief in night] Then the seventh angel poured out his bowl into the air, and a loud voice came out of the temple of heaven, from the throne, saying, "It is done!" (Rev. 16:17)

There are other examples which point to the fact that the book of Revelation is arranged thematically rather than chronologically. In Revelation 16 we read that God remembered Babylon and judged her. It seems so brief, and would be almost understated if chapters 17 and 18 did not give fuller details.

"And" versus "Then" in Revelation

We first need to discover that the word "then" which begins the verse in the *New King James Version*[39], *New English Translation*[40], and many other translations, is not actually in the underlying Greek text. The *New English Translation* Bible notes that "Here καί (*kai*) has been translated as "then" to indicate the implied sequence within the narrative." Though the difference is subtle, it does make a difference in how we read the book of Revelation. John is seeing a lot of visions that he connects, not necessarily in a sequence (with the word "then"), but rather with the word "and". The difference is that he is simply telling us the things he saw. He is not suggesting anything about the order in which the events will necessarily occur.

The word "then" implies that first comes A, then comes B, and then comes C, etc. Whereas, "and" simply suggests he saw A and B and C, and the order in which they would come to pass is not stated. The Greek word καί means "and, even, also" – which carry the same meaning. There is, therefore, no justification for translating the word "*kai*" in Revelation, where it begins a sentence, with the word "then" rather than "and."

The Greek word is *kai* [Καὶ] which simply means "and." *Thayer's Greek-English Lexicon*, defines the word as "and, also, even, indeed, but"[41]. According to the *Liddell-Scott-Jones Lexicon of Classical Greek*, it defines "καί": Conjunction, copulative, joining words and sentences, '**and, also**' Adv., '**even, also, just**'"[42] (emphasis mine). The word is almost always translated as "and" in the many other passages where it appears.

- *And* [Καὶ] *he will turn many of the children of Israel to the Lord their God.* Luke 1:16
- *And* [Καὶ] *Zacharias said to the angel, "How shall I know this? For I am an old man, **and** [καὶ] my wife is well advanced in years."* Luke 1:18
- *And* [Καὶ] *the Word became flesh **and** [καὶ] dwelt among us, **and** [καὶ] we beheld His glory, the glory as of the only begotten of the Father, full of grace **and** [καὶ] truth.* John 1:14
- *And* [Καὶ] *He found in the temple those who sold oxen **and** [καὶ] sheep **and** [καὶ] doves, **and** [καὶ] the money changers doing business.* John 2:14

The Greek word *kai* "and" is used all together 5,222 times in the New Testament with the majority occurring in Luke (850 times, 16%), followed by Matthew (720 times 14%), and the book of John coming in fifth place (545 times 10%).

There is another word for "then." If John had wanted to indicate "then" he could have used the word *tote* [Τότε] "Then; at that time," which is used 155 times in the Greek New Testament. It is the simplest way to indicate the transition from one event to another. Out of those 155 times, 89 times the word appears in the book of Matthew, which is 57% of all the New Testament uses.

- ***Then*** [Τότε] *Herod, when he had secretly called the wise men, determined from them what time the star appeared.* Matt. 2:7
- *But Jesus answered and said to him, "Permit it to be so now, for thus it is fitting for us to fulfill all righteousness." **Then** [τότε] he allowed Him.* Matt. 3:15
- *And Jesus said to them, "Can the friends of the bridegroom mourn as long as the bridegroom is with them? But the days will come when the bridegroom will be taken away from them, **and then** [καὶ τότε] they will fast.* Matt. 9:15

The abundance of "then" in Matthew is fairly significant. According to the *Fragments of Papias*, "Matthew put together the oracles [of the Lord] in the Hebrew language, and each one interpreted them as best he could."[43]

In Hebrew, the use of the word "and" (Hebrew "*ve*" written the letter *vav/waw*) is very common; therefore, so is the word "and." The question, then is, why didn't the translators render καί as "and" if that is the translation?

CHAPTER TEN
Paul's Two Scheme Dimensional System
- Chris Steinle

Paul provides enough information throughout his epistles to understand the technical aspects of the rapture and to explain why he chose the Greek word which has been translated as "rapture." The authors reject the proposition that the rapture was something first revealed to the Apostle of the Gentiles. Nevertheless, a wisdom was given to Paul by revelation about how the spiritual realm operates. Peter admitted that some of Paul's teachings were hard to understand. But we need to understand some of his deeper insights in order to view the rapture from Paul's perspective. Spiritual concepts are not necessarily complex; but they are contrary to worldly thinking, so that certain definitions and rules we might be accustomed to using could need to be redefined.

Paul's concepts of material and spiritual existence were far different from the Dualistic ideas made popular by the Greek Philosophers. To appreciate the weight of the Greek influence upon first century Christians, just remember that Paul's epistles were originally written in Greek. The rapture is easier to visualize once we realize that Paul described the same dimensional system throughout his writings. When Paul commented on different forms of existence, he was sharing his knowledge of ontology. According to *Wikipedia*, "Ontology is the philosophical study of the nature of being, becoming, existence or reality, as well as the basic categories of being and their relations."[44]

The Apostle John made an ontological observation in his statement on what "we shall be" in his first letter. *Beloved, now are we the sons of God, and it doth not yet appear what **we shall be**: but we know that, when he shall appear, **we shall be** like him; for we shall see him as he is.* 1 John 3:2

This verse contrasts two forms of appearance. Both of these forms have, or will be, seen. "Appear", by definition, means that something is observable. Because Jesus will appear in glory, we understand that these appearances represent existence in both the natural realm, and in a form beyond the natural realm.

Although the word "metaphysics" has taken on a negative aspect through association with religious spiritualism and existential philosophy, metaphysics examines the form and substance of objects that exist beyond the physical world. We might say - outside of this dimension. This is the very sort of ontological discussion we need to become familiar with in order to recognize and interpret dozens of New Testament verses dealing with the seen and unseen; the natural and the spiritual. Appearances, forms, and schemes are mentioned throughout the gospels and epistles.

The resurrection - the reconstruction and resuscitation of decayed and scattered molecules - is a miracle. But the rapture involves the transition from one state of existence to another. From the natural (physical, material), to the spiritual (glorious) state of existence; nevertheless, retaining some type of metaphysical bodily form.

When the Bible speaks of a spiritual body, it does not mean to imply that the spirit will escape from bodily form and become a disembodied spirit. Platonism, Gnosticism, and Dualism all pit a theoretical perfect spirit against the imperfect elements (matter). Within these philosophies, spirit is nothing more than the opposite of matter. The Gnostics insist that the spirit is real and that the material is less than real. Whereas, modern humanists believe matter to be real, and the spiritual realm to be nothing more than superstition – something that is a matter of personal choice. But the living God of the Bible is Spirit, and He is infinitely more than the opposite of matter.

When we think of body, soul, and spirit, it is logical to contrast the human body, which has form, with the human spirit, which has no visible form. *The Spirit Himself bears witness with our spirit that we are children of God.* Rom. 8:16 Only a few times in the Bible does the Holy Spirit appear to take on a representative form; such as smoke, flames of fire, or the dove at Jesus' Baptism. But generally, when we think of spirit, we have no form or image associated with either the Spirit of the Godhead or the spiritual component of man. So a spiritual body would seem to be an oxymoron.

But spiritual form, or embodiment, is the very concept that the Apostle Paul was expressing when he wrote about the spiritual bodies that we will receive in the instant of the rapture.

Spiritual bodies are heavenly objects, possessing real substance. This spiritual substance is (usually) unseen to the physical eye but is just as real, and even more substantial, than the substance of material things. The spiritual form has an appearance, a form that can be manifested into the material world. Jesus began to manifest His glorified (spiritual) body at the time of the transformation. Yet He showed Himself in a more natural form to a select few after his resurrection.

Now that we have established the biblical concept of spiritual form, we should address some of the errant philosophies plaguing the Christian church today. The spiritual realm is not merely a nebulous World of Souls dwelling in some ethereal cloud. The heavenly state consists of some type of media or substance. Dimensionality of some type will define our heavenly habitat. Otherwise, how might beings in the spiritual realm know where their identity ends and another person or object begins? How would they communicate or have community? Heaven must have dimensionality or else Moses could not have been shown the pattern of the heavenly tabernacle – the heavenly realities.

Carrying this logic further, for activity to occur in heaven, something must move or change. Some recognition of time over which change can be observed is necessary to recognize that something has happened. Life without measurable activity would resemble our definition of death, not the abundant life promised by Christ.

Chapter 15 of First Corinthians devotes several verses to contrasting natural and spiritual bodies. The spiritual form is the more substantial, more enduring, *appearance* of things.

Schemes, Forms, and Appearances

In the following verses Paul described the natural world as a "scheme." The first verse refers to a future transformation of the world - from the natural scheme into another appearance. The second verse comments on the humility of Christ when He took on the scheme of this world.

For the <u>form</u> (Gr. σχῆμα, **schēma**) of this world is passing away. 1 Cor. 7:31b; (also interpreted as; the world in its present form is passing away.)

And being found in <u>appearance</u> (σχήματι, **schēmati**) as a man, He humbled Himself and became obedient to the point of death, even the death of the cross. Phil. 2:8

The appearance (form) of Jesus was changed from His original glorious appearance, to the form of a bondservant (natural man). Jesus took on the scheme of nature. The natural and spiritual schemes are both very real and apparent forms of embodiment.

In the verses above Paul referred to the present natural form of existence as the scheme of this world. Both examples describe a change in outward appearance based on the assumption there is more than one scheme of existence.

Paul also used another term that can be interpreted as "form" or "appearance". It is the Greek word *morphē*. Morph is the root of the English word, metamorphosis; "to change in form or appearance." Both Matthew and Mark use the word μετεμορφώθη *(metemorphōthē)* to describe Jesus' transfiguration. This expression for one of Paul's two schemes of existence is also found in Paul's Letter to the Philippians.

Let this mind be in you which was also in Christ Jesus, who, being in the <u>form</u> μορφῇ (**morphē**) of God, did not consider it robbery to be equal with God, but made Himself of no reputation, taking the form of a bondservant, and coming in the likeness of men. Phil. 2:5-7

This passage, through the end of the third chapter, is a key section for understanding Paul's schemes of existence. We will see shortly that this passage even contains the Greek word which has been interpreted into English as "caught up!"

Mark also used the Greek stem "morph" in his account of the road to Emmaus encounter. *After that, He* (Jesus) *appeared in <u>another form</u>* ἑτέρᾳ μορφῇ *(hetera **morphē**) to two of them as they walked and went into the country.* Mark 16:12

Now we can look at *schēmati* and *morphē* used together to describe our transformation into the spiritual scheme of Jesus' glorified body. Paul calls this a "trans-schematic" transformation.

Who will transform μετασχηματίσει (meta**schēmati**sei) our lowly body that it may be conformed σύμμορφον (sym**morphon**) to His glorious body, according to the working by which He is able even to subdue all things to Himself. Phil. 3:21

Not to belabor the reader with exhaustive Greek studies, please consider the significance of just one more word used prolifically in the New Testament. In the preceding verse we read, "He appeared in another form..." The Greek word for "appeared" is ἐφανερώθη *(ephanerōthē)*. The root word, "***phan***," is where we get the word "phantom." In English we are used to thinking of a phantom as an apparition - something less than real - perhaps like a vision.

But in the nine occurrences of "appeared" (ἐφανερώθη) below, every single one of them relates to a very real transformation between the spiritual and the natural forms of bodily existence.

> Mark 16:14 Afterward He appeared (ephanerōthē) to the eleven
>
> John 21:14 that Jesus was manifested (ephanerōthē) to the disciples
>
> Col. 1:26 but has now been manifested (ephanerōthē) to His saints
>
> 1 Tim. 3:16 God was manifest (ephanerōthē) in the flesh
>
> 1 John 1:2 and the life was manifested (ephanerōthē), and we have seen
>
> 1 John 1:2 was with the Father and was manifested (ephanerōthē) to us
>
> 1 John 3:5 You know that He appeared (ephanerōthē) in order
>
> 1 John 3:8 Son of God was manifested (ephanerōthē), that
>
> 1 John 4:9 In this was manifested (ephanerōthē) the love of God

To conclude this preliminary study of bridging the dimensions, we must not neglect the most famous references to Christ's appearing to the material world; stated below as "appearing" ἐπιφάνειαν *(epiphaneian)*. (Obviously, this is where we get the word "epiphany".)

2 Tim. 4:1 I charge you therefore before God and the Lord Jesus Christ, who will judge the living and the dead at His appearing (epiphaneian) and His kingdom

2 Tim. 4:8 Finally, there is laid up for me the crown of righteousness, which the Lord, the righteous Judge, will give to me on that Day, and not to me only but also to all who have loved His appearing (epiphaneian).

Titus 2:13 looking for the blessed hope and glorious appearing (epiphaneian) of our great God and Savior Jesus Christ.

Above we looked at the two forms of appearance, and the transition from glory into the physical state. Now we will begin to look at the essence of the rapture. We could call the rapture our "transfiguration" into glory; or our transition into the glorious state.

When Christ who is our life appears, then you also will appear with Him in glory. Col. 3:4

For I consider that the sufferings of this present time are not worthy to be compared with the glory which shall be revealed in us. Rom. 8:18

Moreover whom He predestined, these He also called; whom He called, these He also justified; and whom He justified, these He also glorified. Rom. 8:30

Power, Resurrection, and Subjection

What kind of power will be asserted by God when He transforms corrupted matter from a state of entropy - the fallen state - to the state of glorious immortality? This power to manipulate the very fabric of the universe was the most powerful force imaginable in Bible times, and is still being pursued by scientists today. The prophets and Apostles referred to God's exceeding great power as the force by which He would overcome and subdue both the fallen creation and the waywardness of men and angels.

Tethered to the power of the resurrection and the rapture is the power of God to assert His authority over areas of creation that have had, or were perceived to have had, free-wheeling autonomy. Just as decay and mortality will be subdued, that is to say, conformed to its perfect state; God's creatures and creation will be subdued and submit to God's will. This is the very thing we pray for in the Lord's Prayer; *Thy kingdom come, Thy will be done - on earth, as it is in heaven.* Matt. 6:10

The chart below shows the obvious connection between the revealing of God's mighty power, the resurrection/rapture, and the establishment of God's government on the earth. Our corrupted mortal bodies will be subdued under the same divine power. The fact that these three factors appear repeatedly within adjacent passages would also support the conclusion that they occur at the same time; or at least during the same event. The left and center columns are the focus of this chapter on the presence of God's power during the time of the resurrection and rapture.

Correlation of: God's Power, The Resurrection, and Subjection to God's Authority			
Passage	*Power / Working / Ability*	*Resurrection / Transformation*	*Subjection / Authority*
Rom. 1:4	declared to be the Son of God with **power**	…by the **resurrection** from the dead	
1 Cor. 6:14	…by His **power**	God both **raised up** the Lord and will also **raise us up**	
1 Cor. 15:4-58		…**resurrection**…	He puts an **end to all rule and all authority and power**… till He has put all enemies **under His feet**… Now when all things are made **subject to Him**…
Eph. 1:19-22	what is the exceeding greatness of His **power** toward us… according to the working of His mighty **power** which He **worked**	…in Christ when He **raised Him from the dead**…	…far above all principality and power and might and dominion… He put all things **under His feet**

Passage	Power / Working / Ability	Resurrection / Transformation	Subjection / Authority
Phil. 3:10-21	that I may know Him and the **power**... ... according **to the working** by which He is **able**	of His **resurrection**... I may attain to the **resurrection** from the dead... who will **transform** our lowly body... **conformed** to His glorious body	...even to **subdue** all things to Himself
Col. 2:12	through faith in the **working** of God	...in which you also were **raised** with Him ... who **raised** Him **from the dead**	
Rev. 11:17	You have taken Your great **power**		and have begun to **reign**
Rev. 12:10	Now the salvation, and the **power**		the **kingdom** of our God and the **authority** of His Christ have come

Several of these verses apply to the resurrection, but Phil. 3:20, 21 refer expressly to the transformation of our lowly bodies - the very transformation of our bodies that will take place at the resurrection/rapture.

For our citizenship is in heaven, from which we also eagerly wait for the Savior, the Lord Jesus Christ, who will transform our lowly body that it may be conformed to His glorious body, according to the working by which He is able even to subdue all things to Himself.

For those who are in Christ, the forfeiting of mortality in order to be conformed to the image of Christ has only positive connotations. But verse 21 above indicates that from Jesus' perspective, the process involves power and authority going forth from Him in order to subdue our lowly bodies.

We are reminded here of the healing of the woman with the issue of blood by whom Jesus perceived that power had gone out from Him. God's subduing of all of His enemies means rectifying all that was damaged because of sin. The corrupted mortal body of sin must be overcome/subdued by the power of God.

The book of Revelation describes the destructive forces that God will bring upon the earth before its restoration. The appearance of the glory of the Lord will be accompanied by destructive forces such as the world has not known since the beginning. In Romans Chapter Eight, Paul says that creation has been subjected in the hope of being restored. But even though creation has been corrupted by the fall of man into sin, the world must still undergo a final contortion before its regeneration. The plundering of the planet prior to the Second Coming was prophesied in the 24th Chapter of Isaiah.

> 24:1 Behold, the Lord makes the earth empty and makes it waste, distorts its surface...
> 24:3 The land shall be entirely emptied and utterly plundered, for the Lord has spoken this word.
> 24:6 Therefore the curse has devoured the earth, and those who dwell in it are desolate.
> Therefore the inhabitants of the earth are burned, and few men are left.
> 24:19 The earth is violently broken, The earth is split open, the earth is shaken exceedingly.
> 24:20 The earth shall reel to and fro like a drunkard, and shall totter like a hut;
> Its transgression shall be heavy upon it, and it will fall, and not rise again.

If we equate this time with Revelation's bowls of wrath, it would appear that this plundering is more of a process then an event. But in Chapter 15 of First Corinthians, Paul describes a similarly destructive process which seems to be required as the natural body is exchanged or transformed into the spiritual body. Transformation into the spiritual body demands that whatever remains of the natural body undergo the death of mortality itself – the swallowing up of death.

The destructive element in this dimensional change, from the physical state to the spiritual, will be discussed further when we study First Corinthians 15:54 near the end of this chapter.

Just as Psalms 22 and Isaiah 53 expound upon the events during Christ's crucifixion, First Corinthians Chapter 15 gives the details about the resurrection and the rapture which are only mentioned briefly in First Thessalonians Chapter Four. In the latter half of the 15th chapter, Paul ventures beyond his own hypothetical question of "How are the dead raised up?" in order to discuss the technical details of the glorification process. We might ask today, "What is the rapture in technical terms?" Or in our common vernacular, "What will it look like?"

The Rapture in Technical Terms – 1st Corinthians 15

35 But someone will say, "How are the dead raised up? And with what body do they come? 36 Foolish one, what you sow is not made alive unless it dies.

Paul states that a death - a destruction of some sort - is necessary in the resurrection process. This requirement is a mystery in the same sense that God's vicarious sacrificial system also required the death of the offering. We could infer from Peter's statement that death is required in order to take on spiritual form. *For Christ also suffered once for sins, the just for the unjust, that He might bring us to God, being put to death in the flesh but made alive by the Spirit.* 1 Pet. 3:18. And Jesus' example of the seed was both a prophecy about the fruitfulness of His crucifixion and a statement that resurrected life requires a foregoing death. *But Jesus answered them, saying, "The hour has come that the Son of Man should be glorified. Most assuredly, I say to you, unless a grain of wheat falls into the ground and dies, it remains alone; but if it dies, it produces much grain."* John 12:23, 24

In the following verses Paul explains "How?" and "What body?" because it is ultimately stated that *we will all be changed*. Presumably, all means all; both the living and the resurrected dead must be changed. This assumption will also prove to be in agreement with First Thessalonians 4:17, which says that the dead in Christ which have been resurrected will be changed *together* with the living to meet the Lord in the air.

PAUL'S TWO SCHEME DIMENSIONAL SYSTEM

1 Cor. 15:38-41: *But God gives it a body as He pleases, and to each seed its own bod All flesh is not the same flesh, but there is one kind of flesh of men, another flesh of animals, another of fish, and another of birds. There are also celestial bodies and terrestrial bodies; but the glory of the celestial is one, and the glory of the terrestrial is another. There is one glory of the sun, another glory of the moon, and another glory of the stars; for one star differs from another star in glory.*

Paul demonstrates in preceding verses that God is able to create different life forms and various celestial objects with unique bodily forms. These examples provide support in the following verses, that God is the creator of both the natural (mortal) body, and the spiritual (immortal) body.

1 Cor. 15:42 So also is the resurrection of the dead. The body is sown in corruption, it is raised in incorruption. 43 It is sown in dishonor, it is raised in glory. It is sown in weakness, it is raised in power. 44 It is sown a <u>natural body</u> (σῶμα ψυχικόν - soma psuchikon), it is raised a <u>spiritual body</u> (σῶμα πνευματικόν - soma pneumatikon). There is a natural body, and there is a spiritual body...

The existence of the *soma psuchikon*, the natural body, is self-evident. Paul expects the reader to concede the existence of the *soma pneumatikon* based on the existence of the natural body and based upon faith in what is not seen by his redundant assertion that there is both a natural body and a spiritual body in this passage. This argument is strikingly similar to Paul's assertion in First Thessalonians 4:14 If we believe that Jesus died and rose again, we believe that God will bring with Jesus those who are alive and remain at His coming. Paul states what is known to be fact, and then what we as Christians should believe by faith also to be true.

1 Cor. 15:45 And so it is written, "The first man Adam became a living being." The last Adam became a life-giving spirit. 46 However, the spiritual (pneumatikon) is not first, but the natural (psuchikon), and afterward the spiritual (pneumatikon). 47 The first man was of the earth, made of dust; the second Man is the Lord from heaven. 48 As was the man of dust, so also are those who are made of dust; and as is the heavenly Man, so also are those who are heavenly. 49 And

as we have borne the image of the man of dust, we shall also bear the image of the heavenly Man. 50 Now this I say, brethren, that flesh and blood cannot inherit the kingdom of God; nor does corruption inherit incorruption.

Just as flesh and blood cannot withstand the consuming fire of God's glory, in order to lay "physical" hold on the more enduring possession we must be transformed into the spiritual state. Jesus told Nicodemus in John 3:6; *That which is born of the flesh is flesh, and that which is born of the Spirit is spirit.*

51 Behold, I tell you a mystery: We shall not all sleep, but we shall all be changed...

Only some people will be left alive at Christ's coming, but all, whether previously dead or alive, must be changed. (This point has been well established above.)

52 in a moment (ἐν ἀτόμῳ - en atoma)... in the twinkling of an eye...

The Greek word, *"tom"* means "to cut." Therefore, *a-tom* means "un-cuttable." This word is meant to imply the smallest indivisible particle. When referring to time, ἐν ἀτόμῳ describes a segment of time that cannot be measured - an instant.

52 Continued... at the last trumpet. For the trumpet will sound, and the dead will be raised incorruptible, and we shall be changed.

Because this study will develop by logic its own witness for the timing of the rapture, we will not investigate the rapture in relationship to the sounding of the trumpet at this time.

At this point we must take note of how many times in Chapter 15 Paul has reiterated that we all must be changed. This change encompasses every aspect of man's mortality:

Death to Life – from the temporal to the eternal

Corruption to Incorruption – from the degenerative to permanence, from entropy to indestructibility

Dishonor to Glory – from what is shameful, dark and dull to what is glorious, illuminated, and brilliant

Weakness to Power – from tiredness and fatigue to inexhaustible ability

Natural to Spiritual - we do not yet know what we shall be or how we will appear

Earthly to Heavenly – from dust, born of flesh and blood, to the regenerated heavenly form

Image of Adam to Image of Christ – from the image of the first man, to appear as Jesus appears, for we shall be like Him

53 For this corruptible must put on incorruption, and this mortal must put on immortality.

Here Paul reiterates his argument from verse 50. That is, the necessity, whether once dead or alive, for the *soma psuchikon* to be destroyed and replaced by the *soma pneumatikon*.

54 So when this corruptible has put on incorruption, and this mortal has put on immortality, then shall be brought to pass the saying that is written: "Death is swallowed up in victory."

The Greek word for "swallow" in the original language is *katapino*, literally, "to drink down." *Katesthio* and *kataphagein* can be literally translated, "to eat down," and are used extensively in the Greek Septuagint to mean, "devour" or "destroy."

In the same epiphany in which it was revealed to Job that he would see his Redeemer, it was also revealed that Job's natural body would be destroyed by force. But then, in some type of resurrected body, Job would see his Redeemer.

Job 19:24-27 Oh, that my words were written! Oh, that they were inscribed in a book! That they were engraved on a rock with an iron pen and lead, forever! For I know that my Redeemer lives, and He shall stand at last on the earth; and after my skin is destroyed . . . this I know, that in my flesh I shall see God, whom I shall see for myself, and my eyes shall behold, and not another. How my heart yearns within me!

Job didn't describe the destruction of his flesh as a natural process. The word Job used to depict the destruction of his flesh is *Strong's* 5362, נָקַף *nâqaph, naw-kaf'*; a primitive root; to strike with more or less violence (beat, fell, corrode); by implication (of attack) to knock together, i.e. surround or circulate:—compass about, cut down, destroy, go round (about).[45]

It appears that Job anticipated a sudden, violent attack upon his bodily remains; followed by a reconstitution of his body which would enable him to behold his Redeemer with his own eyes. In fact, such a supernatural "redemption of the body" would be entirely dependent upon the existence of a Redeemer. Job's was under the conviction that God was able, and would indeed raise Job from the grave in some type of body; and that Job himself would behold the One responsible for his regeneration - who would Himself be standing on the earth in some type of bodily form. Paul echoed a similar observation when he asked the rhetorical question; *Who will deliver me from this body of death?* To which Paul acknowledges the Redeemer who is able to accomplish this supernatural feat; *I thank God—through Jesus Christ our Lord!*

Paul expounds further in Second Corinthians 5:1-5; that because God's plan for man includes such a supernatural transition, God has also prepared us to undergo this change.

For we know that if our earthly house, this tent (the soma psuchikon), is destroyed, we have a building from God, a house not made with hands, eternal in the heavens (the soma pneumatikon). For in this we groan, earnestly desiring to be clothed with our habitation which is from heaven, if indeed, having been clothed, we shall not be found naked. For we who are in this tent groan, being burdened, not because we want to be unclothed, but further clothed...

We don't want to be found naked; that is, we don't long to become disembodied spirits. We want to be further clothed; to have an even more enduring body. And God has not prepared us to be mentally comfortable with the prospect of life outside the mortal body. That was never God's plan for the ultimate glorification of man. Instead, death will be the process by which the saints will become further clothed. . . *that mortality may be swallowed up* (devoured, destroyed) *by life.*

...Now He who has prepared us for this very thing is God, who also has given us the Spirit as a guarantee.

What is "this very thing" that has been guaranteed? For which our earthly tent must be destroyed? Once again, this *thing* is the destruction of the natural body, and its replacement with the spiritual body. We have the Spirit as a guarantee that this replacement process will be completed at some time in the future.

Job 19 made a direct connection between the Redeemer and the resurrection of Job's body. Paul's discourse on the restoration of the creation in Romans Chapter Eight also describes this glorification of "we ourselves" as the *redemption of the body*. Here, the first fruits of the Spirit stand as our guarantee.

For we know that the whole creation groans and labors with birth pangs together until now. Not only that, but we also who have the first fruits of the Spirit, even we ourselves groan within ourselves, eagerly waiting for the adoption, the redemption of our body. Rom. 8:22, 23

We who have the first fruits of the Spirit know that our spirits have already been redeemed, because we *"have received the Spirit of adoption by whom we cry out Abba, Father."* Rom. 8:15 We are, nonetheless, still waiting for the *redemption of the body*. From Paul's letters to the Corinthians, we derive that this event, *this thing* that has been guaranteed by the Spirit, consists of the ablation of the *soma psuchikon* and the creation of habitation from heaven (the *soma pneumatikon*). And, *He who has prepared us for this very thing is God, who also has given us the Spirit as a guarantee.*

In Ephesians Chapter One, Paul adds further assurance of the coming redemption of the body; stating that the Spirit is, Himself, both a promise and a guarantee of the coming redemption.

In Him you also trusted, after you heard the word of truth, the gospel of your salvation; in whom also, having believed, you were sealed with the Holy Spirit of promise, 14 who is the guarantee of our inheritance until the redemption of the purchased possession, to the praise of His glory. Eph. 1:13, 14.

Paul's most concise statement on the future glorification guaranteed by the indwelling Spirit is given in Colossians 1:27; *Christ in you, the hope of glory.* The hope of a ransom from sin was realized when Jesus laid down his life for the sins of the world. This hope has already been realized in the forgiveness of sins, the deliverance from judgment, and Christ's righteousness imputed to those who believe. But there is another hope which has not yet been realized, the hope of glory. This unrealized hope in a future transformation into the glorious state of existence is part of the knowledge of our salvation. *For we were saved in this hope, but hope that is seen is not hope; for why does one still hope for what he sees? But if we hope for what we do not see, we eagerly wait for it with perseverance.* Rom. 8:24, 25

The Indwelling Spirit Promising the Redemption of the Body			
Passage	**Indwelling, Spirit**	**Sealing, Promise, Guarantee**	**Redemption, Glory**
Rom 8:22,23	we also who have the first fruits of the **Spirit**		eagerly waiting for the adoption, the **redemption of our body**
2 Cor 5:1-5	who also has given us the **Spirit**	as a **guarantee**	if our earthly house, this tent, is destroyed, we have a **building from God**
Eph 1:13,14	with the **Holy Spirit**	you were **sealed**...of **promise**...who is the **guarantee** of our inheritance	until the **redemption** of the purchased possession
Eph 4:30	And do not grieve the **Holy Spirit** of God	by whom you were **sealed**	for the day of **redemption**
Col 1:27	**Christ in you**		the hope of **glory**

Paul concludes his discourse on the transformation from death and mortality to life and immortality, by quoting two Old Testament prophets. He begins with Isaiah 25:8; *Death is swallowed up in victory.* And then he alludes to Hosea by asking; *O Death, where is your sting? O Hades, where is your victory?*

Hosea 13:14 reads;

> I will ransom them from the power of the grave
> I will redeem them from death.
> O Death, I will be your plagues!
> O Grave, I will be your destruction!

This verse implies that both death and the power of death will be conquered. The bodies of the dead will be raised from the grave, and the bodies of the living will not go down to the grave. This comprehensive verse covers the altruism that *we will all be changed* and that there are two distinct groups that will experience the Thessalonians resurrection/rapture - the dead in Christ and the living, respectively.

In conclusion, Paul's First Thessalonians rapture will be a dimensional change with the meeting/gathering to follow. The rapture will be the physical realization of putting off the old man and putting on the new man. When "this tent" is destroyed (notice: not when we die, or breathe our last breath) we will immediately be clothed with our heavenly habitation which has been prepared for us, and for which we have been prepared.

CHAPTER ELEVEN
The Veil Between Heaven and Earth
- Doug Hamp

The transformation known as the rapture will occur, as we are told by Paul in First Thessalonians Chapter Four, at the time of Christ's coming/descending. We have already established from our study of the "unmysterious" verses relating the rapture/gathering to the Second Coming, the day of the rapture will also be the day when God will rend the heavens and come down. The return of Jesus from heaven is in fact the Day of the Lord. God will come down as the Son of God in His glory. This is His glorious appearing. But what does it mean to "rend the heavens?" This chapter will explore what the Bible says about this supernatural process and when it will occur.

When Do the Heavens Pass Away?

The question of, "When do the new heavens come about?" has to do with "When do the current (old) heavens pass away?" According to Revelation 6:14, the sky, the heavens (in Greek "sky" and "heavens" are the same word – *ouranos*) will roll up one day like a scroll.

Then the **sky** [ouranos οὐρανὸς] receded as a scroll when it is rolled up, and every mountain and island was moved out of its place. Rev. 6:14

That event takes place in the context of the tribulation and **not** after the thousand year reign of Jesus. Those inside the event, who are witnessing it, claim that it is the day of the Lord.

And the kings of the earth, the great men, the rich men, the commanders, the mighty men, every slave and every free man, hid themselves in the caves and in the rocks of the mountains, and said to the mountains and rocks, "Fall on us and hide us from the face of Him who sits on the throne and from the wrath of the Lamb! For the **great day** of His wrath has come, and who is able to stand?" Rev. 6:15-17

Peter also mentioned the monumental event of the heavens passing away, which he says will occur in the day of the Lord, in the context of the tribulation, not after the thousand year reign of Jesus.

But the **day of the Lord** will come as a thief in the night, **in which** the **heavens** will **pass away** with a great noise, and the elements will melt with fervent heat; both the earth and the works that are in it will be burned up. 2 Pet. 3:10

We will consider the question, "What is the day of the Lord?," which comes as a thief in the night, in a later chapter. However we will note here that it is in that day that the heavens pass away. According to Peter the heavens will pass away with a great noise in conjunction with the return of Jesus, not after the thousand years. God first revealed what the passing away of the heavens would look like in the book of Isaiah;

the heavens shall be rolled up like a scroll. Isa. 34:4 He also said; The **heavens** will vanish away like smoke, the earth will grow old like a garment, and those who dwell in it will die in like manner; but My salvation will be forever, and My righteousness will not be abolished. Isa. 51:6

The timing of the heavens vanishing away like smoke is when the earth dwellers die – a reference to the tribulation when massive deaths will occur, not after the thousand years of peace and righteousness. Commentators have by and large been unable to appreciate this because, in some cases, they have interpreted the Bible allegorically; or they have been persuaded that the book of Revelation is a chronologically arranged book. The thematic arrangement of the Revelation is examined in another chapter. Adam Clark, for example, allegorizes it to mean pagan worship: "The **whole system of pagan** and idolatrous worship, with all its spiritual, secular, and superstitious influence, was blasted, shriveled up, and rendered null and void, as a parchment scroll when exposed to the action of a strong fire."[46] (emphasis mine) Albert Barnes, who is a fairly conservative scholar, interprets the passage in the same fashion. He stated that the passing of the heavens is nothing more than symbolic phraseology and cannot be interpreted literally of the physical realm:

"This, too, is a **symbol**, and we are **not** to suppose that it will **literally** occur. Indeed it **never can literally occur**; and we are not, therefore, to look for the fulfillment of this in any physical fact that would correspond with what is here said. The **plain meaning is**, that there would be changes **as if such an event would happen**; that is, that revolutions would occur in the high places of the earth, and among those in power, **as if** the stars should fall, and the very heavens were swept away."[47] Theologian Harry Ironside, conservative commentator on the Scriptures of last century, likewise interprets the passing away of the heavens in a figurative sense. He says that "the **heavens, symbolizing the ecclesiastical powers of every description, will depart as a scroll when it is rolled up**. The whole fabric of Christendom will be wound up as something obsolete and out of date."[48] The passing away of the heavens is clearly described in graphic detail. And yet, as we have seen from this small sampling of mainline commentators, it is commonly and unfortunately explained away as being figurative language. Once we shift our focus then it becomes apparent that the sixth seal of Revelation is the event of the passing away of the heavens, which happens at the end of the tribulation, the day that Jesus returns.

Heaven and Earth Fled Away

As careful students of the Bible, we must consider a passage that would seemingly contradict our entire thesis that the heavens and earth passing away would come at the beginning of the Millennium. In his visions of heavenly things to come, John *saw a great white throne and Him who sat on it, from whose face the **earth and the heaven fled away**. And there was found no place for them.* Rev. 20:11 This passage comes right after John sees the vision of Satan cast into the Abyss for one thousand years, and his subsequent release and final destruction when the fire comes down from heaven and destroys him. John said; *and I saw a great white throne...* The One on the throne judges the nations and then even Hades and death are done away with. Immediately following this vision, John says that he saw a new heavens and new earth. Therefore, it would appear obvious that the new heavens and new earth must come after the thousand year reign of Jesus. How can we reconcile our new paradigm with this verse? We need to take another look at Revelation 20:11.

THE VEIL BETWEEN HEAVEN AND EARTH

Then I saw a great white throne and Him who sat on it, from whose face the earth and the heaven fled away. And there was found no place for them. Rev. 20:11

This verse has been generally interpreted that the earth and heaven will flee away at that moment, after the thousand year reign of Jesus and just before the final judgment, followed by the eternal state. In other words, that would mean that John saw the heavens and earth flee away at that moment that he looked at the One on the throne. However, it is better understood as an adjectival-parenthetical statement, that is, the statement is adjectival and <u>not</u> verbal. It describes a significant feature of the person and not an action that happened at the moment. John is not describing the passing of the earth and heavens **at the moment**, but **describing** the one sitting on the throne. Thus, the one on the throne is the one from whose face heaven and earth fled away.

The word "flee" [*ephugen* ἔφυγεν] is the aorist indicative which means that it happened in the past. The aorist tense in Greek is past tense with no aspect assigned. There is another past tense (imperfect) that does include aspect. We use aspect all the time in English to explain not the time of an event, but the event happened. For example, "I studied," is in the simply (aorist) past. "I was studying," is imperfect. There are variations of this as well. It is also possible for the aorist to act as (the English equivalent of) the pluperfect. The Aorist Indicative is frequently used in narrative passages of a past event which precedes another past event mentioned or implied in the context. "The Greek Pluperfect (Aorist) is used of any past event which is conceived of simply as an event (or as entered upon, or as accomplished), regardless alike of the existence or non-existence of an interval between itself and the moment of speaking, and of the question whether it precedes or not some other past action. It affirms nothing respecting existing result."[49]

Imagine that you saw Neil Armstrong at the mall one day and you wanted to tell a friend but couldn't remember Neil's name. You would say: "I saw the astronaut who walked on the moon today." It would be obvious to both of you that Neil Armstrong did not walk on the moon at the time you saw him. You were simply using his most salient feature to describe him. So, too, when John says that he "saw a big white throne and the One sitting on it **(from whose face the earth and the heaven** fled and for them no place was found)" (Rev. 20:11, translation mine).

130

The words in parentheses in my translation serve as the predicate. The predicate says something about the subject, which in this case is the "the one sitting." John is giving a long description of who is the one sitting on the throne; and he is not saying what action was happening at that very moment. We already know when the earth and heaven fled – at the second coming of Jesus. That is when the heavens receded like a scroll with a great noise. That was the time that God tore the heavens and came down and startled the nations. Thus, Revelation 20:11 cannot be used to prove that the timing of the new heavens and earth comes after the thousand years. The phrase is being used to describe just exactly who is sitting on the big throne and what makes Him so special as compared to the other thrones and those who sat on them to whom judgment was committed (Rev. 20:4).

There is a Veil Between Heaven and Earth

The passing away of the heavens will be very much like the tearing of the veil in the temple. In fact, Isaiah yearns for the day when God would cause the heavens to pass. *Oh, that You would **rend** the heavens! That You would come down! That the mountains might shake at Your presence.* Isa. 64:1 The notion that the heavens will pass away is difficult to comprehend. What did both Isaiah and John see so that caused them to write that the heavens rolled up like a scroll? What did Peter intend when he revealed that the heavens would pass away with a great noise? What did Jesus mean when He said the heavens and earth would pass away? The answers to these questions lie in the reality of the veil between heaven and earth.

There is a veil between heaven and earth that God will one day tear open and come down. Isaiah stated that when God does this, *the mountains will quake at [His] presence—just as fire sets twigs ablaze and the fire causes water to boil.* Isa. 64:1, 2 The ultimate effect would be *to make known your name to your enemies, yes, to your enemies before you, so that the nations might quake at your presence!"* Isa. 64:2 ISV He was literally calling for God to break, or tear, the heavens and come down. He may have yearned for that based on God's revelation to him earlier in his book: *And He will destroy on this mountain the **surface** of the covering cast over all people, and the **veil** that is spread over all nations.* Isa. 25:7

THE VEIL BETWEEN HEAVEN AND EARTH

The opening of the veil is referred to as the heavens opening. There were several times when the veil was pulled back, allowing some to see behind it. As Stephen was being stoned, he *"gazed into heaven and saw the glory of God... and said, 'Look! I see the **heavens opened** [the veil] and the Son of Man standing at the right hand of God!'"* Acts 7:55-56 Ezekiel had a similar experience as he was sitting among the captives in Babylon by the Chebar River. He said, *the **heavens were opened** [the veil] and I saw visions of God. Ezek. 1:1* At the immersion (baptism) of Jesus, *the **heavens were opened** [the veil] to Him, and He saw the Spirit of God descending like a dove. Matt. 3:16* John also saw *heaven opened.* Rev. 19:11

It is like there is a giant stage curtain between the domain of heaven and the domain of earth. All humanity is the audience waiting for the show to start. Occasionally a few people have been able to look through the crack between the curtains and see backstage. The return of Jesus will be the time when the curtains open once and for all.

The word "revealed" in Greek is *apo-kalypsis* [Ἀποκάλυψις *apokalypsis*]. It literally means to unveil or uncover. The book of Revelation is not simply a book that reveals secrets of the future. It is more precisely the book of the unveiling of the Lord Jesus. We could call it 'the disclosure of Jesus'. That reality is demonstrated by Paul's statement in Second Thessalonians One;

when the **Lord Jesus is revealed** [ἀποκαλύψει *apokalypsei*] **from heaven** with His mighty angels, in **flaming** fire taking vengeance on those who do not know God, and on those who do not obey the gospel of our Lord Jesus Christ. 2 Thess. 1:7, 8

Several other Scriptures demonstrate that Jesus will be unveiled, uncovered [*apokalypsei*] at His second coming.

- *... that the genuineness of your faith...may be found to praise, honor, and glory at the **revelation** [ἀποκαλύψει apokalypsei] of Jesus Christ,* 1 Pet. 1:7
- *...that when His glory is **revealed** [ἀποκαλύψει apokalypsei], you may also be glad with exceeding joy.* 1 Pet. 4:13
- *...eagerly waiting for the **revelation** [ἀποκάλυψιν apokalypsin] of our Lord Jesus Christ...* 1 Cor. 1:7

First John 3:2 provides the same description yet with another word which underscores the manifestation, or disclosure, of Jesus; *...when He is revealed, we shall be like Him, for we shall see Him as He is.* 1 John 3:2 In the Hebrew Scriptures (Old Testament) we see this as well; *Then the glory of the Lord will be revealed [וְנִגְלָה venigla], and all humanity will see it at once..."* Isa. 40:5 ISV The Hebrew word *"gala"* means to uncover something. Thus the heavens receding like a scroll is literally the moment when Jesus is uncovered, unveiled. That is to say, when the veil between heaven and earth is removed. When this happens there will no longer be any atheists on the earth. All who had convinced themselves that there was no God will be rudely awakened to the reality that there is a God. In fact, they will see Him coming down to the planet in His fiery-lightning glory.

Then the kings of the earth, the important people, the generals, the rich, the powerful, and all the slaves and free people concealed themselves in caves and among the rocks in the mountains. They told the mountains and rocks, "Fall on us and hide us from the face of the one who sits on the throne and from the wrath of the lamb. For the **great day of their wrath has come**, and who is able to endure it?" Rev. 6:15-17 ISV

When the veil is removed there will no longer be any doubts about Jesus. There will no longer be any doubts about who is the King. The removal of the veil which was protecting them from God's fiery-lightning presence will leave everyone exposed to His power. They will suddenly realize that they are not able to endure it, which is why they run into the caves and call for the rocks to fall upon them. The veil, which was the very thing making man's arrogance possible, will finally be removed the day Jesus comes back. At that time, *"The **haughty looks of mankind** will be brought low, the **lofty pride** of human beings will be **humbled**, and the Lord alone will be exalted at that time."* Isa. 2:11 ISV The heavens passing away, therefore, is not the destruction of the sun, moon, and stars; or even the entire universe passing away (because they are eternal), but is the protective barrier between heaven and earth being removed once and for all.

The Two Veils

The veil between heaven and earth was even modeled for us by the tabernacle and its two veils. The tabernacle, we must remember, was *the copy and shadow of the heavenly things, as Moses was divinely instructed when he was about to make the tabernacle. For He said, "See that you make all things according to the pattern shown you on the mountain."* Heb. 8:5 The first veil was the gate or main door to the entire compound of the tabernacle. *Behind the* **second** **curtain** *[veil] was the part of the tent called the Most Holy Place.* Heb. 9:3 ISV In other words, the second veil was the inner most veil inside the structure where the Ark of the Covenant was. Therefore, there are two veils above. One is the general veil between the two realms just like the first veil or door to the entire tabernacle compound. The other is the inside veil to the Holy of Holies (not the acacia-gold-covered doors of the structure itself). At the death of Jesus the outer most veil in front of the temple tore *in two from top to bottom, the earth shook, rocks were split open,* Matt. 27:51 ISV indicating the beginning of the return to the unveiled relationship between the two realms.

This had been part of God's secret plan that He set forth in the Messiah to usher in the fullness of the times and to bring together in the Messiah **all things in heaven and on earth**... Eph. 1:9, 10 ISV

Doing the work necessary on the cross was in large part to reconcile the two realms which Paul states in Colossians;

Through the Son, God also reconciled all things to himself, whether things on **earth or things in heaven**, thereby making peace through the blood of his cross. Col. 1:20 That was the hope, firm and secure like an anchor for our souls, [which] reaches behind the curtain. Heb. 6:19 ISV

Therefore, just as there were two veils in the earthly tabernacle, so too there are two veils in the spiritual realm. In conjunction with the return of Jesus to the earth, the temple/tabernacle of God in Heaven will be opened.

Then the **temple of God** was **opened in heaven**, and the ark of His covenant was seen in His temple. And there were lightnings, noises, thunderings, an earthquake, and great hail. Rev. 11:19 The **temple** was filled with smoke from the **glory of God** and from His power, and **no one was able to enter** the **temple** till the seven plagues of the seven angels were completed. Rev. 15:8

The opening of the temple/tabernacle of God in heaven is the inner veil. Jesus tearing the veil between heaven and earth is the outer veil of the tabernacle. When those two are opened, then the fiery-lightning presence of God will be revealed (unveiled) for all mankind to see. The response to that event will be nothing short of terror for those who dwell on the earth for the heavens/sky/veil will disappear and Jesus will be unveiled as He returns in flaming fire (2 Thess. 1:7, 8).

Then the **sky** receded as a scroll when it is rolled up, and every mountain and island was moved out of its place. And the **kings of the earth**, the great men, the rich men, the commanders, the mighty men, every slave and every free man, hid themselves in the caves and in the rocks of the mountains, and said to the mountains and rocks, "Fall on us and **hide us from the face of Him** who **sits on the throne** and from the wrath of the Lamb! For the **great day of His wrath has come**, and who is able to stand?" Rev. 6:14-17

The veil in the tabernacle was a copy of the things in heaven (Heb. 8:5). The tearing of the first veil (not in the Holy of Holies) is a picture of the literal veil that will be torn (Isa. 64:1) and rolled up (Isa. 34:4; 2 Pet. 3:10) at Jesus' return.

We Are Like the Boy in the Bubble

Many of us have heard the story of David Vetter, better known as the boy in the plastic bubble, who had to live his entire twelve years of life in a bubble to protect him from the germs of the outside world because his immune system did not work properly. We can think of ourselves as that boy and God. Our loving Father is outside the bubble, longingly looking in. Parents can easily imagine the grief that David's parents must have felt looking through the protective plastic veil between them and their son. On the one hand, the plastic barrier between them meant that their son could live.

On the other hand, it meant that they could not be intimate with their dear and precious child. The only hope was that someday his body could be healed, and they could all be in the same space without the bubble.

This is essentially the relationship that we currently have with our Father. Like the plastic between David and his parents, the veil between God's domain and ours (inside the bubble) is what protects us from Him. Due to our infirmity, caused by the eating of the forbidden fruit, we and our Father cannot be together. We have a problem of compatibility. Before the fall of Adam and Eve there was no problem and no need for a veil between heaven and earth. The veil came about as a result of the fall. God used to come to the Garden of Eden and walk there. The first thing that Adam and Eve feel compelled to do after eating of the fruit of the tree of the knowledge of good and evil is to cover themselves. In my book, *Corrupting the Image*[50], I demonstrate how Adam and Eve were covered in light prior to the fall, and as such were compatible with the fiery-lightning presence of God.

Adam and the *Adamáh*

The big event was nothing other than the Fall of Adam. God created Adam from the *"adamáh"* (earth, the dirt, the soil). Adam was literally the earth-man. We could actually call him Mr. Dirt, or Dusty, for short. He was the federal head of all creation. In Genesis 1:2 we learn that the earth was temporarily in a liquid, amorphous state. From that material (water), God formed the earth, the ball of dirt that we are standing on today. The heavens and planet in the beginning were perfect; there was no corruption, no decay, etc. When Adam ate from the fruit, thereby committing evil, he entered into a state of degeneration and decay because he was physically linked to the *adamáh*. Then it had to endure the same fate.

At the sentencing of Adam in the Garden, God declared, and appears to have activated, the degenerative, decay-death reaction that Adam triggered (Gen. 2:17). The earth and material cosmos started to decay, wear out, and eventually fall apart. Things were going from a higher state of order to a lower state of order; such as the process we see when a piece of metal becomes oxidized, rusted (Rom 8:20, 21).

Everything began decaying and dying, from the invisible world of cells and DNA, to all the animals, birds, and fish which God had formed out of the *adamáh*. They shared the fate of Adam and the *adamáh*. Degeneration and corruption ensnared everything, permeating the entire creation. The principle of rust entered the world where only a moment before, no such oxidation was ever known. Metals, and every material, would have remained intact forever. Even the rocks became degenerative from the release of alpha particles leaving them slightly radioactive. This is something students of the earth are only recently discovering. The discovery of the alpha particles is testimony to ruin at the Fall, when the Earth became corrupted.

The Earth is now longing to be liberated (not destroyed) into the glorious liberty of the sons of God (Rom. 8:19-22), which will come about in conjunction with the resurrection and the return of Jesus, when the sons of God (believers) receive their new bodies. The decay (corruption) latent in the earth will be reversed so that we will live on the same ball of dirt as God created in the beginning.

CHAPTER TWELVE
The Veil -Vignette
- Doug Hamp

This vignette finds Ben and Kristiana, part of the remnant of Israel, observing, with the angels, past moments in time as events unfold following the disobedience of Adam and Eve.

Ben and Kristiana saw Michael, Gabriel and all of the Angels surrounding the Garden watching tensely to see how Adonai would resolve the crisis of degeneration which had been triggered.

Adonai looked tenderly at his son Adam; grief overwhelmed him because of the words he had to utter that would activate what Adam put in motion. They had lost Adonai's breath and the glow from his light was fading quickly. Soon they would not be able to endure his presence whatsoever. "The *adamáh* will now degenerate and decay," Adonai said. "In time, because you are *adamáh* and were taken from it, to *adamáh* you will return because of what you have done."

Immediately there was a deep rumble, like the groaning of a million voices at the point of death, which reached a climax. All at once, a burst, a pulse of radiation emitted from the atoms of every tree, from every flower, from every blade of grass, from every rock and from the very soil itself. It started in the dirt under Adam's feet and then spread throughout the whole planet and eventually the entire cosmos. The complete composition of everything had changed. The earth and material cosmos started decaying, wearing out, and finally fell. Everything began decaying and dying from the invisible world of cells and DNA to all animals, birds, and fish which Adonai had formed out of the *adamáh*. They shared the fate of Adam and the *adamáh*. Even the rocks became degenerative from the release of alpha particles leaving them slightly radioactive. Degeneration and corruption ensnared all things, permeating the entire creation. The principle of rust entered the world where only a moment before, no such oxidation was ever known; metals and every material would have remained intact forever.

Adam sighed looking at the ground, and kneeling down, he took some dirt into his hands and stared at it for several moments. "I am made from the dust of the *adamáh* and to it I shall return," he whispered finally realizing how when Adonai formed him from the *adamáh*, he made him the living, federal head of all created matter. He then let the dirt slip through his fingers, contemplating the relationship he had with it. "We are one and our fates are one. My fate determines the fate of everything in the material cosmos; the vitality of everything is linked and dependent on my life."

"Father!" Adam sobbed as he and Eve looked back with tears in their eyes at the Garden of Eden and at Adonai as it all began to disappear before their eyes like a scroll being unrolled before them; they were unaware that it was the last time in their lives they would be face to face with their father. As it unrolled, the domain of Adonai and all the Angels, those good and evil, disappeared from their vision forever; everything of that domain was completely cloaked from their sight. Like a great curtain closing in front of them, the world behind it was blocked from their sight like a one-way mirror, transparent on one side and opaque on the other; those behind it could still see through to the other side. Spatially, they were practically on top of one another, but were separated dimensionally by a wall or veil, like a membrane, barring passage between the domains.

"Oh for the day when the Promised One comes, destroys Lucifer who beguiled us, and restores Adonai's spirit and the glorious light that flowed from us," Adam sighed longingly.

"How will the Promised One," Eve asked in tears, "have the power to restore us when the corruption now touches every fiber of our being and that of our sons?" Adonai's promise of the one who would crush the head of Lucifer lingered in Adam's mind because freedom from death was his heart's desire. "I don't know," he answered despondently. "I don't know. Yet maybe there is hope after all."

Lucifer and the rebellious Angels watched everything happening on the other side of the veil. "Let them languish in their pain!" Lucifer scoffed. "Though we have been stripped of our beauty and fire, they are now cast out from Adonai's presence forever!" Lucifer turned around smiling deviously at the others who were intently staring at his disfiguration as well as their own. "We are free! We are free from the oppression of Adonai and free from serving the little worm he created," he said relishing in his victory against Adonai.

"Your ingenious plan to cause Adam to murder himself was a great success," one of the rebel Angels, later called Watchers, praised him.

"Now we will never be required to serve the speck of dust that he is," Lucifer answered. "There is no hope for Adam or any sons that come after him for none will by any means be able to repurchase a brother, nor give to Adonai a ransom for that brother, for the redemption of their souls is costly. None will continue to live eternally, and not see the Abyss," he exclaimed. "I was also right in my assessment that causing Adam to defy the directive of Adonai would force Adonai into a self-imposed exile lest his consuming fire, which is like a stream of brimstone, destroy the earth and everything on it. I calculated that Adonai, in all of his compassion, would sooner divorce himself from the earth rather than utterly destroy everything by his fiery-lightning presence. I have successfully separated the abode of Adonai from the abode of Adam. The earth is ours forever!"

"That is not true, the earth and all its fullness will forever be Adonai's!" The same Watcher countered. "How can you suggest that it is ours?"

"The answer is simple, brother," Lucifer said haughtily. "Because Adonai cannot touch the earth and because Adam, the true benefactor, has forfeited his right of dominion over the earth, I have become the de-facto ruler of this world. You are correct, however, that it shall always 'technically' be Adonai's but he will never be able to possess it, nor can Adam ever regain his dominion over it. We have adversely taken possession of the earth which was created by Adonai and benefited to Adam. I rightly deduced that once death entered into Adam, then he and his descendants would necessarily forfeit their possession and Adonai could not have it either because his glory would destroy it, which he clearly would never allow. It is just too much for any degenerative mortal to endure. It will be ours forever because Adam cannot undo death, no matter what, and so there will never be any one of his sons authorized, acceptable or legitimate who can undo Adam's action. Hence I will remain the ruler of the world indefinitely and you all shall possess part of it."

"Yet for all that, we are left disfigured and barren," one of the rebel Watchers snarled viciously motioning to his body. "I am here because I share your conviction that we should not be subservient to Dusty, yet now we are left desolate. You apparently did not foresee that Adonai could remove his fire from all of us. Even now I feel the drain of power in myself," he said feeling the need to consume something for the very first time. "What have we gained if we are never satiated?" he continued. "The removal of Adonai's fire and power has left us disconnected from the source of life, leaving me craving a life-essence that I can devour!" the Watcher bellowed greedily with a look in his eyes like a hungry lion. "Adam is still able to derive energy and food from the earth and though he is dying, when he is hungry he simply needs to take of the produce of the *adamáh*. Even in its state of degeneration the *adamáh* will still produce enough to nourish him until his death because he was taken from it. Even the animals might be eaten since they too were derived from it. What can I consume to placate the ravenous void inside me?"

"You are correct that unlike Adam," Lucifer stated, "we cannot gain any energy from the *adamáh*, for our bodies are trans-dimensional and hence will never fail like Adam's, yet we still need an input of energy. Adonai has already instituted what we need: the creature which Adonai caused to come up out of the *adamáh*, whose blood, life-force was given in exchange for Adam, Eve and their progeny to be in close proximity to him, cannot actually reverse the effect of the treason committed. The Covering is nothing more than a force field, a shield of energy which covers a person or object from the fiery-lightning of Adonai. Because it will last only one year and will have to be continually repeated, we can take our nourishment from the life-force of any creature, including the sons of Dusty himself." He smiled slyly. "The life-force is of a trans-dimensional nature and does nothing for the terrestrial bodies of Adam and Eve but will sustain us quite nicely," he said smugly.

"And how do you propose that we obtain blood since we are on this side of the veil?" yet another Angel inquired, sensing the futility of Lucifer's suggestion. "Have you not seen that an impassable barrier has been placed between the domain of Adam and the domain we exist in? Do you think that we can just pass over it without any retaliation from Adonai?"

"Here is what we will do," Lucifer responded coolly to the rebel Angel which had snickered.

"Though we despise the Adamites, they will willingly offer up blood of another creature in our honor and then we will receive nourishment from the life-force in the blood. However, because Adonai created Adam in his image, they are therefore of greater value than animals, and hence they will be more delectable treats. Let me explain how we will now rule the earth and be energized at the same time. Adam and Eve had a limited understanding of the City of Adonai, which is now cloaked behind the veil," Lucifer said. "You must realize the incredible power our knowledge of those things 'above' give us over the Adamites living 'below' on the other side of the veil. Our secrets of the world behind the veil will make us into gods! We shall use it to exploit the Adamites who will have a deep yet unconscious yearning to return to the Mountain-City of Adonai. We will exploit this longing for restoration to entice them to commit even greater acts of evil than their father Adam has committed."

"We will distract them with empty promises," one of the rebel Watchers interjected, "so that rather than seeking to commune with Adonai by way of the Covering, the rebellion against Adonai will only increase and will become so bad that even calling on his name will be profaned. Instead of calling on his name as a blessing, it will become a curse and Adonai will further distance himself from men until he is grieved that he even created them."

"And as their memory fades with each passing day," Lucifer continued, "the sons of Dirt will be more easily convinced that we are in fact 'gods' and they must earn our favor by giving blood, the life-force of another," he said excitedly, and then transformed himself once again into a glorious Angel. "We shall convince them to practice every sort of abomination that Adonai hates."

"Since we are hidden behind the veil," another Watcher said, "consulting our knowledge will be known as divination because they will believe we are divine and our powers will be considered sorcery. Through war and murder and horrors of great magnitude committed by the Adamites in our honor we shall be completely satisfied."

"Finally, brothers," Lucifer said, regaining control of the disclosure of the big idea, "there is one more delight that we shall partake of; you shall be satiated when we convince the Adamites to do something utterly repugnant, something which Adonai never commanded nor did it even come into his mind! We shall seduce them to offer up their sons and daughters in fire; and we shall do so until they are slaughtering their children to us under every spreading tree, in the ravines, and under the clefts of the rocks. When this occurs, then your hunger shall be abated and you shall be satisfied in the most delectable way."

"What about the Promised One who Adonai said would crush your head and ours too?" another Watcher questioned anxiously. "How do you propose to overcome that?"

"When the time is right," Lucifer responded, "then some of you will mingle yourselves with the seed of Adam and corrupt the ways of all flesh on the earth. When Adam was created there was no death, decay or degeneration whatsoever in him. When they have offspring, then the degeneration, the record of the event of the Fall, will be passed virtually identically from Adam to all of his sons perpetual transmission of death, inherent in the seed, from generation to generation. Hence, when our seed is mingled with theirs, then our seed will be passed from generation to generation. Then the Promised One will be one of us and if he is one of us then he cannot be the one to restore Adam."

The rebels cheered in shrill voices at the even more insidious intentions of their leader.

CHAPTER THIRTEEN
Reclaiming the 1st Thessalonians Rapture Narrative
- Chris Steinle

Paul stated in First Corinthians 15; *Behold, I tell you a mystery: We shall not all sleep, but we shall all be changed - in a moment, in the twinkling of an eye, at the last trumpet. For the trumpet will sound, and the dead will be raised incorruptible, and we shall be changed.* 1 Cor. 15:51, 52 This passage on the resurrection and "change" is the big sister to the rapture narrative found in First Thessalonians Chapter Four.

But I do not want you to be ignorant, brethren, concerning those who have fallen asleep, lest you sorrow as others who have no hope. For if we believe that Jesus died and rose again, even so God will bring with Him those who sleep in Jesus. For this we say to you by the word of the Lord, that we who are alive and remain until the coming of the Lord will by no means precede those who are asleep.

For the Lord Himself will descend from heaven with a shout, with the voice of an archangel, and with the trumpet of God. And the dead in Christ will rise first. Then we who are alive and remain shall be caught up together with them in the clouds to meet the Lord in the air. And thus we shall always be with the Lord. Therefore comfort one another with these words. 1 Thess. 4:13-18.

This passage is proof of the rapture. But the details of these verses have, unfortunately, been overlooked by Pre-Tribulation rapture theologians, authors, and movie-makers.

In accordance with basic (inductive) Bible interpretation guidelines, the very first step in determining the meaning of this passage is to establish its single main theme. If these verses above were to be bound as a stand-alone booklet, what would it be called? What was Paul's primary motive for conveying these thoughts?

The first and last verses are focused on giving comfort to those who had lost their loved ones. The first verse also implies that the bereaved would be less grieved and more hopeful if they were more informed about the things that Paul is about to share with them. Paul didn't want those who had lost their loved ones to think that they had perished and would miss out on the Lord's return. It also brings to mind the remorse of Mary and Martha; "Lord, if you had been here, our brother Lazarus would not have died." The overall objective of the Thessalonians citation is comfort. Comfort through education. An appropriate title might be something like, *"Paul's Words of Comfort to the Bereaved."*

For if we believe that Jesus died and rose again, even so God will bring with Him those who sleep in Jesus. 1 Thess. 4:13

This verse takes the form of an "if – then" statement. "If" we believe that Jesus died and rose again; then (even so), or (thus) – *"God will bring with Him those who sleep in Jesus."* The independent conditional statement is that "one believes in the death and resurrection of Jesus." If we believe in the death and resurrection of Jesus, *even so* we should also believe what Jesus has promised to His followers; *"because I live, you will live also."* John 5:25 says, *"Most assuredly, I say to you, the hour is coming, and now is, when the dead will hear the voice of the Son of God; and those who hear will live."* The dead will hear the voice of Jesus and rise. First Thessalonians 4:14 ties these two resurrections together. We believe in the death and resurrection of Jesus; and even so, we believe that God will raise those who have fallen asleep.

For this we say to you by the word of the Lord, that we who are alive and remain until the coming of the Lord will by no means precede those who are asleep. 1 Thess. 4:15

"by the word of the Lord."

We have already demonstrated by citing numerous Scriptures (the word of the Lord) that the resurrection will precede the gathering. According to Paul's statement, the resurrection of the dead must occur before the rapture of the living. Stated from the other perspective, the rapture cannot occur before the resurrection.

"By no means" is formed by two negative Greek words. In English this would be a double negative. But in the Greek it has the meaning, "It absolutely won't happen." This fact, expressed in the Greek's most emphatic negative expression, implies that the living cannot possibly experience the rapture at the Lord's return in advance of the resurrection of the dead.

The Coming of the Lord

"Until the coming of the Lord."

Notice that it does not say, "Until a calling from the Lord." This distinction will be amplified further in the next verse.

For the Lord Himself will descend from heaven with a shout, with the voice of an archangel, and with the trumpet of God. And the dead in Christ will rise first. 1 Thess. 4:16

This verse contains so many important elements that we need to examine each phrase individually. The first phrase identifies three different arguments which would persuade the Thessalonians that Paul was describing the second coming of Christ.

"For the Lord Himself"

There is an additional Greek word in the original texts. The Greek word – *hoti*[51] (that) appears before "Himself." The Online Interlinear translation of this verse captures the meaning of this phrase as, "For that same Lord."[52] Another good translation would be, "For that self-same Lord." By using these words, anyone familiar with the Book of Acts would tend to associate them with "that same Jesus" from Luke's record of the ascension in Acts 1:9-11.

Now when He had spoken these things, while they watched, He was taken up, and a cloud received Him out of their sight. And while they looked steadfastly toward heaven as He went up, behold, two men stood by them in white apparel, who also said, "Men of Galilee, why do you stand gazing up into heaven? This same Jesus, who was taken up from you into heaven, will so come in like manner as you saw Him go into heaven."

Because Paul has just mentioned "the coming of the Lord," it would appear that Paul is deliberately calling to mind the mental image of the Lord's bodily return. Although this may not provide conclusive evidence that this "coming" is the bodily second coming of Christ; please consider the next two phrases as further supporting evidence.

"Will descend"

The Lord – that same Lord, will descend; *katabesetai*[53] (will descend). This exact word is used in Romans 10:7 asking the question, *"Who will descend into the abyss?" Katabas*[54] is usually translated *"come down,"* as in the Gospel of John where Jesus referred to Himself as the one who *"comes down from heaven,"* and, *"the bread that came down from heaven."* Paul first referred to this event as *"the coming of the Lord"* in verse 15. Verse 16 reinforces the fact that Jesus is *"coming,"* and that He's *"coming down"* – *"descending."*

"From heaven"

Here the operative word is *"from."* This is a common word in the Greek pronounced *"apa."*[55] The point in examining this word is to differentiate what this preposition is not saying. It does not mean *"in,"* or *"near,"* or *"around."* The Greek has other words that mean those things. *Apa* (from), conveys a separation between two positions. Just like its use in English, *"from"* generally implies departure and distance. An object was there, and now is here; the object came *from* its former position.

This study seems mundane except that it is necessary in order to express the precision of the original Greek text. *"From heaven"* means that Jesus has distanced Himself *from* heaven. He was in heaven, and now he has separated Himself *from* heaven. He's not merely coming *in* heaven, or descending *in* heaven. He's going to descend *from* heaven. He's not going to get up from His throne and walk a few steps - and call to the church. No. He is, once again, going to depart from His place in heaven and *descend.*

"For the Lord Himself will descend from heaven."

What Paul has written affirms that the same Jesus who has ascended will also come down from heaven – *"in like manner as you saw Him go into heaven." "In like manner"* means that the same processes will recur; except that they will occur in a reverse manner. When Jesus was taken up to heaven he ascended from the earth. When Jesus returns from heaven, he will descend to earth. When Jesus ascended into heaven he disappeared from sight. When Jesus descends He will reappear; and *this* is the blessed hope. *Looking for the blessed hope and glorious appearing of our great God and Savior Jesus Christ.* Titus 2:13

Let's put this all together now. From verse 15: *"the coming of the Lord."* From verse 16: *"the self-same Lord," "will come down," "from heaven."* Let's take a closer look at these observations about the station of Lord Jesus:

1. He is coming / will come down.
2. He is the same Lord. (Himself, or self-same)
3. He is descending.

He is coming. He is no longer seated in heaven - He is not merely calling or commanding the saints to rise and join Him in heaven. He is coming.

For the Lord Himself. Paul is not being redundant. Jesus is, "the self-same Lord." Once again this points to a physical second coming, as foretold by the angels in the Book of Acts. As He ascended, He will descend. In what manner? In bodily form.

He is Descending. Jesus cannot be sitting and descending at the same time. He is either sitting at the Father's right hand or He is descending. Paul says He is descending.

"With a shout, with the voice of an archangel, and with the trumpet of God."

The Bible describes a truly *glorious appearing* at Christ's return - which every eye will witness. This celebration, once again, lends itself to the conclusion that Paul is describing the bodily return of Jesus.

These verses are primarily given as counsel to the living regarding their dead. They're going to burst forth from their graves. They're not going to miss out on anything. So you don't have to sorrow as those who have no hope. Isn't it interesting that verse 17 (the part about the rapture) is presented in books and movies without a depiction of the resurrection of the dead? Images portray the saints as though they were ascending straight into heaven with no appearing of the Lord. In most cases there are no voices, no trumpets, and no descending Christ; and certainly no graphic imagery of the resurrection of the dead. The authors and screenwriters *have* studied these verses. They know *exactly* what they're doing. But they don't want the audience to think about the fact that the resurrection of the dead occurs first - even though that information is presented in the text three times.

This concealment is most certainly made because the Bible places the resurrection of the dead at the end of the age, after the time of the Great Tribulation. People who are trying to force the idea of the Pre-Tribulation rapture of the church either can't use this verse (which is the only verse in the English Bible that actually refers to this meeting in the air as the rapture); or, they must strip it of its context and show the rapture scene by itself. If they present the rapture verse in its context, it becomes obvious that it's not a Pre-Tribulation rapture at all. It's a rapture following the resurrection of the dead.

And the dead in Christ will rise first

The dead in Christ will include all who have died in faith. There is only one faith. Whether these who died in Christ were baptized in the name of the Trinity, baptized in the sea, or baptized into that Rock which was Christ; there is only one baptism. As stated earlier, and based on Paul's qualification here, this resurrection immediately preceding the rapture appears to be what is called the resurrection of the righteous, also known as the resurrection of the just.

Now we come to verse 17 of First Thessalonians Four - the rapture verse. Here we will slow down and take a word-by-word approach based on our hypothesis that the rapture is comprised of three distinct events; the resurrection, the rapture, and the gathering.

The precision of the Greek words used by Paul will allow us to examine the rapture sequence on the microscopic level. This will also provide the opportunity to apply all of the ontological concepts employed by Paul in his other epistles.

There are no textual variants in verse 17 in any of the Greek texts from which major English Bible versions are translated. Each Greek letter of each word is consistent throughout the sea of ancient Greek manuscripts. The words are identical in the Byzantine, Alexandrian, Western, and majority text-types. The Greek words presented below are used as the base text in the *King James*[56], *New King James*[57], *New International*[58], *American Standard(s)*[59], and other modern paraphrased versions. The reader may be completely unfamiliar with the Greek language. Nevertheless, it is beneficial to view the 2,000 year-old Greek with one's own eyes.

Translating the Rapture Verse

First let's examine the common Greek-to-English equivalent of each word or phrase so that we can start with the literal Greek meaning expressed by the original language. Commentary is inserted where English words are added, or where English translations depart from the literal Greek equivalent. (Greek words and phrases from Verse 17 are in bold)

Verse 17: ἔπειτα ἡμεῖς (*epeita haemeis*); Then we.

Verse 17: οἱ ζῶντες (*hoi zontes*); the ones alive.

Verse 17: οἱ περιλειπόμενοι (*hoi perileipomenoi*); the ones left behind

These "ones" are typically translated into English as; "the living survivors," or "those alive and remaining."

The word commonly used in the New Testament for "remain" is the Greek word μένω (*meno*); to remain, abide. Therefore Paul's choice to use a different word reflects a peculiar aspect about these living ones.

Strong's NT 4035: περιλείπω (*peri-leipo*)

From *peri* and *leipo*; to leave all around, i.e. (passively) survive - remain.

Greek; *peri*; about, around

Greek; *leipo*; to be destitute, lack.[60]

According to Thayer's Greek Lexicon:

περιλείπω: present passive participle περιλειπόμενος (cf. περί, III. 2); to leave over; passive, to remain over, to survive: 1 Thessalonians 4:15, 17. (Aristophanes, Plato, Euripides, Polybius, Herodian; 2 Macc. 1:31.)[61]

The Complete Word Study Dictionary of the New Testament by Spiros Zodhiates begins its definition of *perileipo* by noting the Classical Greek meaning as; "those who survived, and therefore remained, or were left behind."[62] Specifically referring to First Thessalonians 4:17, Zodhiates translates οἱ περιλειπόμενοι (*hoi perileipomenoi*) as; the surviving ones.

St. Paul described these ones remaining as a remnant of survivors who will not merely be alive and abiding, but they will be literally leftover or left about.

Paul was echoing the ideas expressed in the fourth chapter of Isaiah. The Greek Septuagint uses the same root words as Paul used in First Thessalonians 4:17:

και εσται το υπολειφθεν εν σιων και το καταλειφθεν εν ιερουσαλημ αγιοι κληθησονται παντες οι γραφεντες εις ζωην εν ιερουσαλημ (Isa. 4:2)[63]

In that day the Branch of the Lord shall be beautiful and glorious; and the fruit of the earth shall be excellent and appealing for those of Israel who have escaped [death]. And it shall come to pass that he who is **left (LXX; hupo-leiph-then)** in Zion **and remains (LXX; kata-leiph-then)** in Jerusalem will be called holy - everyone who is recorded **among the living** [those left alive] in Jerusalem. Isa. 4:2, 3

Verse 17: ἅμα (*hama*); together / at the same time, or simultaneously.

Verse 17: σὺν αὐτοῖς (*sun autois*); with them. - *The Spirit testifying that they should not be made perfect apart from us.* Heb. 11:40 may apply here as to why we must be glorified together. The dead, together with the living, at the same time, will both experience the change described by the following verb.

Harpagēsometha

Verse 17: ἁρπαγησόμεθα (*harpagēsometha*)

Paul used a word for rapture that is so unique in form that this exact word doesn't occur anywhere else in the Greek New Testament or in the *Greek Septuagint* version of the Old Testament. Yet the Pre-Tribulation rapture theory has pinned its hopes and built a media empire upon this one word. The internet is replete with images of being "caught up" - the English translation of the word *"harpázō."* But there is a Greek word even closer to *harpagēsometha* than *harpázō*. The Greek word *"harpagē"* is so close to the word Paul used for "rapture" that it is actually part of the word, **harpagē**sometha.

Harpázō, and *harpagē* are closely related; but do they mean the same thing? And more importantly, which one of these words expresses the meaning intended by Paul?

The Greek stems of these words are; *harpas* (Gr. ἁρπασ), and *harpag* (Gr. ἁρπαγ). Using Latin characters, the only difference is the last letter of each stem - sigma (sometimes taking the phonetic forms z or dz). And gamma (g). These two words have slightly different definitions and are designated by Strong's as; GS724 and GS726.

GS724 *harpagē* har-pag-ay' from 726; pillage (properly abstract):-- extortion, ravening, spoiling.[64]

GS726 *harpázō* har-pad'-zo from a derivative of 138; to seize (in various applications):--catch (away, up), pluck, pull, take (by forces).[65]

Strong's indicates that *harpagē* is derived from *harpázō*. And the origin of *harpagēsometha* has been attributed to both of these lexical entries. But, as can be seen above, the words do not mean the same thing. Nevertheless each of these two words can be shown to support the authors' conclusions about the rapture and its timing.

As stated by Strong's above, *harpázō* is translated into English in a variety of ways. But whether the Greek word means; take away, carry off, catch up, tear up, rend, ravish, or seize, *harpázō* usually signifies the use of force. There are other Greek words commonly used to convey that someone or something has been taken, lifted up, or carried away. But *harpázō* implies that the object which is being taken will be, or has been, seized or violated by force.

Force is precisely what we would expect to be present at the Lord's second coming. The exceeding great power of God will forcefully subdue death, including the mortality of our lowly bodies, at the time of the resurrection/rapture.

The rapture will occur at the time of Christ's plundering of the devil's power, which he continues to hold over death. When Jesus was accused of relying on the power of Beelzebub, He used the occasion to talk about the triumph of His kingdom (house) over the household of Satan. *Or how can one enter a strong man's house and plunder ἁρπάσαι (harpasai) his goods, unless he first binds the strong man? And then he will plunder διαρπάσει (di-arpasei) his house. Matt. 12:29* (See also Mark 3:27.)

Harpagē means; pillage, plunder, or spoil. Above in Matthew's gospel, some English translators have rendered *harpasai* as "plunder." Could there be any greater indicator that Christ has overcome His last enemy (death), than at the resurrection of the dead where death is swallowed up in victory?

Inasmuch then as the children have partaken of flesh and blood, He Himself likewise shared in the same, that through death He might destroy him who had the power of death, that is, the devil. Heb. 2:14 (emphasis added)

Harpagē conveys the same forceful aspect of *harpázō*, but actually fits the First Thessalonians rapture narrative better than *harpázō*. Based on the assumption that the purpose of the rapture is to remove the church from the planet, popular theologians have asserted that *harpagēsometha* is the first person plural future passive indicative of the word *harpázō*. [We] (first person plural) shall (future) be seized/caught/snatched (passive indicative).

But if *harpagēsometha* is formed from *harpázō*, why does the stem contain the gamma ending? Why does it contain the very word, *harpagē*? This obvious *harpagē* connection has been conveniently explained away by asserting that the passive voice of "seized" somehow becomes equivalent to the word "plundered." But changing "to seize" into "to be seized" does not make "seize" an interchangeable equivalent of the word "plunder." The passive form of "to plunder" would be "to be plundered."

Dr. Spiros Zodhiates recognized that *harpagēsometha* is formed from the root word, *harpagē*. It is not merely the future passive indicative of *harpázō*. It is, in fact, the future indicative of *harpagē*.

"724. ἁρπαγή *harpagē*; gen. *harpagēs*, from *harpázō* (726), to seize upon with force. Robbery, plundering. Zodhiates provides synonyms such as; *skulon* (4661), in the plural meaning spoils, arms stripped from an enemy; *akrothinion* (205), the top of a heap [of plunder], the choicest spoils of war."[66] (emphasis added)

"To seize upon," does not mean "seized." Likewise, a person being robbed or plundered of their possessions is not an equivalent expression for taking the whole person away; whether they be caught up, taken away, or carried off.

The authors agree with Zodhiates that Paul intended *harpagēsometha* to be the first person plural future indicative of *harpagē* rather than a derivative form of *harpázō*. As a verb, *harpagē* denotes the act of plundering, a forceful change of ownership. But unlike *harpázō*, *harpagē* does not involve the abduction of the person himself. The contrast between taking someone away, and taking something away from its owner, is paramount if you happen to be the person involved. That is why our analysis of *harpagē* must go so much deeper than the casual observance that *harpagēsometha* would seem to come from the word "*harpázō*."

The future passive indicative of *harpázō* would indeed be "shall be seized." But the future passive indicative of *harpagē* is "shall be plundered." English translators have bypassed the literal meaning of *harpagēsometha* simply because they have not understood how "plundered" fits into the rapture scenario. The pre-tribbers have missed the point that Paul was trying to communicate because it doesn't fit into their own narrative. Paul used the word "plunder" because he was describing the transformation that will occur when mortality is overpowered at Christ's appearing. Great force will be present at the time of the resurrection/rapture.

Furthermore, if Paul had used a form of *harpázō* to mean "seized;" he would have been implying that the force of God will be released for the purpose of gathering the saints against their will. The notion that God's people would resist drawing near to their Savior is reminiscent of the words of the Psalmist;

Do not be like the horse or like the mule, which have no understanding, which must be harnessed with bit and bridle, else they will not come near you. Psa. 32:9

Rather, Paul was acknowledging the power of God to transform our lowly bodies. Immediately after this forceful rapture the saints will peacefully, joyfully, meet the Lord in the air.

The chart on the following pages shows the overall consistency with which *harpázō* and *harpagē* are used in the biblical texts. Because *harpázō* has almost become a household word among students of eschatology, examples of its use are presented first. Included are some exceptions where the words have been used interchangeably.

There are dozens more examples of *harpázō* and *di-arpázō* in the *Greek Septuagint* that could have been listed in the chart. But the chart is representative of the results of the larger study.

An online article at *PreceptAustin.org* sites 34 uses of *harpázō* in the non-apocryphal Septuagint (LXX) (Gen. 37:33; Lev. 6:4; 19:13; Deut. 28:31; Jdg. 21:21, 23; 2 Sam. 23:21; Job 20:19; 24:2, 9, 19; Ps. 7:2; 10:9; 22:13; 50:22; 69:4; 104:21; Isa. 10:2; Ezek 18:7, 12, 16, 18; 19:3, 6; 22:25, 27; Hos. 5:14;6:1; Amos 1:11; 3:4; Mic. 3:2; 5:8; Nah. 2:12)

The article continues; "A number of the uses of *harpázō* in the LXX translate the Hebrew word meaning to tear (*taraph*; 2963) (as of beasts of prey, tear to pieces – Gen. 37:33, Ps. 7:2, 50:22, Hos. 5:14, 6:1) which brings out the <u>violent aspect of *harpázō*</u> ." The article concludes; "<u>None of the LXX uses of *harpázō* convey the same sense of rapture as found here in 1 Thessalonians.</u>"[67]

Uses of *Harpázō* and *Harpagē* in the Bible and Apocrypha

Verse	Verses including the Gr. stem *harpas*	English Translation	
		snatch, take away, seize	rob, spoil, plunder
Leviticus 19:13	You shall not cheat your neighbor nor rob ἁρπάσεις (*harpaseis*) him.		X
Deuteronomy 28:31	your donkey shall be violently taken away ἡρπασμένος (*haerpasmenos*)	X	
Judges 21:21	and every man catch ἁρπάσετε (*harpasete*) a wife for himself from the daughters of Shiloh.	X	
Judith 16:9	Her sandal caught (fig. captured) ἥρπασεν (*haerpasen*) his eye	X	
Matthew 13:19	the evil one comes and snatches ἁρπάζει (*harpasei*) away what was sown	X	
Nahum 2:12a	The lion caught ἥρπασεν (*haerpasen*) enough for his whelps	X	
John 10:12	and the wolf snatches ἁρπάζει (*harpasei*) them	X	
John 10:28	no one will snatch ἁρπάσει (*harpasei*) them out of My hand.	X	
Acts 8:39,40	the Spirit of the Lord caught ἥρπασεν (*haerpasen*) Philip away	X	
Revelation 12:5	and her child was caught up ἡρπάσθη (*hērpasthē*) to God	X	

Verse	Verses including the Gr. stem *harpag*	snatch, take away, seize	rob, spoil, plunder
Leviticus 6:2	If anyone lies ... about a robbery ἁρπαγῆς (harpagēs)		X
Isaiah 3:14	the plunder ἁρπαγὴ (harpagē) of the poor is in your houses.		X
Isaiah 42:22	This is a people despoiled and plundered διηρπασμένος (di-haerpasmenos)... For plunder ἅρπαγμα (harpagma), and no one says, "Restore!"		X X
Isaiah 61:8	I hate robbery ἁρπάγματα (harpagmata) for burnt offering.		X
Nahum 2:12b	and his den with rapine ἁρπαγῆς (harpagēs).		X
2 Corinthians 12:2-4	such a man was caught up ἁρπαγέντα (harpagenta) to the third ... was caught up ἡρπάγη (hērpagē) into Paradise	X X	
Matthew 23:25	outside of the cup and dish, but inside they are full of robbery ἁρπαγῆς (harpagēs) and self-indulgence		X
Luke 11:39	but your inward part is full of robbery ἁρπαγῆς (harpagēs) and wickedness.		X
Philippians 2:5,6	being in the form of God, did not consider it robbery ἁρπαγμὸν (harpagmon)		X
Hebrews 10:34	and joyfully accepted the plundering ἁρπαγὴν (harpagēn) of your goods		X

After reviewing the table above we can see that nearly without exception, *harpázō* is translated into English as "snatch", "take away", "seize", etc.; and *harpagē* is translated as; "rob", "spoil", "plunder", etc. Such consistent usage of the two words and their translations adds further support that *harpagēsometha* should be translated as "shall be robbed, spoiled or plundered."

John Jeffrey Dodson's lexicon which harmonizes the work of Abbott-Smith, Berry, Souter, and Strong, gives the concise meaning of *harpagē* as; "the act of plundering, plunder, spoil."[68]

Based on the assumption that *harpagēsometha* is the future indicative of *harpagē*, what has, since the King James era, been translated as "caught up," could justifiably be translated "plundered." But would this translation make sense within the context of the verse? Yes! Using "plundered" in verse 17 of First Thessalonians Chapter Four brings out more detail and adds even more weight to Paul's argument for the timing of the resurrection.

The next thing to consider is why two of the exceptions in the table above were made when translating Paul's use of *harpagē* into English. Paul may have used *harpagē* with the specific purpose of magnifying the ambiguity of whether, in fact, he had been taken in bodily form, or just caught away in a vision.

A bolder position as to why *harpagē* has been translated as "caught up," (as if it were the Greek word *harpázō* used in Revelation Chapter 12) is based on the possibility that the English translation has missed Paul's intent; and that he meant "plundered" in all instances of *harpagē*. Paul, knowing that flesh and blood cannot enter into the real presence of God, may have used *harpagē* in recognition that his mortality would have needed to be transformed into a spiritual body; if indeed, Paul had actually been translated into a spiritual body.

But to say that the English interpretation should vary from its typical meaning in First Thessalonians 4:17 simply because English interpreters have interpreted a previous verse as an anomaly, would base the translation of *harpagē* in First Thessalonians on circular reasoning. On the other hand, if "plunder" can be shown to work within the context of verse 17, then there is no need to rationalize why an atypical rendering of the word would yield a more accurate interpretation of the verse.

As a technicality, we will find when we implement *harpagē* to First Thessalonians Four that "up" may be implied, but is not expressed in texts of either Second Corinthians 12:2-4 or First Thessalonians 4:17. More on this in a moment.

Then we who are alive and remain shall be shall be plundered/robbed/spoiled. Our goods (our natural body, our mortality) will be plundered. The *purchased possession* spoken of by Paul in Ephesians 1:14 will be redeemed. Instead of being snatched away, God will rob us of our *soma psuchikon* (the natural body) and further clothe us with our *soma pneumatikon* (spiritual body). This glorification process requires the destruction, the plundering, of the old body. The saints are not being carried off at the instant of the "rapture." The resurrected dead and those who are Christ's at His coming will be *changed in a moment, in the twinkling of an eye.*

The plundering is not the removal of the body, but the redemption of the body. Paul's employment of this single Greek word does not establish, by itself, the foundation for an eschatological system. But there are enough examples of the customary Greek usage of *harpadzo* and *harpagē* to support the conclusion that *harpagē*, found in First Thessalonians 4:17, depicts the moment of change promised in First Corinthians 15:23, 50-58. *Harpagēsometha* supports the idea that those who are Christ's at His coming will be transformed. This change will occur before both the living survivors and the resurrected saints are gathered to be with the Lord.

The main purpose of First Thessalonians 4:13-18 is to present such a precise order of events at the time of the Lord's return so as to comfort to the living. If Paul had used *harpázō*, he would have been skipping over the moment of the change. This would have blurred the precision of the discrete realities which he was hoping would comfort the bereaved.

What's Up with "Caught Up"?

There are no directional Greek words in verse 17. Neither do the English expressions below have anything to do with elevation.

Act up	Beat up	Blown up	Bottle up
Brush up	Buckle up	Buff up	Buy up
Clean up	Clogged up	Close up	Divide up
Drum up	Fed up	Finish up	Fix up
Heat up	Held up	Lighten up	Live it up
Loosen up	Making it up	Plugged up	Roll up
Seal up	Set up	Sewn up	Shake up
Shut up	Stack up	Start up	Stitch up
Stopped up	Straighten up	Take up (space)	Tidy up
Tied up	Tighten up	Wake up	Wash up
Use up	Wind up	Wise up	Wrap up

So how did we end up with "caught up?" And, why bring it up?

Many Greek words or prefixes could have been used to express the direction "up"; such as; *ana, anabaino, egeiro, hupsoo*, etc. Just as there is no *harpázō*, the verse lacks any root, prefix, or adverb for "up." The fact that the Pre-Tribulation "rapture" theory was first popularized in the British Isles may well be directly "bound up" in the English translation of *harpagaesometha*. Indeed, the Pre-Tribulation doctrine was scarcely insinuated by the Greek-speaking Early Church, Byzantine Church, or later Eastern Orthodox Churches. The very use of the phrase "caught up" may have coloured the imagination of modern English theologians.

The English translation of John 19:30b reads; *And bowing His head, He gave up His spirit.* Once again, "up" is not found in the ancient Greek texts. *"Paredoken"*; Gr. παρέδωκεν, is the word translated into English as, "gave up." But the Greek word παρέδωκεν, means; "delivered, given over, or handed over". Yet English translations often contain the colloquialism "gave up."

Apparently, around the time of the King James era, the appendage, "up," was popular in Great Britain, in the same way that "on" has been adopted for some of the idioms of today; e.g., hold on, right on, carry on, bring it on, full on, etc.

Looking back to earlier English Bible translations provides evidence that *harpagēsometha* represents a disruption from the normal course, not a rescue from difficult circumstances. John Wycliffe's translation (1382 - 1395) of First Thessalonians 4:17 reads as follows:

Afterward we that lyuen, that ben left, schulen be rauyschid togidere with hem in cloudis, metinge Crist `in to the eir.[69] (Note, the correct translation of those who have "ben left", the survivors.)

Wycliffe translated the Greek word, *harpagēsometha* (ἀρπαγησόμεθα), as *"rauyschid."* Rauyschid is found one other time in the *Wycliffe Bible*. Acts 27:15 describes how Paul's ship was obstructed by the wind as it left the port of Phoenix, Crete. The ship was prevented from rounding the island toward a safer winter harbor.

Wycliffe: *And whanne the schip was <u>rauyschid</u>, and myyte not enforse ayens the wynde . . .*[70]

NKJV: *So when the ship was <u>caught</u>, and could not head into the wind . . .*

Notice that, according to the *New King James Version*, the ship was not "caught up," nor did it escape from the storm. The ship was overcome by the wind and was prevented from sailing in the desired direction. In fact, it was apparently being blown backward. Being *rauyschid* marked the beginning of the shipwreck course to Malta. Recalling the chart showing the connection between God's power, the resurrection, and the subduing of Christ's enemies, being overcome or subdued is exactly what we would expect to encounter in the First Thessalonians rapture passage.

Where Do We Go from Here?

Verse 17: ἐν (*en*); in / into. There is no definite article, no "the." Notice once again the accuracy of Wycliffe's translation. "schulen be rauyschid togidere with hem <u>in cloudis</u>." Not; in *the* cloudis. John Spencer has also commented on the absence of the definite article as well as the fact that "caught up" is missing from the original text.

"Because in the original Greek there is no definite article before, "clouds," the phrase can most literally be translated 'seized in clouds.'"[71]

Verse 17: νεφέλαις (*nefelais*); clouds. We shall be seized/plundered in clouds. Clouds are often mentioned in scripture during a transition between the physical and the spiritual states. Clouds were present during the transfiguration and the ascension; and Jesus will return in clouds. Clouds and dark smoke filled the Temple. These instances do not represent natural clouds or smoke, but a supernatural phenomenon. They are present during divine interventions between the heavenly and earthly realms. This transitional zone - this blur between two different dimensions - appears as clouds, vapor, or smoke. Once again, the only directional words in First Thessalonians 4:13-18 refer to the Lord descending and the dead rising.

Verse 17: εἰς (*eis*); for / to

Verse 17: ἀπάντησιν (*apantaesin*); from *apantao*[72], to meet from different directions. To further support the resolve that Jesus is coming and not merely planning a fly-by, we need only study the word "*meet*." *Apantesin*[73] (meet). This word is used in Matthew 25:6, Acts 28:15, and here in First Thessalonians. In every instance it is used to describe a greeting party, not a departure. Let's look at its usage in Matthew because of the striking similarity between Paul's usage and its usage by our Lord Jesus.

Then the kingdom of heaven shall be likened to ten virgins who took their lamps and went out <u>to meet</u> the bridegroom. Now five of them were wise, and five were foolish. Those who were foolish took their lamps and took no oil with them, but the wise took oil in their vessels with their lamps. But while the bridegroom was delayed, they all slumbered and slept. And at midnight a cry was heard: 'Behold, the bridegroom is coming; go out <u>to meet</u> him!' Then all those virgins arose and trimmed their lamps. And the foolish said to the wise, 'Give us some of your oil, for our lamps are going out.'. But the wise answered, saying, 'No, lest there should not be enough for us and you; but go rather to those who sell, and buy for yourselves.' And while they went to buy, the bridegroom came, and those who were ready went in with him to the wedding; and the door was shut. Afterward the other virgins came also, saying, 'Lord, Lord, open to us!' But he answered and said, 'Assuredly, I say to you, I do not know you.' Watch therefore, for you know neither the day nor the hour in which the Son of Man is coming. Matt. 25:1-13

This passage is often used to support the pre-tribulation rapture theory. But look at this meeting more closely. In verses one and six of Matthew Chapter 25, were the 10 virgins going out to be taken away by the Lord? Or, were they going out meet Him with the intention of escorting Him back to the bride? The answer is obvious. Their lanterns were lit specifically for the purpose of leading the bridegroom back to where the virgins had come from.

Once again, the greeting nature of this word for "meet" is clarified in Acts 28:15. *And from there, when the brethren heard about us, they came to meet us as far as Appii Forum and Three Inns. When Paul saw them, he thanked God and took courage.*

These believers from Italy were not going out to meet Paul with any thought of returning with him to Malta. Their meeting was nothing more than a greeting. *Apantesin* is also used several times in the Greek Septuagint version of the Old Testament; I Sam. 9:14, I Chron. 12:17, Jer. 41:6.

The reader who is thorough enough to investigate these Old Testament passages will only find further support that *apantesin* is a meeting and not a one-way departure.

Paul has now given a sufficient description of Christ's descent as the bodily Second Coming. Nothing in First Thessalonians Four says He's returning back up into heaven at the time of this meeting.

Verse 17: τοῦ Κυρίου (*tou Kuriou*); the Lord

Verse 17: εἰς (*eis*); in / into

Verse 17: ἀέρα (*aera*); air - the first heaven, above the ground. "In air" does not indicate that the glorified saints will be venturing beyond the atmosphere. The meeting in the air is nonspecific in terms of location. Paul could just as easily have used the word "heaven" or "heavens." Meeting in air is yet one more indication that Christ has descended from heaven at the time of the rapture. We will meet the Lord somewhere in [the] air. This meeting is the same gathering mentioned by Paul in his second letter to the Thessalonians.

We shall be changed. We shall be robbed of our physical bodies – plundered.

We will not be taken away immediately, but something will first be taken from us. Something that has already been purchased and merely waits for its redemption. The purchased possession is our mortal bodies.

Or do you not know that your body is the temple of the Holy Spirit who is in you, whom you have from God, and you are not your own? For you were <u>bought at a price</u>; therefore glorify God in your body and in your spirit, which are God's. 1 Cor. 6:19-20

Therefore comfort one another with these words. I Thess. 4:18

More about Paul's comfort to the Thessalonians will be discussed in the chapter on Christ's last enemy. The intent of this chapter has been to show that the rapture describes the transition in bodily form that will occur to enable the gathering of God's people into the presence of Christ.

The moment that we see Him as He is, we shall be like Him. The rapture is not God's people going to heaven; it is God's people becoming heavenly.

CHAPTER FOURTEEN
Tree of Life - New Body Transformation Vignette
- Doug Hamp

In this vignette Ben and Kristiana, part of the remnant of Israel, come to understand the true meaning of the Tree of Life from the time of Adam through to the moment they stood before it.

"To enter the city," Yeshua said, "you still need to be transformed from your bodies of flesh and blood to bodies like the Angels, glorious and not comprised of dust; yours must be conformed to my own glorious body and become partakers of my divine nature, free of corruption. You must be born again by taking of the Tree of Life and be transformed like Antipas and all of your clan that came before them." Pointing to the Tree of Life, which lined the river, each individual tree connected at the roots, he said with a big smile, "Now, both of you, stretch out your hands and take and eat leaves from the Tree of Life which are for your healing, and live forever!"

Kristiana's heart leapt with joy as she stretched out her hand and plucked off a leaf from the same Tree of Life which had been in Eden with Adam and Eve!

Ben stared intently at the leaf; his thoughts drifted back to the original Tree and amazingly it was as if he and Kristiana were holding the AEFOD again, back in the Chronicles: "Adam, where are you?" He felt the weight of Adonai's sadness on that day so long ago when he looked longingly for the last time at his dear children, from whom he was obligated to remove himself, and from the earth lest his splendor and radiance destroy it. Ben understood: his desire had been to walk with Adam and his sons as an expression of love. He wanted to make his home with them and share his heart; he wanted them to be where he was because he had always desired to live and walk among them, to be their King and Father, and they his people. He thought of how Adonai was forced to abandon the earth, putting up a veil of separation lest his own glory, like a stream of brimstone, destroy that which he had created. Because of Adonai's great mercy and love for his creation he had to go into a self-imposed exile rather than let everything become a lake of fire.

All of a sudden, they both saw and felt Michael and Gabriel standing next to the Tree of Life, surrounded by the four cherubim, which appeared like blazing torches. They passed from one to another the fiery whirling sword with such speed that it looked like lightning and became an impenetrable wall of fiery-lightning.

"Lucifer's strategy worked, despite his humiliation," Michael said in shock. "Death is now permanent and irreversible according to Lucifer's scheme. Will Adonai ever be able to undo it? I can only wonder what hope there is for Adam and Eve and their race now that the way to the Tree of Life is blocked. So long as Adam and his sons are separated through degeneration, Adonai can never reassert his presence on the earth because of his unequaled power, fire, and lightning."

Kristiana looked again at the leaf in her hand. It was so powerful it could transform a person from a constitution of dirt, *adamáh,* to one of spirit – like an Angel. The transformation could not be undone, however, and whatever state a person was in when they partook of the fruit, such would be their permanent state forever and ever. It was for that reason that Adonai had placed the cherubim around the tree to guard it at all costs. Therefore, the mortals could not eat from the Tree of Life until they had washed their garments, had bathed in the water of life, and had drunk from it. Once they had washed their robes, however, they had the right to the Tree of Life, and could enter through the gates into the City of Adonai because they possessed a body made of spirit, like the Angels.

For the first time, Ben understood why Adonai so quickly guarded Adam and Eve from eating from the tree. Had Adam taken of its fruit, he would have forever been in a state of death. Ben understood that adding the state of life from the Tree of Life to the state of death incurred by eating of the Tree of the Knowledge of Good and Evil, would have equaled an infinite state of incompatibility, like opposite forces. Had Adam eaten from the tree, he would have been transformed into the likeness of an Angel, though rebellious and accursed like Lucifer and the rebellious Angels.

He would have lingered in the gloom of shades and shadows, constantly in death, yearning to be free of its grip, yet with no hope of remedy from his dire existence.

Ben looked back at the river of life clearly understanding the predicament which Lucifer had created and which Yeshua had overcome through his sacrifice and his restoration of hope to the hopeless. Only now was there a way for an Adamite to transition from dirt body to spirit body, allowing entrance into the presence of Adonai. First, by bathing and drinking of the water of life which only Adonai could provide for the cleansing and healing of their bodies. And, then by eating of the Tree of Life completing the transformation and making them compatible with life in Adonai's kingdom.

Ben and Kristiana ate the leaves; in a mere moment they felt their entire composition change from the inside out. Every cell in their bodies, which was made of carbon, was transformed. The *adamáh*, planet, soil, dirt, which was their base composition was transformed into spirit, immortal, and resplendent bodies. They both looked at each other and then at their own new glorious body which death would never inhabit, which no weakness would ever plague. They were radiating light – the light coming from Adonai. They were new creations; no longer comprised of the *adamáh* but of the immaterial, created directly by Adonai. Their bodies at last conformed to his because they would always be in the light of his presence with no veil between them anymore. They at last had their wedding garment – their garment of *Yeshuáh*.

Ben looked over at Kristiana, whose body looked like a dazzling gem and who had rays of light emanating from her face, creating a glorious crown of life, sparkling like crystal with the color of emeralds shining brightly, with topazes, gems, and yellow pearls. Her feet and arms were shining like gleaming metal and her clothing was shining whiter than any snow; a shine like that of the stars of heaven, sparkling like the rays of the sun. Truly, she had been conformed to the image of the glorious body of Adonai and had become a partaker of the divine nature; she would never die and was truly a daughter of Adonai.

Ben sensed the same thing in his own body. The newness of his body stunned him so much that he grabbed one hand with the other to see how his new hands felt. The sensation of touch was just as real.

TREE OF LIFE – NEW BODY TRANSFIGURATION VIGNETTE

His body was tangible and "physical" but no longer made of dust. It was an altogether new mode of existence. But there was more, he seemed to have this special connection to all around him. Not only could he see Kristiana's beautiful new body but he could actually look into her heart. He knew her as she also knew him to the very depths of their souls. They each knew the history of the other. Instantly, Ben understood that this is the way it would be with all in Yeshua's kingdom, knowing and being known by all.

CHAPTER FIFTEEN
Christ's Last Enemy and the Rapture
- Chris Steinle

Why the Lord Tarries

Most Christians have used the phrase, "if the Lord tarries." The Bible tells us one of the reasons for Jesus' delay is that God *is longsuffering toward us, not willing that any should perish but that all should come to repentance.* But there is another reason why Jesus is waiting. The writer of Hebrews explains; *But this Man [Jesus], after He had offered one sacrifice for sins forever, sat down at the right hand of God, from that time <u>waiting till His enemies are made His footstool</u>. Heb. 10:12, 13.*

The fact that Christ's position at the right hand of the Father has a finite duration, and a condition upon which His retention in heaven depends, establishes an eschatological milestone - a technical marker establishing its own witness to the onset and order of end time events.

We have already shown the relationship between the resurrection/rapture and the physical realization of God's authority on earth. The chart from a previous chapter is presented again below to show the subjection involved in the transformation process.

Recall from our study of first century expectations that the Messianic epoch should begin with the *last tribulation and perplexity.* As any mature Christian can attest, affliction is effective to bring about humility and a heartfelt submission to God's will. Even so, the earth will be humbled in that Day.

> They shall go into the holes of the rocks,
> And into the caves of the earth,
> From the terror of the Lord
> And the glory of His majesty,
> When He arises to shake the earth mightily. Isaiah 2:19

The Correlation of God's Power, the Resurrection, & the Realization of God's Authority

Passage	*Power / Working / Ability*	*Resurrection / Transformation*	*Subjection / Authority*
Rom. 1:4	declared to be the Son of God with **power**	…by the **resurrection** from the dead	
1 Cor. 6:14	…by His **power**	God both **raised up** the Lord and will also **raise us up**	
1 Cor. 15:4-58		…**resurrection**…	He puts an **end to all rule and all authority and power**… till He has put all enemies **under His feet**… Now when all things are made **subject to Him**…
Eph. 1:19-22	what is the exceeding greatness of His **power** toward us… according to the **working** of His **mighty power** which He **worked**	…in Christ when He **raised Him from the dead**…	…far above all principality and power and might and dominion… He put all things **under His feet**
Phil. 3:10-21	that I may know Him and the **power**… … according to **the working** by which He is **able**	of His **resurrection**… I may attain to the **resurrection** from the dead… who will **transform** our lowly body… **conformed** to His glorious body	…even to **subdue** all things to Himself

Passage	Power / Working / Ability	Resurrection / Transformation	Subjection / Authority
Col. 2:12	through faith in the **working** of God	…in which you also were **raised** with Him … who **raised** Him **from the dead**	
Rev. 11:17	You have taken Your great **power**		and have begun to **reign**
Rev. 12:10	Now the salvation, and the **power**		the **kingdom** of our God and the **authority** of His Christ have come

Based on the correlations in the table above we could logically assert:
- If Christ must remain in heaven until all enemies are subdued, and,
- If the forces of heaven must be unleashed to bring mankind into subjection,
- Then Jesus cannot return until after the time of great tribulation, because He must sit at the Father's right hand till His enemies are subdued.

First Corinthians 15:24-26 provides another witness to the timing of the rapture. Paul stated;

Then comes the end, when He delivers the kingdom to God the Father, when He puts an end to all rule and all authority and power. For He must reign till He has put all enemies under His feet. The last enemy that will be abolished is death.

*The last enemy that will be abolished **(katargeitai)** is death.* 1 Cor. 15:26 Subduing death must be distinguished from the destruction (ἀπόλλυται, *apollytai*) of death. The Greek texts do not say the last enemy that will be "destroyed" is death.

Katargeitai and *apollutai* do not have the same meaning. There is a difference between subduing and destroying.

Thayer's Greek Lexicon:

"STRONG'S NT 622: ἀπόλλυμι destroy, i.e. to put out of the way entirely, abolish, put an end to, ruin..."[74]

A form of *katargeo* occurs in the following verse and has also been translated as "destroyed." But according Thayer's Greek Lexicon, death is overcome, not destroyed.

Inasmuch then as the children have partaken of flesh and blood, He Himself likewise shared in the same, that through death He might <u>bring to naught</u> (καταργήσῃ, katargēsē) him who had the power of death, that is, the devil. Heb. 2:14

Thayer's Greek Lexicon:

"STRONG'S NT 2673: καταργέω
to render idle, unemployed, inactive, inoperative: τήν γῆν, to deprive of its strength, make barren (A. V. cumber), Luke 13:7; to cause a person or a thing to have no further efficiency; to deprive of force, influence, power (A. V. bring to naught, make of none effect)"[75]

In ancient times, victory over an enemy was sometimes dramatized by placing the defeated authority's head or neck under the foot of the conquering king. The conquered king's personal plight was in the hands of the victor. The defeated king may, or may not, be executed (destroyed) subsequent to his subjection.

The death which Paul was referring to as the last enemy is the "state of being dead," which is holding the dead in their graves. It is the *power of death* that is being overcome; and God will *bring to naught* the power of death in the resurrection of the dead. Jesus will have mastered death when, at His command, the dead hear His voice and rise to life. At that time, the enemy of death will become the footstool of Christ. After the millennial reign, when every soul is emptied from Hades, Hades will have no more purpose. At that time, death will be destroyed. But Christ's technical victory over death will have already been realized at the *resurrection of the dead*.

Then Comes the End

Then comes the end... The end of what? Paul tells us this end comes at the time *when He puts an end to all rule and all authority and power.* That would be the time when all of Christ's enemies have been subdued, because, *He must reign till He has put all enemies under His feet.* Therefore, *"Then comes the end"* refers to the end of Jesus' station at the Father's right hand. Then comes the end of waiting for the subjection of Christ's enemies.

"Then" Jesus will be released to descend from heaven and return to earth. Hebrews 2:8 says, *But now we do not yet see all things put under him.* "Then comes the end," announces the time when we DO SEE all things put under Him. And most particularly according to Paul, we see His last enemy, death, put under Him. Paul makes a direct connection between the completion of Jesus' time at the Father's right hand and the subduing of death.

The subjection of the last enemy, death, will be realized on earth as the resurrection of the dead, in much the same way as Christ's government on earth will be realized during Christ's Millennial Reign. Jesus will return immediately upon the resurrection of the dead to transform the living and those raised in the resurrection.

It is reasonable to assume that Paul shared this same resurrection discourse in-person while he was with the Thessalonians that he had written to the church at Corinth. Because of the association between the resurrection and the subduing of Christ's last enemy, Paul's comfort to the bereaved Thessalonians took the form of the following syllogism:

- The subjection of death will be realized on earth by the resurrection of the dead.
- Christ will reside in heaven until His last enemy (death) is overcome.
- Therefore, Christ's coming/descending from the Father's right hand cannot precede the resurrection of those who have fallen asleep.
- And, those left alive will not be changed until they see Him as He is, when Christ descends from heaven.

So now with all of the information available we can articulate the resurrection/rapture/gathering in detail. Jesus will call forth the dead from their graves while seated at the Father's right hand or during His descent from heaven, but at least simultaneously with the subduing of death. According to Paul, the dead must rise first, so the living will remain unchanged until after the resurrection. Then, the resurrected dead, together with the living, will be transformed in the redemption of the body. Then the glorified saints will meet Jesus in the air and participate in the Gathering.

We have already reviewed Paul's quotation from Isaiah 25 and Hosea 13 that death will be swallowed up in victory. But where is the witness in Scripture to the fact that death will be Christ's last enemy? Does the Bible disclose any of Christ's other enemies? The twelfth chapter of Daniel could have provided the basis for the order of end time events mentioned by Paul in his Corinthian and Thessalonian letters.

Daniel and the Thessalonians Connection

The table below compares events found in Daniel Chapter 12 with similar events used by Paul to teach the order of end time events. The Last Enemy, labeled "Z," was established in First Corinthians 15. Suggested enemies "X" and "Y" must obviously be encountered before the last enemy – death. We also have corroborating passages from Revelation 19 and 20 that Satan is only overcome and bound (subdued) at the Second Coming. Satan will survive as the last enemy, after the Beast and False Prophet have been thrown into the lake of fire.

Christ's Enemies Based on the Chronology of Daniel Chapter 12			
Daniel 12 Passage	**Messianic Age Event**	**2nd Thessalonians Reference**	**Enemies of Christ**
Vs 1. Michael and the Time of Distress	Last Tribulation		
Vs 7. when the **power of the holy people** has been **completely shattered**	Perplexity	Vs 3b. the **falling away** comes first	Enemy (X) Forces of Wickedness? The Fourth Beast?
Vs 11. **daily sacrifice is taken away**, and the **abomination of desolation**	Hostile Powers?	Vs 3c, 4. **man of sin** is revealed, **opposes** & **exalts, sits as God in the temple of God**	Enemy (Y) Son of Perdition Lawless One False Prophet
Vs 13. go your way **till the end**; for **you shall rest, and will arise** to **your inheritance** at the end of the days	Resurrection of the Just Gathering of the Dispersed	Vs 1. **coming of our Lord Jesus Christ** and our **gathering together to Him** Vs 2. as though the **day of the Lord (Christ)** had come	Last Enemy (Z) Death Satan (the Power of Death) The Dragon

If, in fact, the False Prophet is also the Lawless One, Paul states that he will be destroyed by the brightness of His coming - which could be a reference to God as a consuming fire. But in this case also, Satan would be allowed to survive the Lawless One. We'll discuss the identity of the Beast in relation to the time of Perplexity near the end of this chapter.

Because death is the last enemy to be subdued, all other enemies would have to be subdued first. These other enemies might be thought of as the next-to-the-last enemies. The associations shown in the table may have been precisely what Paul had taught the Thessalonians when he was with them. He may have simply been teaching the Thessalonians from the Book of Daniel – a book dear to the heart of the Pharisees because of its witness to the resurrection.

Paul stated in First Thessalonians Four that the resurrection would be the last prophetic event before, or at the time of, Christ's return. We have already demonstrated logically that, if the resurrection is last, then Christ's victory over death would likewise be last. But the resurrection is also the last event, in the last verse, of the last chapter of Daniel. Could Paul's chronology of end time events have been based on this placement of the resurrection in the prophetic Book of Daniel? We find strong evidence for such a conclusion in the second chapter of Paul's second letter to the Thessalonians. In order to establish this connection to Daniel, it will be necessary to review the opening verses of Second Thessalonians Chapter Two.

1 Now, brethren, concerning the coming of our Lord Jesus Christ and our gathering together to Him, we ask you, 2 not to be soon shaken in mind or troubled, either by spirit or by word or by letter, as if from us, as though the day of Christ had come. 3 Let no one deceive you by any means; for that Day will not come unless the falling away comes first, and the man of sin is revealed, the son of perdition, 4 who opposes and exalts himself above all that is called God or that is worshiped, so that he sits as God in the temple of God, showing himself that he is God.

5 Do you not remember that when I was still with you I told you these things? 6 And now you know what is restraining, that he may be revealed in his own time. 7 For the mystery of lawlessness is already at work; only he who now restrains will do so until he is taken out of the way.

8 And then the lawless one will be revealed, whom the Lord will consume with the breath of His mouth and destroy with the brightness of His coming. 9 The coming of the lawless one is according to the working of Satan, with all power, signs, and lying wonders, 10 and with all unrighteous deception among those who perish, because they did not receive the love of the truth, that they might be saved. 11 And for this reason God will send them strong delusion, that they should believe the lie, 12 that they all may be condemned who did not believe the truth but had pleasure in unrighteousness. 2 Thess. 2:1-12

We are not told in the verses above what kind of report had been circulated. Jesus warned His disciples that deceivers would come, saying; *"Then if anyone says to you, 'Look, here is the Christ!' or 'There!' do not believe it."* What we do know is Paul described the Second Coming in several ways to make it perfectly clear which day he was talking about: *The coming of our Lord Jesus Christ; our gathering together to Him; the day of Christ.*

An important observation to note for the purpose of linking this passage to Daniel Chapter 12 is that Paul started from endpoint, Christ's coming - the final event in the table above. Then Paul submitted two end times signs that must occur before the Second Coming. Both of these signs can be found in Daniel Chapter 12.

The first sign, *the falling away,* refers to the condition of God's people, but will likely be the result of sinister forces. The second sign, the revealing of *the man of sin*, refers specifically to *the Son of Perdition*. Both of these signs take place in Daniel during a season - *"At that time"* - which is a time of great distress.

Some explanation of the layout of the Book of Daniel is necessary in order to understand why the Thessalonians would have recognized these two signs by their brief descriptions in Paul's letter. Daniel Chapter 12 comes at the end of a vision that began in Daniel Chapter 10. Chapter 12 could be compared to Revelation Chapter Six in that they both contain an overview of each book. But rather than being symbolized by the seals at the opening of Revelation, the Book of Daniel places the overview of Daniel's dreams and visions at the end of the book.

Daniel Chapter 12 contains two condensed summaries of the time of the end. Verses 1-3 present a poetic version of the summary; then verses 7-13 give a final explanation of the time of the end.

We will look at the time of tribulation in the opening summary of Daniel 12 first, because it provides several links between Daniel and Second Thessalonians Chapter Two. These associations require a little digging to discover; but once the background for these associations is developed, the connections become so obvious that they can't be ignored.

> 1 At that time Michael shall stand up,
> The great prince who stands watch over the sons of your people;
> And there shall be a time of trouble,
> Such as never was since there was a nation,
> Even to that time.
> And at that time your people shall be delivered,
> Every one who is found written in the book.
> 2 And many of those who sleep in the dust of the earth shall awake,
> Some to everlasting life,
> Some to shame and everlasting contempt.
> 3 Those who are wise shall shine
> Like the brightness of the firmament,
> And those who turn many to righteousness
> Like the stars forever and ever.

The first verse attributes the time of trouble to the archangel Michael. Revelation Chapter 12 explains how this struggle in the spiritual realm results in woe to the inhabitants of the earth.

> And war broke out in heaven: Michael and his angels fought with the dragon; and the dragon and his angels fought, but they did not prevail, nor was a place found for them in heaven any longer. So the great dragon was cast out, that serpent of old, called the Devil and Satan, who deceives the whole world; he was cast to the earth, and his angels were cast out with him. Then I heard a loud voice saying in heaven, "Now salvation, and strength, and the kingdom of our God, and the power of His Christ have come, for the accuser of our brethren, who accused them before our God day and night, has been cast down. And they overcame him by the blood of the Lamb and by the word of their testimony, and they did not love their lives to the death. Therefore rejoice, O heavens, and you who dwell in them! Woe to the inhabitants of the earth and the sea! For the devil has come down to you, having great wrath, because he knows that he has a short time. Rev. 12:7-12.

Michael's victory over Satan would certainly be counted as a measure of Christ's enemies being subdued. But this victory is not the end of Satan. Angels are often depicted by artists as wrestlers. So in modern terms we might think of this wrestling bout as Satan getting thrown into the stands. Gabriel and Michael could be described as two members of a heavenly wrestling team. Daniel's vision in chapters 10-12 contains the following references supporting the imagery of angelic wrestlers.

"But the prince of the kingdom of Persia withstood me twenty-one days; and behold, Michael, one of the chief princes, came to help me, for I had been left alone there with the kings of Persia." - Daniel 10:13.

"No one upholds me against these, except Michael your prince." Daniel 10:21b.

"Hold" is a wrestling term still used today. Wrestling holds are used to restrain one's opponent. The reader may be familiar with this line of reasoning and be completely convinced that the restrainer of Second Thessalonians is the Holy Spirit or the Church. But there is nothing in the Greek text to support this conclusion. And there is far more support for connecting the restrainer to Michael. The authors are both well aware of, and have been fully trained in, the arguments from the Dispensational and Pre-Tribulational points of view.

But let's take a look at the facts that we do know. Some Bible publishers have capitalized (deified) the personal pronoun, "he," in Second Thessalonians 2:7 in order to support the Dispensational doctrine. No such capitalization exists in the original manuscripts and there is no mention of the Holy Spirit in this passage. Paul expected the Thessalonians to understand what was restraining based on a prior conversation.

Because the ancient manuscripts do not identify the pronouns in verses five and six, the Protestant Reformers believed the one restraining to be the Roman Empire, and the one being restrained to be the Roman Papacy. Consider a few short quotes that will demonstrate the ambiguity of the pronouns in question.

- "And now what withholdeth... Let my readers now consider which of the two is the probable - either that Paul declared that the light of the gospel must be diffused through all parts of the earth before God would thus give loose reins to Satan, or that the power of the Roman Empire stood in the way of the rise of Antichrist..."[76] *Commentary of the Second Epistle to the Thessalonians* by John Calvin.

- "And now ye know what withholdeth that he might be revealed in his time. What hinders and stops...He foretells that when the empire of Rome is taken away, the seat that falls away from God will succeed and hold its place, as the old writers, Tertullian, Chrysostom, and Jerome explain and interpret it. He who is now in authority and rules all, that is, the Roman Empire."[77] *The Geneva Bible*

- "Something hindered or withheld the man of sin. It is supposed to be the power of the Roman Empire, which the apostle did not mention more plainly at that time."[78] *The Matthew Henry Commentary*

- "And now ye know - By what I told you when I was with you. That which restraineth - The power of the Roman emperors. When this is taken away, the wicked one will be revealed."[79] *John Wesley*

Hopefully the Christian reader would place as much confidence in the scholarship of these sources as in the opinion of a modern commercial Bible publisher. These quotes are presented solely for the purpose of showing that the pronoun, "he" is non-specific based on the text; not for the purpose of endorsing antagonism toward the politics or religion of Rome. So now, hopefully, the reader can investigate the identity of the restrainer somewhat objectively.

6 And now you know what is restraining, that he may be revealed in his own time. 7 For the mystery of lawlessness is already at work; only he who now restrains will do so until he is taken out of the way. 8 And then the lawless one will be revealed,

What restrains? What situation or predicament? In the original Greek text, the word for "restrains" is κατέχον (*katechon*)[80], from the Greek word, *echo*, "to hold." This is also the word used in the Greek Septuagint to express restraint in Daniel's vision. *"No one holds with me against these, except Michael your prince."* But would the assumption that Michael is the one holding make sense within the context of Paul's letter? The answer is; "Absolutely!"

The mystery of lawlessness was already working in the world at the time of Paul's letter. But the full manifestation of Satan's power will not be realized in the physical realm until Satan has been fully restricted from the spiritual realm. Satan's presence in heaven is restraining the fullness of his power on earth. The wrestling has been ongoing at least since the time of Daniel. Please consider the following interpretation of the pronouns. He (Michael) will continue holding (restraining) until he (Satan) is taken down (out of the way from heaven's perspective). Then the full force of Satan, *according to the working of Satan, with all power, signs, and lying wonders* will cause the time of woe to the inhabitants of the earth known as the Great Tribulation.

As expected from the time of the Second Temple, the last tribulation will be a time of perplexity. Because Satan is a deceiver and the father of lies, a spirit of deception will encompass the world. The books of Daniel and Revelation attribute the consternation of humanity to the boastful and blasphemous words being disseminated by the one given eyes and a mouth to speak pompous words. Those who do not love the truth of God will be given over to strong delusion to believe the lie.

During this period of perplexity two discrete entities will appear. One is a re-emergence of Daniel's Fourth Beast who *"shall devour the whole earth."* And the second entity is the Little Horn, who would seem from his profile to be the False Prophet of Revelation; and, according to Second Thessalonians, also the man of sin, the Lawless One, or the Son of Perdition.

Because the falling away is a condition apparently brought about during the time of delusion, and because the Beast is a kingdom, it is the Son of Perdition who will be the human incarnation of Satan once he is cast out of heaven. Thus, we have come full circle in showing the relationship between Daniel 12:1 and Second Thessalonians Chapter Two.

Paul doesn't mention the Beast, but clearly alludes to the time of deceit and the manifestation of Satan (the dragon) in human form.

Verses 7, 11, and 13 listed in the table above are from the last section of Daniel 12. We have now demonstrated how each of these verses could have been the source for Paul's chronology for both of his letters to the Thessalonians. The remote probability of finding such a tight correlation within the span of a few verses supports the conclusions drawn in this chapter. But there are still two more points of interest in these last chapters of Daniel.

Gabriel told Daniel that the information he was sent to share was *"noted in the* Scripture of *Truth" Daniel 10:21*. Could this have been the truth that those perishing had no love for? In addition, the prophecy imparted at the end of the Book of Daniel in verses 7-13 was given by a *"man clothed in linen."* In Daniel Chapter 10, at the beginning of the vision, Daniel described this man clothed in linen by the attributes of the Son of God in His glory. This would imply that this final summary of the events of the end were spoken "By the word of the Lord." Could this also be why the angel told John near the end of the Apocalypse, For the testimony of Jesus is the spirit of prophecy. Rev. 19:10

The fact that Paul used the falling away and the man of sin as precursors to the Lord's coming indicates that he did not anticipate the onset of the time of distress to be a recognizable sign in itself. If Paul thought there would be an obvious beginning to the Tribulation, he could have merely stated the absence of tribulation as proof that the Lord had not already come. The implications of this observation call for a revision in the church's expectation regarding the onset of the Great Tribulation. What if, as Jesus stated, the time of tribulation begins gradually - like the birth pangs of labor?

Daniel Chapter Twelve begins with the words, "At that time." To understand the things that will happen when we enter that time we must look back to the previous chapters of Daniel. Indeed, verses 7, 11, and 13 of Daniel Twelve also look back to the details of the prior chapters. It is beyond the scope of this study to comment on the entire Book of Daniel, so we will only make a few general observations.

1. Wicked rulers are raised up by vicarious powers.
2. Pomp, blasphemy, cunning, and deceit characterize their reigns.
3. Various rulers and nations war against one another.
4. The saints are persecuted and slain.
5. The Fourth Beast will devour the whole earth.
6. The King of the North will take away sacrifices and set up the abomination in the sanctuary.

The first four of these circumstances have been fulfilled during multiple waves throughout history. But the last two are yet to be fulfilled; although, some might argue that one or more Beasts (heathen nations) have already devoured the earth.

So based on Paul's writings, what will be the signs indicating the time of the Great Tribulation has begun? First of all, deceit and delusion will swell to the point that even the elect will be tempted to doubt what is true. This time of strong delusion will be a sign that the end has begun. Paul had apparently already told the Thessalonian Church to expect this sign because he was reminding them of the details of their former conversation.

In the midst of this time of perplexity, the King of the North (or a type of the King of the North) will rise up after the fashion of Antiochus Epiphanies. Jesus and Paul both told believers to watch for a final occurrence of this event.

In conclusion, the sign of the falling away will be recognized by a level of perplexity and deception unequaled in human history. The disinformation broadcast by evil leaders will very likely be responsible for the state of lawlessness and the abounding of sin. Such a state of delusion, accompanied by the setting up of an actual abomination in the sanctuary, would fulfill the prerequisites of Paul based on the Book of Daniel. These signs will precede the rapture. The rapture is not the sign.

CHAPTER SIXTEEN
Putting It All Together: What Happens on the Day of the Second Coming?
- Doug Hamp

When we think about the end times, we often think about the Antichrist, about the changes in the weather, about the failing economy - things that are touching our lives. This makes sense because we all have lives to live. But there is a day coming that we know as, "The Second Coming." This chapter presents a graphic look at the second coming of Jesus Christ to the earth. This chapter will also point to scriptural proof that the second coming will occur at Armageddon.

The reader is familiar with the second coming, and has probably heard of the battle of Armageddon; but there are actually a lot of misconceptions about Armageddon. For example, think for a moment about where you believe the battle of Armageddon is going to take place. Maybe you have taken a Bible class where you saw that it was up north. We will demonstrate that the actual location is in Jerusalem. This, and other, exciting revelations will open the reader's eyes to a new perspective on the events of the second coming of Jesus Christ, and the battle of Armageddon.

Questions we might have concerning this time period might include:

1. What are the conditions on the Earth before Jesus comes? We should consider this question because the earth is going to be quite a mess when Jesus returns.
2. What will it look like when the heavens pass away? What is the scriptural evidence for this dramatic event?
3. What happens to the earth at Jesus fiery return? This will definitely be an exciting event. We will discover that the earth is going to be destroyed beyond repair.
4. What will be the location of the battle of Armageddon? As was briefly stated, it will be closer to Jerusalem than one might have previously considered it to be.
5. How will Jesus fight when He comes back? We know He is coming on a white horse, but will He do any more than that? We will examine this in great detail.

PUTTING IT ALL TOGETHER

What are the conditions of the earth before the second coming? There will be an ash cloud that blankets the earth, blocking the sun and the moon. Billions would have been killed by the two hundred million demonic horsemen that come out of the pit (Rev. 9). All the oceans, rivers, lakes etc. are blood instead of water. The earth at this time is not a place that we would want to be. Satan and the fallen angels in actual bodily form are on the earth.

Smoke will darken the sky before the day of the Lord (Rev. 9:2). This is about the midpoint of a seven year period which is traditionally called "The Great Tribulation". It can be argued, however, that The Great Tribulation is technically a three and a half year period, but this argument is beyond the scope of this particular book. *And he opened the bottomless pit, and smoke arose out of the pit like the smoke of a great furnace. So the sun and the air were darkened because of the smoke of the pit. Rev. 9:2* This is the same darkening of the sun referenced in Isaiah 13:10; *For the stars of heaven and their constellations will not give their light; the sun will be darkened in its going forth, and the moon will not cause its light to shine.* Why will it not cause its light to shine? Because ash has filled the sky.

Some years ago we had some forest fires here in California. I remember looking up at the sky in the evening with all the ash in the sky; and I saw that the moon was actually blood red. When it is observed through a layer of ash, it looks blood red. There is also a phenomenon, known as a lunar eclipse, where the earth comes between the sun and the moon and casts a red shadow on the moon. This is called a "blood moon". This darkening of the sun and moon will be a constant state of reality during that three and a half year period due to all that ash that is going to come out of the pit when Satan opens it up.

Revelation 16:10 says; *Then the fifth angel poured out his bowl on the throne of the beast, and his kingdom became full of darkness; and they gnawed their tongues because of the pain.* Again, why is it dark? Is it just some mysterious kind of darkness? Or could it be from the ash that has come out of the pit? This author believes the red moon is caused by the ash. As an example, there are pictures of an ice filled sky in Iceland showing that the sun is not giving the fullness of its light because it has been blocked out by ice particles. If thick, dark ash were to cover the sun, it would look like sack cloth had covered it.

Revelation tells us that the earth is going to be laid waste. *Then the second angel poured out his bowl on the sea, and it became blood as of a dead man; and every living creature in the sea died. Then the third angel poured out his bowl on the rivers and springs of water, and they became blood.* Rev. 16:3, 4 Imagine all of the water in the entire world has become full of blood. It says in Isaiah 26:21, *The earth will also disclose her blood, and will no more cover her slain.* We believe this verse says that all the blood that was ever shed from the days of Abel, up until the very last person to be murdered, will come back and come out in the oceans and rivers. The angel of the waters will say, *You are righteous, O Lord, the One who is and who was and who is to be, because You have judged these things. For they have shed the blood of saints and prophets, and You have given them blood to drink. For it is their just due.* Rev. 16:5, 6 Those who shed innocent blood on the earth will have blood to drink as their just reward.

We know that the fallen angels are going to be bodily on the earth at this time. It says in Revelation 12:9, *So the great dragon was cast out, that serpent of old, called the Devil and Satan, who deceives the whole world; he was cast to the earth, and his angels were cast out with him.* This will happen at the mid-point of the seven year period. Notice also in Revelation 12:4 that it says, *His tail drew a third of the stars of heaven and threw them to the earth.* He is called "the great dragon", the "serpent of old", "the Devil" and "Satan." The image of him as a dragon is used when depicting his tail drawing a third of the stars of heaven and throwing them to the earth. Here we see that the angels are called stars. In Revelation 8:10, 11; *And a great star fell from heaven, burning like a torch, and it fell on a third of the rivers and on the springs of water. The name of the star is Wormwood.*

One might ask, "How can it be that events in Revelation 12 and events in Revelation Eight are happening at the same time?" Revelation is a thematically organized book and not a chronological book. The Gospel of John, for example, is also laid out thematically. It groups like-kind events together. A historian documenting a certain period of history might arrange events in chronological order, or in a thematic manner. A chronological time line would begin with year one and relate events as they happened. This approach can be difficult to follow at times.

PUTTING IT ALL TOGETHER

It is often beneficial to group things together according to relationships and circles, as it were. This is essentially what John has done in Revelation. He grouped events together. Obviously he wrote according to the way he received the revelations, but really, God is the one who gave us these events in a thematic way.

So rather than looking at the chapter and verse to say what comes first and what comes second, look at the events themselves and if they pair up in any way. It could be argued that if there are three points in common, one would have a very strong connection between the two events. This approach is similar to triangulation. If one has a cell phone, and if there are three towers around the cell phone location, one can triangulate his/her position. This is essentially what we are doing. I have named this principle, "Biblical Triangulation". It is this principle that is used here in Revelation, and other passages in the Bible.

Then the fifth angel sounded: and I saw a star fallen from heaven to the earth. To him was given the key to the bottomless pit. Rev. 9:1 Here is a star that is falling. When did this star fall? He fell back in Revelation 8:10, *And a great star fell from heaven, burning like a torch.* Who is this star? We discover who this star is in Revelation 12:4, *His tail drew a third of the stars of heaven and threw them to the earth.* As previously mentioned, this is a reference to Satan. So in Revelation 8:10, when it says, *a great star fell from heaven*, this seems to be a reference to Satan himself, not a meteorite.

It is basically different camera angles. In Revelation Chapter 12, the camera is up here in heaven, now looking down. One could think of Michael with his cell phone, filming what's going on and then he puts it up on *YouTube* or something. At the same time, the people on the earth have their cell phones, as it were, and they're watching as Satan falls to the earth. What would he look like to them? He would look like a great star falling from heaven. Revelation 9:1 says that the star fallen from heaven was already on the earth. Stars are being interpreted as angels. We see this in other places as well. For example, when Jesus has the seven stars in His right hand, which are the seven angels to the seven churches (Rev. 1:20). Revelation Chapter Eight also references angels when discussing some of the host of heaven being cast down and some of the stars being cast down to the ground and trampled.

There are symbols in scripture and there are keys to unlocking our understanding of the symbols. The Bible can be taken literally once one understands the key for unlocking the symbols. Scripture tells us that stars are, in fact, angels. Daniel Chapter Eight talks about the Antichrist rising up to the host of heaven. This is a description of the angels, and then also of the stars. We have in Revelation 6:13, *And the stars of heaven* (that is, fallen angels) *fell to the earth, as a fig tree drops its late figs when it is shaken by a mighty wind.* And Isaiah 34 says, *All the host of heaven shall be dissolved, and the heavens shall be rolled up like a scroll; all their host shall fall down, as the leaf falls from the vine, and as fruit falling from a fig tree.*

Now think about it for a second; is this is really talking about stars? Stars are very, very far away. It would take them a long time to get here. Or, is it talking about the star closest to us, the sun? If it is talking about the sun, and then the sun falls to the earth, the earth is gone; right? Then the book of Revelation is over. There are really no more events for Revelation to convey to us if everything has just ended. So it can't be talking about actual stars like our sun. It is talking about the angels; those are fallen angels that have fallen to the earth because they are going to pass through the veil.

The veil between heaven and earth is a very important principle that I did not even know about until a couple years ago when I began discovering it. But there it was, in the Bible, all along. It is an exciting discovery! The book of Revelation is literally the unveiling of the Lord Jesus Christ. In the Greek we have the words *apo kalupsi. Apo* means "away from" and *kalupsis* means "a veil". So *apo kalupsi* means: "the uncovering", "the unveiling", or the "revelation".

In First John 3:2, when He is revealed, uncovered, unveiled, we shall see Him. *We shall be like Him, for we shall see Him as He is.* In Isaiah 40, verse 5 tells us that the glory of the Lord will be revealed and all of humanity will see it at once. Before the fall of Adam, the terrestrial realm and the spiritual realm were really one. Today, we cannot see beyond the veil on any given day.

But before the fall, God was in perfect harmony with man and man was in perfect harmony with God. That's why when God came walking in the garden there was no issue, until Adam and Eve took a bite of that fruit. As a result, God had to cast them out because they could no longer be in His presence. Why couldn't they be in His presence?

PUTTING IT ALL TOGETHER

Was God suddenly kind of snobbish? Perhaps with an attitude of," I'm sorry I'm just too good for you guys now. You didn't obey me, so now we can't be friends anymore." No. That really wasn't, and still isn't, the issue. The issue is, understanding what is God really like.

As Christians we have a fair understanding of God's characteristics, such as love. But what does He look like? Scriptures clearly tell us that He has fire from His waist up and from His waist down, and it's mingled with electricity. The word in Hebrew is *Ashman*, which means "electricity." In Greek, it's *electros*, again "electricity." We see in other places that it's lightning. So you have this fiery, lightning, kind of God that cannot have sin or corruption in His presence, not because He doesn't like us, but just because we're incompatible. Daniel says His throne was a fiery flame, its wheels a burning fire; a fiery stream issued and came forth from before Him. Imagine being in the presence of God and all of His blazing fire. Now imagine going up to God and giving Him a hug. How would that feel? That would really be the end of your day, wouldn't it? Because you cannot do that, I cannot do that, we are incompatible with God.

It is similar to the story of the boy in the bubble. He could not be exposed to the outside world. Now imagine you're his mother or you are his father. How would you feel? Wouldn't you want to just climb in there and give your son a hug because you love him so much? You would want to squeeze him and tell him how wonderful he is and that you want to be with him. But instead you must say, "Honey, I can't come in there because if I do, if I go beyond this veil between us, you will die. So you have to stay in there until we find a solution for you." God knew what the solution was, but He could not fulfill that until the appropriate time.

So God put a veil between heaven and earth, until that time. Actually, God is the one who left the Garden and lets us be on planet Earth. But on occasion, that veil was opened so that people could see through. Stephen, when he was being stoned, gazed into heaven and saw the glory of God. He said, *Look! I see the heavens opened and the Son of Man standing at the right hand of God! Acts 7:56* Now this isn't the kind of "stoned" that can happen here in California! He was actually being stoned with real rocks and he was able to see beyond the veil. This is just one occasion when God allowed people see beyond that veil. John says in Revelation, *Now I saw heaven opened. Rev. 19:11*

Ezekiel sitting by the river Chebar says, *the heavens were opened and I saw visions of God.* Ezek. 1:1 As Jesus was coming up out of the water, *the heavens were opened to Him.* Matt. 3:16

There were so many places where the heavens are opened and people were able to see just through a little bit. When Elisha and his servant were surrounded by the Syrians, Elisha prayed that God would open his eyes and then he saw horses and chariots of fire (2 Kings 6:17). It was like Elisha's servant put on his decoder glasses, could then see beyond into that other realm and he could see what was behind the veil. God's desire has always been to dwell with men openly, without any kind of a veil, with nothing between us, and completely exposed, one to another. This is His great desire. The day is coming; and it will happen at the Second Coming. God wants to dwell with man. *And he who sits on the throne will dwell among them* (Rev. 7:15). *The tabernacle of God is with men, and He will dwell with them, and they shall be His people. God Himself will be with them and be their God.* Rev. 21:3

And the heavens shall be rolled up like a scroll. Is. 34:4 This is another one of those passages that I couldn't figure out. What would it look like for the sky to recede like a scroll? This is a reference to the veil that will eventually pass away. It doesn't mean the sun, the moon and the stars will one day go away. Those will never depart. God promised His continued faithfulness toward Israel, based on the continued existence of the sun, moon and stars. So the heavens passing away, the heavens rolling up like a scroll, are because the veil is going to go away. *Then the sky receded as a scroll when it is rolled up, and every mountain and island was moved out of its place.* Rev. 6:14 This is a pretty major phenomenon when this happens; in fact, I see this as the end. We have come now to the end of all things. There is nothing more that's going to happen as far as the kingdom of Antichrist.

This is the time when the veil goes away and Jesus comes back. Isaiah writes it this way;

And He will destroy on this mountain the surface of the covering cast over all people, and the veil that is spread over all nations. He will swallow up death forever, and the Lord God will wipe away tears from all faces; the rebuke of His people He will take away from all the earth; for the Lord has spoken. And it will be said in that day:

PUTTING IT ALL TOGETHER

"Behold, this is our God; we have waited for Him, and He will save us. This is the Lord; we have waited for Him; we will be glad and rejoice in His salvation." Isa. 25:7-9

The Lord God will swallow up death forever and wipe away tears from all faces. The surface of the covering cast over all people, and the veil that is spread over all nations, will go away when the Lord comes back. Notice that death will be swallowed up at that point. For those who are in the city, or in the temple, on the mountain of God, it will pass away. Isaiah also says it this way; *Oh, that You would rend the heavens! That You would come down!* Isa. 64:1 He wants the heavens to be broken so that God himself would come down.

The veil is like a curtain. When it opens, out comes Jesus - ta da! "Here I am". Everyone will take notice. No longer will they be pretending that He does not exist. There are many atheists in the world today. There will not be any atheists on the day that the veil opens up, when the heavens pass away, because every eye will see Him. People will say, as they go running into the caves and the clefts of the rocks, *"Fall on us and hide us from the face of Him who sits on the throne and from the wrath of the Lamb!* Suddenly everyone will realize that this is the big day; *For the great day of His wrath has come, and who is able to stand?* Rev. 6:17

Perhaps it will be like a one way mirror. A one way mirror enables people on one side to look through, but people on the other side cannot see through. Right now we cannot see through that one way mirror, but those on the other side can see through. Perhaps the one way mirror will break at that time. We don't know exactly what it will look like when the veil is removed, but it will pass away. Then the two domains; the domain of mankind with planet Earth, and the domain of God and the angels - and even the demons, will not be separated. When the veil between the two domains passes away, the two shall become one again.

The heavens are going to open and Jesus will come. His return will be a fiery return. Everyone will see Him coming in flaming fire. Every mountain will be shaken, moved and gone. Every island will be shaken, moved and gone. The elements and the mountains will begin to melt at that time. This will be unmistakable. Don't worry - you will know when the Second Coming is! You will know when Jesus comes back. That is why He told his disciples, if someone says, *'I am the Christ'*, don't believe it because you will know when the Christ comes (Matt. 24:5).

Why do we believe Jesus' second coming will be a fiery return? We read in Isaiah 66:15 and 16, *For behold, the Lord will come with fire and with His chariots, like a whirlwind, to render His anger with fury, and His rebuke with flames of fire. For by fire and by His sword The Lord will judge all flesh; and the slain of the Lord shall be many.*

In Second Thessalonians, it says, *when the Lord Jesus is revealed from heaven with His mighty angels, in flaming fire taking vengeance on those who do not know God, and on those who do not obey the gospel of our Lord Jesus Christ.* 2 Thess. 1:7, 8 I plan to be riding on a horse behind Him in my new body at that point. If you are one of the rebels who are fighting against Him, it will not be a very pleasant day for you.

Jesus says that, *Heaven and earth will pass away, but My words will by no means pass away. But of that day and hour no one knows, not even the angels of heaven, but My Father only* Matt. 24:35, 36. Some believe this scripture refers to the rapture. I disagree. Though I don't know the day and the hour of the rapture, I believe this reference is to the passing away of the heavens and the earth. We see this in other scriptures.

> Of old You laid the foundation of the earth,
> And the heavens are the work of Your hands.
> They will perish, but You will endure;
> Yes, they will all grow old like a garment;
> Like a cloak You will change them,
> And they will be changed. Psa. 102:25, 26

The day of the Lord, is the day that Jesus comes back. It's not the entire seven year period. It's not the three and half year period. The second three and a half year period is called "the time of Jacobs's trouble". It will be a time of great distress for the nation of Israel and also for the world at large.

On that day the ancient hills are going to collapse. *Behold, the day of the Lord comes, cruel, with both wrath and fierce anger, to lay the land desolate.* Is. 13:9 When Jeremiah said, *I beheld the earth, and indeed it was without form, and void; and the heavens, they had no light.* Jer. 4:23, he used the same word that is used in Genesis 1:2 (*tu voo va vo*).

PUTTING IT ALL TOGETHER

Jeremiah used the phrase (*Tu vo vavoo*) to describe this amorphous liquefaction of the mountains because they will become like *Jell-O*™. They will fall down and become nothing. *And every mountain and island was moved out of its place.* Rev. 6:14 Also in Revelation 16:20, *Then every island fled away, and the mountains were not found.* When every island moves away and every mountain goes away, that's what I call Epic. That is essentially the movie *2012* where the entire earth just begins to fall apart.

But it will probably be even worse than that because it will be a day unlike any other. This is the day that Jesus comes back and that's why it's called "The Day of the Lord". Some events will unfold before the Day of the Lord; but on the Day of the Lord, many things are going to happen. You might wonder how there will be enough time for so many events to take place on the day of the Lord.

It says in Habakkuk Chapter 3:11, *the sun and the moon stood still in their habitation*. There was another time when the sun and the moon stood still in their habitation. It was during the long day of Joshua. This is very interesting because on that day he said he was fighting the Amorites. The Amorites were Nephilim. I describe this in detail in my book, *Corrupting the Image*[81]. So Joshua was fighting against the Nephilim. I believe Jesus will also be fighting hybrids because people that have taken the mark of the Beast would have mingled themselves with demons. The world will believe them to be aliens, but that is all a ruse to deceive the nations. The Day of the Lord will be a long day because Jesus has a lot of work to do on that day.

We are told that the earth is violently broken. Again, if all of the islands and all of the mountains flee away, the earth is violently broken. The earth will be split open and exceedingly shaken. Isaiah says, *The earth shall reel to and fro like a drunkard, and shall totter like a hut; its transgression shall be heavy upon it, and it will fall, and not rise again.* Isa. 24:20 Please understand that at this point, because the earth is so incredibly devastated, it's over. The earth is down for the count, crying "uncle"; or, maybe it's just plain dead. The Earth becomes completely uninhabitable. *For the day of the Lord of hosts shall come upon everything proud and lofty.* Isa. 2:12

The day of the Lord is when the earth moves.

And there were noises and thunderings and lightnings; and there was a great earthquake, such a mighty and great earthquake as had not occurred since men were on the earth. Rev. 16:18

Therefore I will shake the heavens, and the earth will move out of her place, in the wrath of the Lord of hosts and in the day of His fierce anger. Isa. 13:13

Here we see "the day of the Lord" once again. It's not the seven year period of the Lord. It isn't even the three and a half year period, as bad as those will be. It is "the day" that Jesus, the Christ, the Savior, comes back to redeem His people. He will intercede on behalf of Israel who has finally cried out to Him, "*Baruch haba beshem Adonai*". *Blessed is He who comes in the name of the Lord.* Psa. 118:26 Welcome Jesus; finally, we are welcoming you.

Paul says; *But concerning the times and the seasons, brethren, you have no need that I should write to you. For you yourselves know perfectly that the day of the Lord so comes as a thief in the night.* 1 Thess. 5:1, 2 This has often been interpreted to speak about the rapture, but it isn't speaking about the rapture. It is speaking of the day that Jesus comes back.

You see, God has a plan. He is going to launch a surprise attack on the Antichrist. He will say, "Here I am!"; and everyone will run like cockroaches into dark places. *But the day of the Lord will come as a thief in the night, in which the heavens will pass away with a great noise, and the elements will melt with fervent heat; both the earth and the works that are in it will be burned up.* 2 Pet. 3:10 Jesus says it this way, *Therefore if you will not watch, I will come upon you as a thief, and you will not know what hour I will come upon you.* Rev. 3:3 He says this in Revelation 16:15; *Behold, I am coming as a thief. Blessed is he who watches, and keeps his garments, lest he walk naked and they see his shame.*

This is sandwiched right between the place where Satan, the Antichrist and false prophet have these three spirits that look like frogs that come out of their mouths and go out to all the nations to bring them to battle at the place of Armageddon to make war against Him who sits on the horse. Jesus says, sandwiched between those events, He is warning the world - I am coming as a thief; watch out;

you're not going to realize when I come; you're not going to know what is about to hit you. The day of the Lord, the thief in the night, is when the earth is destroyed in Second Peter 3:10.

But the heavens and the earth, which are now preserved by the same word, are reserved for fire until the Day of Judgment and perdition of ungodly men. 2 Pet. 3:7 But the day of the Lord will come as a thief in the night, in which the heavens will pass away with a great noise, and the elements will melt with fervent heat; both the earth and the works that are in it will be burned up. 2 Pet, 3:10 Nevertheless, we according to His promise, look for new heavens and a new earth, in which righteousness dwells. 2 Pet. 3:13

Notice not only that the day of the Lord comes as a thief in the night, but also that the heavens will pass away with a great noise. The elements melt with fervent heat. We previously discussed verses in Revelation and Isaiah that tell us the sky is going to recede, or roll up, as a scroll. This is the time when the heavens pass away. At the same time, the mountains are going to melt like wax at the presence of the Lord of the whole earth. *Lift up your eyes to the heavens, and look on the earth beneath. For the heavens will vanish away like smoke, the earth will grow old like a garment, and those who dwell in it will die in like manner.* Isa. 51:6

In summary, following are some of the events of the Second Coming:
1. An ash cloud will blanket the earth, blocking sun and moon.
2. The rivers, lakes and oceans will be turned to blood.
3. The veil between the heavens will pass away.
4. Everyone will see Jesus coming in flames of fire.
5. The earth, every mountain and island, is shaken, moved and gone; and the elements, mountains, begin to melt.

This now brings us to the Battle of Armageddon. Traditionally the Battle of Armageddon has been believed to come before the Day of the Lord. I put the Battle of Armageddon in the day of the Lord. That is the time when it will happen - when Jesus comes back - because He is the one who's going to be fighting. The Battle of Armageddon is not a nation-against-nation war. Very often people have gone to a location in the northern part of Galilee called the Jezreel Valley and thought it could be an incredible place for a battle. Napoleon said, "I could see a battle being fought here."

Unfortunately, this is not the location of the Battle of Armageddon. Secondly, this battle will not see the tanks of the world coming together; or the world's infantry divisions fighting one another. This battle won't even feature the high tech weaponry that we have today against other countries. The Battle of Armageddon will be the world united against Jesus and those that He loves. It says in Revelation 16:16, *And they gathered them together to the place called in Hebrew, Armageddon.* Then in Revelation 19 John writes; *And I saw the beast, the kings of the earth, and their armies, gathered together to make war against Him who sat on the horse and against His army.* Rev. 19:19 Again, it's not nation against nation. It's all the nations of the world united together to fight against Jesus.

In addition to understanding who is fighting whom, we will also consider the linguistic understanding of this battle; the sheaves in a harvest motif that we find very frequently, and the idea of stomping on grapes. We will discover that these aspects can be understood very literally. It's just a matter of putting the puzzle pieces in their right places. I have to admit that I broke my head!

In Spanish, a jig saw puzzle is called a *"rompecabezas"* because it breaks your head. I feel that I have been breaking my head trying to put the pieces together. Now, though, I am very excited to share them with you because I believe that the Lord has guided me in discovering how these puzzle pieces fit together. I will let you be the judge, of course, but I think you will see that the pieces fit incredibly well; and that we can take them very literally, which always excites me because God's Word is very literal.

Jesus will stomp on grapes. Blood will go up to the horse's bridle. There's even some imagery that is a repeat of the Exodus crossing of the Red Sea. I think God likes to recycle themes.

This theme will be recycled in a very grand way. God's Word also tells us that a trap will be set by the Antichrist for the Jews. The trap that the Antichrist will set will actually be the trap that he will fall into. There's a proverb that says "he who sets a snare will himself fall into it."

This is exactly what's going to happen to the Antichrist. He will set the snare but he himself will fall into it. These things will happen outside the city. The traditional location of the Battle of Armageddon is in the Jezreel Valley. If one were to tour Israel today,

PUTTING IT ALL TOGETHER

he or she would be sure to visit Armageddon because most people want to see where the final battle is going to take place. The tour would visit the traditional Battle of Armageddon site in the plain of Jezreel at the Tel Megiddo. One can see Tel Megiddo, but it's not a mountain.

A "tel" is not a mountain. Tel is a very ancient word. It actually comes from Acadian, which tells us that the word has been around for long time. A tel is a mound where a city was and then was destroyed, and then they built on top of it, then that city was destroyed, and so on. Eventually, after many centuries, the various destruction layers build up into an artificial mountain that is called a tel. One would not find a mountain in Tel Megiddo today, only a tel. This begs the question, "Where is the mountain?" Where is the city? There is wonderful agriculture in this place, but no city or mountain. One could visit the Jezreel Valley and Tel Megiddo and think to himself, "Wow! This is where the battle is going to happen. But there's nobody here. Why would anybody fight here? Why suddenly here, when all the other places in scripture keep talking about Jerusalem?" Well of course this is the whole point. It is not going to happen here even though we have been taught that this is the location of the battle.

Let's consider the linguistic implications of the Battle of Armageddon. If we read the *King James*[82], or the *New King James*[83], which are based on the *Textus Receptus*[84], we will find that the word "Armageddon" is spelled with two letter "d's." If we look at Armageddon in the *Byzantine Majority*[85] text, the word actually has one delta (d). If we look at the *Alexandrian Vaticanas*[86], it's spelled with one delta, but in the *Textus Receptus*, it is spelled with two. Some people prefer the *Textus Receptus*, and may even have strong feelings against the *Alexandrian Vaticanis*, which is fine. However, I would like to point out that the *Textus Receptus* comes out of the Byzantine family. It is a collection of manuscripts. It is really a handful of manuscripts, somewhere between six to twelve manuscripts were used. It came from a larger tradition called the *Byzantine Majority* text family, which were about five thousand manuscripts. I mention this because there's only one delta in the *Byzantine Majority* text. This is an important clue.

One might think it doesn't really matter if there are one or two deltas but actually it does. The reason is that based on the Hebrew word, the word that we have is *Meg-i-don*, the vowels don't fit for different readings. In the Greek, as it comes to us, we are told that this is a Hebrew word. But we have to look at it through the Greek language which spells it as *Ar-ma-ge-don*, not *me- gi-don*. Clearly the vowels do not match up between the Greek and the Hebrew words, and neither does the double "d". Certainly the double "d" in the *Textus Receptus* would match, but it doesn't match with the other textual evidence that we have.

My assertion is that really, none of these words match the word Megiddo. Megiddo is not the word that should be used. The reason it is important that there is not a mountain in Megiddo is because it is understood that *Ar* means mountain and *Megiddo* is, of course, Megiddo; thus Ar Megiddo (the mountain of Megiddo). Not only is there no mountain in Megiddo; linguistically and phonetically, it does not match properly. Therefore, of all the possible interpretations, Ar Megiddo does not fit.

Some people have suggested that this is "the place of the crowds" and that is what the word means. Perhaps there is an underlying secondary use of that, though I rather doubt it. Dr. Michael Hazer has eloquently posited that this could be *Ar- moed,* meaning "mountain of the appointed meeting time." *Moed* means the appointed meeting time. I think he argued it well. I tend to disagree, though, because I believe the preferable translation is *Ar- ma-ge'don*, which would be "the valley of the judging of the harvested heap (or sheaves)." Here's why. This word *Arema* fits really well. The only vowel that would not fit, that we have to imagine, is the "e" in *Ar-e-ma*. Jeremiah 50 uses this word when he says, "come to her from a far, open up her barns, pile her up like heaps of grain and completely destroy her; don't leave any survivors." When Ruth went to Boaz, he was sleeping on an *Arema*. He was sleeping on a pile of harvested grain. This is from the word *Aram* which means "to be heaped up." It occurs once in the verbal form and we find it other places as a noun, "heap." We also find it in Micah 4:12. *For He will gather them like sheaves to the threshing floor.* God says that He will gather them like sheaves to the threshing floor. He is telling us about the trap He will lay for the Antichrist.

PUTTING IT ALL TOGETHER

My belief is that what happened with the word Armageddon is something called a "metathesis." This is where two letters can switch. There are many examples of this. It isn't common, but it does happen. There are a number of examples where letters have been transposed; they have had a metathesis. Essentially, they have traded places. *Amir*, for example, is a word of the same basic meaning as the word *Arema*. *Amir* says that God will gather them (those who are coming against Jerusalem) like sheaves to the threshing floor. This motif carries through in the Armageddon / Second Coming event.

The word *Ge ana* means "the Valley of the Sun of Inom" (*Gabeninum*). And *Gabeninom* became *Geana* later on. One can see how there's been a reduction of both vowels, and even some of the consonants. There are three different words for "valley" in Hebrew. One is *Bica*. Megiddo is described as a *Bica*. So this is not described as a *Ge*. It is described as an open plain, an open valley; and indeed, that is what it is. There is also the word *Emic*, which means "to be deep." This indicates a valley of wide expanse, fit for agriculture or warfare. Then, there is the word *Gets*, which indicates a lower lot, or valley, or lower flat region. Sacrifices were unfortunately held outside of Jerusalem in Beninum, a valley not far from the Mount of Olives and from the Valley of Jehoshaphat, incidentally.

The last part of Armageddon is *don*. The word *don* comes from the word *dean* and it's very, very similar to the word *shaphat*. The Valley of Jehoshaphat, or Yehoshaphat, is where Yahweh will judge, or "Yahweh judges." So the word *shaphat* is identical to the word *dean*. We are told in Joel Chapter Three;

Let the nations be wakened, and come up to the Valley of Jehoshaphat; For there I will sit to judge all the surrounding nations. Put in the sickle, for the harvest is ripe. Come, go down; for the winepress is full, the vats overflow— Joel 3:12, 13

This imagery is of harvesting, a sickle, and heaped up sheaves. This will be in the Valley of Jehoshaphat, the place where Yahweh judges. So Armageddon is the valley of the judging of the sheaves, or the heap.

Let's go back to the words *dean* and *don*. What is the difference between them? The difference is based on the infinitive absolute.

This is a bi-consonantal word; and in the infinitive absolute, it always has a long "o" sound. *Yacomo*, for example, becomes *com*. In English the word "moot" becomes "moat". This is an example of how a bi consonantal verb actually becomes "a," with that "o" sound in there. Therefore, *dean* could follow this grammatical rule to become *don*. This explains the *don* part of the word Armageddon - the Valley of the judging of the harvested heap or sheaves; and this is going to take place, again, not up north in the Jezreel Valley, but down next to Jerusalem. It's in the Valley of Jehoshaphat between the Temple Mount and the Mount of Olives. This is where Jesus is going to come back, near to the Temple and to the Mount of Olives, which faces the city.

Jesus will fight on behalf of Jerusalem. He will fight those nations that are coming against Jerusalem. *Now also many nations have gathered against you, who say, "Let her be defiled, and let our eye look upon Zion."* Micah 4:11. Zechariah 12:2, 3 tells us that the battle location is Jerusalem, not the Jezreel Valley; *"Behold, I will make Jerusalem a cup of drunkenness to all the surrounding peoples, when they lay siege against Judah and Jerusalem. And it shall happen in that day that I will make Jerusalem a very heavy stone for all peoples; all who would heave it away will surely be cut in pieces, though all nations of the earth are gathered against it."* Jerusalem and the Valley of Jehoshaphat is where the action is going to be. Now that we understand linguistically that Armageddon does not mean Ar Megiddo, that it actually means "the valley of the judging of the sheaves", we can see how the Battle of Armageddon will take place in even greater detail.

"Put in the sickle, for the harvest is ripe. Come, go down; for the winepress is full, the vats overflow—for their wickedness is great." Joel 3:13

And the winepress was trampled outside the city, and blood came out of the winepress, up to the horses' bridles, for one thousand six hundred furlongs. Rev. 14:20 The wine press was trampled outside the city, not up in the Valley of Megiddo or the plain of Megiddo; but outside the city of Jerusalem.

Proclaim this among the nations: "Prepare for war! Wake up the mighty men, let all the men of war draw near, Let them come up. Joel 3:9

God is basically saying, "You guys have touched the apple of my eye one too many times and now this means war. Get ready because I'm coming personally. This is no longer business as usual. This is personal. Now I am coming and I am going to decimate you because you have really made me mad this time. So watch out! Get ready for war." *Let all the men of war draw near, let them come up. Beat your plowshares into swords and your pruning hooks into spears.* Joel 3:9, 10 "You don't have a weapon? Well go get one because you're going to need it because I, God, am coming." All the nations will go to the Valley of Jehoshaphat and Jesus will go down and harvest multitudes and multitudes with His sickle in the valley of decision "for their wickedness is great."

Then I looked, and behold, a white cloud, and on the cloud sat One like the Son of Man, having on His head a golden crown, and in His hand a sharp sickle. And another angel came out of the temple, crying with a loud voice to Him who sat on the cloud, "Thrust in Your sickle and reap, for the time has come for You to reap, for the harvest of the earth is ripe." So He who sat on the cloud thrust in His sickle on the earth, and the earth was reaped. Rev. 14:14-16

The Mount of Olives has all these tools on it because the Jews believe that's where the Messiah will come, so they wanted them to be there when He arrived. The Mount of Olives overlooks the Valley of Jehoshaphat. Revelation 14:20 tells us that, *the winepress was trampled outside the city, and blood came out of the winepress, up to the horses' bridles, for one thousand six hundred furlongs.*

Imagine blood coming up about five feet, that's as high as a horse's bridle, in the Valley of Megiddo, or Jezreel Valley. Liquid will always find its own level; so there would have to be blood going on for a very, very, very, very, very long way to have enough to fill that valley. But understanding that the battle location is the Valley of Jehoshaphat, which is a narrow valley, causes this statement to make complete sense. We are still talking about a lot of blood, but it would be more like it was in a pool if it was in a narrow valley. This makes it easier for us to comprehend how blood could run at that height.

Jesus is going to destroy His enemies. He will trample them like grapes. *"I have trodden the winepress alone, and from the peoples no one was with Me. For I have trodden them in My anger, and trampled them in My fury; Their blood is sprinkled upon My garments, and I have stained all My robes.* Isa. 63:3 *For the indignation of the Lord is against all nations, and His fury against all their armies; He has utterly destroyed them, He has given them over to the slaughter."* Isa. 34:2 Isaiah goes on to say in verses three and five, *"Also their slain shall be thrown out; their stench shall rise from their corpses, and the mountains shall be melted with their blood. For My sword shall be bathed in heaven; indeed it shall come down on Edom, and on the people of My curse, for judgment."*

The nations will be trapped in the Valley of Jehoshaphat. *Now also many nations have gathered against you, who say, "Let her be defiled, and let our eye look upon Zion." But they do not know the thoughts of the Lord, nor do they understand His counsel; for He will gather them like sheaves to the threshing floor.* Micah 4:11, 12. I mentioned that this is where Satan and the Antichrist will set a trap to try to destroy the Jews. But God actually has a better plan. He is setting the trap for the Antichrist and his forces in order to destroy them. He will use His winnowing fan. It is in His hand and He will thoroughly clean out His threshing floor. *Behold, the day of the Lord is coming, and your spoil will be divided in your midst. For I will gather all the nations to battle against Jerusalem.* Zech. 14:1, 2 We also read in Zechariah 14 that, *The city shall be taken, the houses rifled, and the women ravished. Half of the city shall go into captivity, but the remnant of the people shall not be cut off from the city.* Zech. 14:2

There will be a remnant of people who are still there, that are waiting expectantly for the Lord Jesus to return. They will be the ones that will finally cry out to Him. Jesus said, *You shall see Me no more till you say, 'Blessed is He who comes in the name of the Lord!* Matt. 23:39

This verse tells us they will finally say, *Baruch haba beshem Adonai.* They are finally going to acknowledge their offense. *I will return again to My place till they acknowledge their offense. Then they will seek My face; in their affliction they will earnestly seek Me.* Hos. 5:15

God says, "I will return again to my place until you acknowledge your offence. It will take a little bit of prodding, shall we say, but when they finally do that, and say, 'Come, Lord Jesus,' I will come."

The remnant now find themselves in the Valley of Jehoshaphat. Somehow they will be forced out into this valley and they will wait for Jesus to come back. Presumably, they will be standing in front of the Mount of Olives, because they know that's where He's going to come back. As they are gathered together in front of the Mount of Olives, they will be surrounded by the forces of Antichrist. Jesus is in route, coming to save them. Scripture says that,

In that day I will make the governors of Judah like a firepan in the woodpile, and like a fiery torch in the sheaves; they shall devour all the surrounding peoples on the right hand and on the left, but Jerusalem shall be inhabited again in her own place—Jerusalem. Zech. 12:6

I just couldn't figure this out for such a long time. I thought; "Now wait a second. You have Jesus coming back and yet you also have these governors doing something." But Jesus says He will do it all by Himself. Still...He will give them some kind of power.

When I started to put all the pieces together I realized that everything will happen very quickly; but they must hold out until Jesus comes. He gives them incredible, supernatural power, and the governors of Judah are going to be like a fire pan in the wood pile and a fiery torch in the sheaves. This power will enable them to devour those on the right hand and on the left. Perhaps the scene will play out something like this:

The remnant is down in the Valley of Jehoshaphat. The forces of Antichrist are coming against them on the right and on the left. Then the governors of Judah who are on the periphery receive special power from the Lord so that they can actually shoot fire out from their sides. Scripture says, *In that day the Lord will defend the inhabitants of Jerusalem; the one who is feeble among them in that day shall be like David, and the house of David shall be like God, like the Angel of the Lord before them.* Zech. 12:8. Habakkuk 3:4 gave me an important piece of the puzzle. *His brightness was like the light; He had rays flashing from His hand, and there His power was hidden.* Jesus has rays of light flashing from His hand.

This is far cooler than any super hero movie we've ever seen, or any villain, or the emperor from *Star Wars™*, who can shoot out electricity. Jesus is far cooler and it appears that He will give them this power. The strong among them will be like the Angel of the Lord before them. And so the scene continues with the remnant imbued with power coming out of their hands to defend themselves until Jesus gets there.

Then the Lord will go forth and fight against those nations, as He fights in the day of battle. Zech. 14:3 Our scene continues: The Jewish remnant that is down in the Valley of Jehoshaphat, the Kidron Valley, is waiting for Jesus. They are fending off hordes of Antichrist attackers who have postured themselves to be able to get to the remnant from either the left or the right. But the remnant are fighting them off and devouring them on the both sides. Then Jesus finally comes back.

Scene Two begins: His feet will touch the Mount of Olives.

And in that day His feet will stand on the Mount of Olives, which faces Jerusalem on the east. And the Mount of Olives shall be split in two, from east to west, making a very large valley; half of the mountain shall move toward the north and half of it toward the south. Zech. 14:4

The word used in the verse for valley is the word, *gae*, just like Ar-ma-gae-don. The touch of Jesus' feet to the Mount of Olives will create a deep ravine, a canyon. *Then you shall flee through My mountain valley,* it says in Zechariah 14:5.

So we now have a new puzzle piece. What does it look like? I believe the Lord showed it to me as a picture of Jesus stepping down onto the Mount of Olives, which then splits. At this point the remnant realizes that they have a way of escape. They flee through that mountain valley that has opened up. The Antichrist forces pursue, following hard behind them. Does this remind us of anything? Was there another time in history when this might have happened? Well, of course there was. God parted the Red Sea so the Children of Israel could cross through it on dry ground.

For Pharaoh will say of the children of Israel, 'They are bewildered by the land; the wilderness has closed them in. Ex. 14:3

PUTTING IT ALL TOGETHER

Pharaoh thought the Children of Israel were trapped, so he changed his mind and pursued them, intent on destroying them completely. Just when it appeared that Pharaoh had won the day, God showed that He had actually led Pharaoh and his armies into a trap in which they were destroyed. This scene plays out in much the same way as the Exodus story. After the Jews have fled through the valley opened up by the Mount of Olives splitting in two, Jesus will interpose himself between the Jews that have fled behind Him and the forces of Antichrist that are coming in like a wave with the intent of destroying them.

Why are they so intent on destroying the Jews? We should keep in mind that the only thing Satan can do is destroy the Jewish people. If he could destroy them, then he could have a standoff with God. God says that He would give the kingdom to the saints. *But the saints of the Most High shall receive the kingdom, and possess the kingdom forever, even forever and ever.'* Dan. 7:18 As long as there is at least one breathing Jew on the planet, then God can still fulfill His promise. However, if there was not a single Jew left on the planet, then God could not fulfill His promise, which makes Him a liar. This explains why Satan is working very hard to destroy the Jews.

Scene Three: Jesus has interposed himself between the Jews and the Antichrist's forces. He has rays of light flashing from His hands and a sword coming out of His mouth, perhaps similar to something like a laser. He will then begin to decimate the attackers that are coming. He starts to hack them in pieces with the rays of light coming from where His power is hidden. According to Habakkuk 3:5, there will be pestilence before Him and fever will follow at His feet. Jesus' coming will confuse His enemies. They will see Jesus and realize they are in trouble. They will try to turn around, but they will not able to.

It shall come to pass in that day that a great panic from the Lord will be among them. Everyone will seize the hand of his neighbor, and raise his hand against his neighbor's hand. Zech. 14:13

In their panic they will begin to kill one another with their own swords. Even every horse will be struck with confusion and blindness because of Jesus (Zech. 12:4). Why blindness? Remember that Jesus is incredibly bright, brighter even than the sun. He is the man of fire. He is a consuming fire. As Jesus stands there before them, keep in mind that He is a fire, He has fiery lightning clothing on Him and He will shoot out rays of light. They will not be able see. They will try to turn around, but He will begin to cut them in pieces and destroy them.

And this shall be the plague with which the Lord will strike all the people who fought against Jerusalem: their flesh shall dissolve while they stand on their feet, their eyes shall dissolve in their sockets, and their tongues shall dissolve in their mouths. Zech. 14:12

Some have proposed that this might be referring to a neutron bomb or a nuclear bomb of some sort; I beg to differ. I suggest that this reference is to the armies being exposed to God's fiery lightning presence. The armies would, at this time, have come into close proximity to Jesus. They would try to get away, but they will not be able to do so.

Why is Your apparel red,
And Your garments like one who treads in the winepress?
"I have trodden the winepress alone,
And from the peoples no one was with Me.
For I have trodden them in My anger,
And trampled them in My fury;
Their blood is sprinkled upon My garments,
And I have stained all My robes. Isa. 63:2, 3

Jesus will do this all by Himself.

I believe we will be on horses behind Jesus. I think our job will be as a group of cheerleaders.

Give me a "J",
give me an "E",
give me an "S",
give me a "U",
give me an "S",
What does that spell? "Jesus!"

I don't believe we will do anything except stand and see the salvation of the Lord. Jesus will advance against the Antichrist's forces, cut them to pieces, and tread on them like grapes. The description we are given is all very literal. Soon there will be a bloody mess so great that the blood will go up to the horse's bridle. There will be corpses everywhere and tons of carnage.

PUTTING IT ALL TOGETHER

I believe this will happen on the day of Yom Kippur. The day of Yom Kippur is when the books are opened and the wicked destroyed.

Incidentally, it just so happens that twice a year there is a massive migration of birds in the spring and in the fall from the north to the south, from Europe and Asia, and down to Africa. Their common route is to fly over Israel. They don't fly over anywhere else primarily, almost completely over Israel. This means there are millions and millions of birds up in the sky who are also very hungry. Everything has been destroyed at this point. All the grass has been burnt up, the trees have been destroyed, and the waters have become blood.

Then I saw an angel standing in the sun; and he cried with a loud voice, saying to all the birds that fly in the midst of heaven, "Come and gather together for the supper of the great God, that you may eat the flesh of kings, the flesh of captains, the flesh of mighty men, the flesh of horses and of those who sit on them, and the flesh of all people, free and slave, both small and great." Rev. 19:17

Matthew 24:27 and 28 always gave me trouble. I could not understand the meaning of these two verses put together until I started putting all these puzzle pieces together.

For as the lightning comes from the east and flashes to the west, so also will the coming of the Son of Man be. For wherever the carcass is, there the eagles will be gathered together.

Now it makes sense. All of these events of Jesus' return are happening at this time; and the judgment has come.

Scene Four: Also at this time, Revelation 19 tells us that the Antichrist and False Prophet are cast into the lake of fire. Then will be the judgment of the sheep and the goats. This happens on Yom Kippur.

I watched till the beast was slain, and its body destroyed and given to the burning flame. Dan. 7:11

Then the beast was captured, and with him the false prophet who worked signs in his presence, by which he deceived those who received the mark of the beast and those who worshiped his image. These two were cast alive into the lake of fire burning with brimstone. Rev. 19:20.

There is a stream of flaming fire coming out from God. His throne was a fiery flame, its wheels a burning fire; a fiery stream issued and came forth from before Him. Dan. 7:9, 10

The Beast and False Prophet are thrown into that fire. It is true they are relegated to a geographical place, but the fire that is hitting them is the fire that is coming out from God Himself. Isaiah 30:33 says, *The breath of the Lord, like a stream of brimstone, kindles it.*

Thousands, thousands ministered to Him, ten thousand times ten thousand stood before Him, the court was seated in the books were opened. Dan. 7:10

This is the day that Jesus will judge. This is the day of Yom Kippur. And also the nations will be gathered before Him. He will separate one from the other, the sheep on His right hand and the goats on His left. *"Then He will also say to those on the left hand, 'Depart from Me, you cursed, into the everlasting fire prepared for the devil and his angels'"* Matt. 25:41 At the same time, Satan and the demons are bound.

Then I saw an angel coming down from heaven, having the key to the bottomless pit and a great chain in his hand. He laid hold of the dragon, that serpent of old, who is the Devil and Satan, and bound him for a thousand years; and he cast him into the bottomless pit, and shut him up, and set a seal on him, so that he should deceive the nations no more till the thousand years were finished. Rev. 20:1-3

Satan and the demons are not destroyed at this point, but they are put into a holding cell where they will remain for 1,000 years.

We see this in Isaiah 24:21, 22;

It shall come to pass in that day
That the Lord will punish on high the host of exalted ones,
And on the earth the kings of the earth.
They will be gathered together,
As prisoners are gathered in the pit,
And will be shut up in the prison.

After many days they will be punished. Satan and the demons will be punished after the 1,000 years. But during the 1,000 years they will remain in prison. Then as Satan descends down into Sheol, to the lowest depths of the abyss, *"Those who see you (Satan) will gaze at you, and consider you, saying: 'Is this the man who made the earth tremble, who shook kingdoms?'"* Isa. 14:16 That will be the end of the Antichrist, the end of Satan, at least for 1,000 years. Then Jesus will usher in the Millennium.

In summary:

1. The Antichrist gathered the nations to destroy Israel, but this when Jesus comes back. He rends the veil and He comes down.
2. The governors of Judah fend off their attackers, briefly, until Jesus puts His feet down upon the Mount of Olives. At that point the Mount of Olives will split in two and the remnant will flee through the resulting valley.
3. Jesus jumps down into that canyon and fights the attackers. He gets all bloody as He squashes them like grapes in a winepress. The blood comes up to the horse's bridle.
4. There are so many bodies and so much carnage that the birds come and feast themselves on the flesh of kings and mighty men.
5. The judging of the sheep and the goats immediately follows.
6. The heavens will pass away. This will literally be the unveiling which will happen the day that Jesus returns.
7. The Day of the Lord is a "thief in the night" event.
8. Armageddon fits better linguistically and logistically with the valley of the judging of the harvest of the sheaves (Valley of Jehoshaphat).
9. Jesus comes personally and fights for Israel.
10. The Biblical imagery is literal.

REFERENCES

1. Hamp, Doug. *The Millennium Chronicles: Road to the Final Rebellion*. Eskaton Media Group, 2013. Print.
2. Lindsey, Hal. *The Rapture: Truth or Consequences*. New York: Bantam Books, 1983. 31. Print.
3. Lindsey, Hal. *The Rapture: Truth or Consequences*. New York: Bantam Books, 1983. 32. Print.
4. LaHaye,Tim. *No Fear of the Storm: Why Christians Will Escape All the Tribulation*. Colorado Springs: Multnomah Books, 1994. 69. Print.
5. LaHaye,Tim. *No Fear of the Storm: Why Christians Will Escape All the Tribulation*. Colorado Springs: Multnomah Books, 1994. 188. Print.
6. Reagan, Dr. David R. "The Mystery of the Rapture". *Lion and Lamb Ministries*. Christinprophecy.org. 2017. Web. 11 July 2017. <http://christinprophecy.org/articles/the-mystery-of-the-rapture/>
7. "THE MYSTERY OF THE RAPTURE OF THE BODY OF CHRIST AT THE END OF THE CHURCH AGE OUTLINE I Cor. 15:51-58, 1 Thess. 4:13-18" *Bible Truth*. Bible-truth.org. 2016. Web. 11 July 2017. <http://bible-truth.org/myst-3.htm>
8. "BELIEVERS WILL ESCAPE GOD'S WRATH – BIBLICAL FORESHADOWS OF THE RAPTURE". *BEGINNING AND END*. Beginningandend.com. 21 Mar. 2012. Web. 11 July 2017. <http://beginningandend.com/believers-escape-gods-wrath-biblical-foreshadows-rapture/>
9. Hitchcock, Mark. *The End: A Complete Overview of Bible Prophecy and the End of Days*. Carol Stream: Tyndale House Publishers, Inc., 2012. 136. Print.
10. "ZOHAR THREE IN ONE". *Artists for Israel International Messianic Bible Society*. Afii.org. 2017. Web. 11 July 2017. <http://www.afii.org/zoharthreeinone.htm>

11. *A Thief in the Night*. Dir. Donald W. Thompson. Mark IV Pictures, Inc., 1972. Film.
12. Fruchtenbaum, Arnold G. *The Footsteps of the Messiah*. San Antonio: Ariel Ministries, 2003. Print.
13. Pentecost, Dr. J. Dwight. *Things to Come: A Study in Biblical Eschatology*. Grand Rapids: Zondervan, 1958. 231. Print.
14. *Englishman's Concordance*: entry for "agiais". *Bible Hub*. Biblehub.com. 2016. Web. 11 July 2017. <http://biblehub.com/greek/agiais_40.htm>
15. *Englishman's Concordance*: entry for "muriasin". *Bible Hub*. Biblehub.com. 2016. Web. 11 July 2017. <http://biblehub.com/greek/muriasin_3461.htm>
16. *Englishman's Concordance*: entry for "agiais". *Bible Hub*. Biblehub.com. 2016. Web. 11 July 2017. <http://biblehub.com/greek/agiais_40.htm>
17. *Englishman's Concordance*: entry for "angeloi". *Bible Hub*. Biblehub.com. 2016. Web. 11 July 2017. <http://biblehub.com/greek/angeloi_32.htm>
18. *Englishman's Concordance*: entry for "angelon". *Bible Hub*. Biblehub.com. 2016. Web. 11 July 2017. <http://biblehub.com/greek/angelo_n_32.htm>
19. *Englishman's Concordance*: entry for "dunameos". *Bible Hub*. Biblehub.com. 2016. Web. 11 July 2017. <http://biblehub.com/greek/dunameo_s_1411.htm>
20. *Englishman's Concordance*: entry for "ares". *Bible Hub*. Biblehub.com. 2016. Web. 11 July 2017. <http://biblehub.com/greek/are_s_142.htm>
21. *Englishman's Concordance*: entry for "tereso". *Bible Hub*. Biblehub.com. 2016. Web. 11 July 2017. <http://biblehub.com/greek/te_re_so__5083.htm>
22. *Englishman's Concordance*: entry for "eteresas". *Bible Hub*. Biblehub.com. 2016. Web. 11 July 2017. <http://biblehub.com/greek/ete_re_sas_5083.htm>
23. *Englishman's Concordance*: entry for "tereso". *Bible Hub*. Biblehub.com. 2016. Web. 11 July 2017. <http://biblehub.com/greek/te_re_so__5083.htm>

24. *Englishman's Concordance*: entry for "ares". *Bible Hub*. Biblehub.com. 2016. Web. 11 July 2017. <http://biblehub.com/greek/are_s_142.htm>
25. *Englishman's Concordance*: entry for "tereso". *Bible Hub*. Biblehub.com. 2016. Web. 11 July 2017. <http://biblehub.com/greek/te_re_so__5083.htm>
26. Gregg, Steve. *Revelation, Four Views: A Parallel Commentary*. Nashville, Thomas Nelson, Inc., 1997. 38. Print.
27. Hitchcock, Mark. *The End: A Complete Overview of Bible Prophecy and the End of Days*. Carol Stream: Tyndale House Publishers, Inc., 2012. 136. Print.
28. *Tanakh. Jewish Virtual Library*. American-Israeli Cooperative Enterprise. 2017. Web. 11 July 2017. <https://www.jewishvirtuallibrary.org/the-tanakh-full-text>
29. *Esdras, The Second (Fourth) Book of; Apocalyptic Ezdras. Bible Study Tools*. Biblestudytools.com. 2017. Web. 11 July 2017. <http://www.biblestudytools.com/encyclopedias/isbe/esdras-the-second-fourth-book-of-apocalyptic-esdras.html>
30. *Apocalypse of Baruch. Bible Hub*. Biblehub.com. 2016. Web. 11 July 2017. <http://biblehub.com/library/deane/pseudepigrapha/the_apocalypse_of_baruch.htm>
31. *Assumption of Moses. Bible Hub*. Biblehub.com. 2016. Web. 11 July 2017. <http://biblehub.com/library/deane/pseudepigrapha/the_assumption_of_moses.htm>
32. Schürer, Emil. *A History of the Jewish People in the time of Jesus Christ*. Edinburg: T&T Clark, 1890. 2nd Div ed. Vol. 2. 154-187. Print.
33. Calvin, John. *Commentaries on the Epistle of Paul to the Philippians, Colossians and Thessalonians. Christian Classics Ethereal Library*, Calvin College Computer Science, 1 June 2005. Web. 11 July 2017. <https://www.ccel.org/ccel/calvin/calcom42.i.html>

34. *Babylonian Talmud: Tractate Sanhedrin Folio 91a. Jewish Virtual Library.* American-Israeli Cooperative Enterprise. 2017. Web. 11 July 2017.
<http://www.jewishvirtuallibrary.org/tractate-sanhedrin-chapter-11>
35. *Babylonia Talmud: Tractate Sanhedrin. Jewish Virtual Library.* American-Israeli Cooperative Enterprise. 2017. Web. 11 July 2017.
<http://www.jewishvirtuallibrary.org/tractate-sanhedrin-chapter-11>
36. *Babylonian Talmud: Tractate Sanhedrin. Jewish Virtual Library.* American-Israeli Cooperative Enterprise. 2017. Web. 11 July 2017.
<http://www.jewishvirtuallibrary.org/tractate-sanhedrin-chapter-11>
37. *Babylonian Talmud: Tractate Sanhedrin 90b. Jewish Virtual Library.* American-Israeli Cooperative Enterprise. 2017. Web. 11 July 2017.
<http://www.jewishvirtuallibrary.org/tractate-sanhedrin-chapter-11>
38. Constable, Dr. Thomas. *Bible Commentaries: Expository Notes of Dr. Thomas Constable; Revelation 6. StudyLight.org.* studylight.org. 2017. Web. 11 July 2017.
<https://www.studylight.org/commentaries/dcc/revelation-6.html>
39. *The Holy Bible, New King James Version (NKJV).* Nashville: Thomas Nelson, Inc., 1994. Print.
40. *New English Translation (NET). NET Bible.* Richardson: Biblical Studies Press, L.L.C., 2006. Print.
41. Thayer, Joseph H. and James Strong. *Thayer's Greek-English Lexicon of the New Testament: Coded with Strong's Concordance Numbers.* Peabody: Hendrickson Publishers, 1995. Print.
42. *LSJ: The Online Liddell-Scott-Jones Greek-English Lexicon. Thesaurus Linguae Graecae.* 2009. Web. 11 July 2017.
<http://stephanus.tlg.uci.edu/lsj/#eid=1&context=lsj>

43. Pamphilus, Eusebius; C. F. Cruse, Translator. *Eusebius Ecclesiastical History*. New York: Merchant Books, 2011. III, 39, 1. Print.
44. Entry for "Ontology". *Wikipedia*. Wikipedia.org. 25 June 2017. Web. 11 July 2017. <https://en.wikipedia.org/wiki/Ontology>
45. *Strong's Exhaustive Concordance*: entry for "5362. naqaph". *Bible Hub*. Biblehub.com. 2016. Web. 12 July 2017. <http://biblehub.com/hebrew/5362.htm>
46. Clarke, Adam. *Bible Commentaries: Adam Clarke Commentary, Revelation 6. StudyLight.org*. studylight.org. 2017. Web. 12 July 2017. <https://www.studylight.org/commentaries/acc/revelation-6.html>
47. Barnes, Albert. *Bible Commentaries: Albert Barnes Notes on the Whole Bible, Revelation 6. StudyLight.org*. studylight.org. 2017. Web. 12 July 2017. <http://www.studylight.org/commentaries/bnb/revelation-6.html>
48. Ironside, Harry A. *Bible Commentaries: Ironside's Notes on Selected Books, Current Book: Revelation. StudyLight.org*. studylight.org. 2017. Web. 12 July 2017. <https://www.studylight.org/commentaries/isn/revelation.html>
49. Burton, Ernest De Witt. *Syntax of the Moods and Tenses in New Testament Greek (Classic Reprint)*. London: Forgotten Books, 2012. 199. < https://www.amazon.com/Syntax-Tenses-Testament-Classic-Reprint/dp/B0098MOO26/ref=sr_1_5?s=books&ie=UTF8&qid=1499871427&sr=1-5&keywords=burton%27s+greek+grammar>
50. Hamp, Douglas. *Corrupting the Image: Angels, Aliens, and the Antichrist Revealed*. Crane: Defender Publishing, LLC., 2011. Print.
51. *Englishman's Concordance*: entry for "oti". *Bible Hub*. Biblehub.com. 2016. Web. 11 July 2017. <http://biblehub.com/greek/oti_3754.htm>

52. *Greek Interlinear Bible (NT). Scripture4All.* Scripture4All Publishing. 2015. Web. 13 July 2017. <http://www.scripture4all.org/OnlineInterlinear/Greek_Index.htm>
53. *Englishman's Concordance*: entry for "katabesetai". *Bible Hub.* Biblehub.com. 2016. Web. 11 July 2017. <http://biblehub.com/greek/katabe_setai_2597.htm>
54. *Englishman's Concordance*: entry for "katabas". *Bible Hub.* Biblehub.com. 2016. Web. 11 July 2017. <http://biblehub.com/greek/katabas_2597.htm>
55. *Englishman's Concordance*: entry for "ap". *Bible Hub.* Biblehub.com. 2016. Web. 11 July 2017. <http://biblehub.com/greek/ap_575.htm>
56. *The Holy Bible, King James Version.* Cambridge Edition: 1769; *King James Bible Online*, 2017. Web. 12 July 2017. <http://www.kingjamesbibleonline.org>
57. *The Holy Bible, New King James Version (NKJV).* Nashville: Thomas Nelson, Inc., 1994. Print.
58. *Holy Bible, New International Version, (NIV).* Colorado Springs: Biblica, Inc., 2011. Print.
59. *New American Standard Bible (NASB)* La Habra: The Lockman Foundation, 1995. Web. 13 July 2017. <https://www.biblegateway.com/versions/New-American-Standard-Bible-NASB/>
60. *Strong's Exhaustive Concordance*: entry for "4035. perileipomai". *Bible Hub.* Biblehub.com. 2016. Web. 12 July 2017. <http://biblehub.com/greek/4035.htm>
61. Thayer, Joseph H. and James Strong. *Thayer's Greek-English Lexicon of the New Testament: Coded with Strong's Concordance Numbers.* Peabody: Hendrickson Publishers, 1995. Print.
62. Zodhiates, Spiros. *The Complete Word Study Dictionary: New Testament,* Chattanooga: AMG Publishers, 1992. Print.
63. *Yeshaiya (Isaiah) 4 :: Septuagint (LXX). Blue Letter Bible.* Blueletterbible.org. 2017. Web. 12 July 2017. <https://www.blueletterbible.org/lxx/isa/4/1/s_683001>

64. *Strong's Exhaustive Concordance*: entry for "724. harpage". *Bible Hub*. Biblehub.com. 2016. Web. 12 July 2017. <http://biblehub.com/greek/724.htm>
65. *Strong's Exhaustive Concordance*: entry for "726. harpazo". *Bible Hub*. Biblehub.com. 2016. Web. 12 July 2017. <http://biblehub.com/greek/726.htm>
66. Zodhiates, Spiros. *The Complete Word Study Dictionary: New Testament*, Chattanooga: AMG Publishers, 1992. 256. Print.
67. *1 Thess. 4:17-18 Commentary. Precept Austin*. Preceptaustin.org. Web. 11 July 2017. <http://www.preceptaustin.org/pdf/59702>
68. Dodson, John Jeffrey. *Dodson Greek-English Lexicon 1.0. BibleSupport.com*. Biblesupport.com. 13 Sep. 2015. Web. 11 July 2017. <http://www.biblesupport.com/e-sword-downloads/file/10038-dodson-greek-english-lexicon/>
69. Wycliffe, John. *John Wycliffe's Translation*. (1382) Northwest Nazarene University. Web. 11 July 2017. <http://wesley.nnu.edu/fileadmin/imported_site/wycliffe/1th.txt>
70. Wycliffe, John. *John Wycliffe's Translation*. (1382) Northwest Nazarene University. Web. 11 July 2017. <http://wesley.nnu.edu/fileadmin/imported_site/wycliffe/Act.txt>
71. Spencer, John R. *New Heaven, New Earth* Lincoln: Writers Club Press, 2002. 189. Print.
72. *Strong's Exhaustive Concordance*: entry for "528. apanteo". *Bible Hub*. Biblehub.com. 2016. Web. 11 July 2017.<http://biblehub.com/strongs/greek/528.htm>
73. *Englishman's Concordance*: entry for "apantesin". *Bible Hub*. Biblehub.com. 2016. Web. 11 July 2017.<http://biblehub.com/greek/apante_sin_529.htm>
74. Thayer, Joseph H. and James Strong. "Strong's NT 622". *Thayer's Greek-English Lexicon of the New Testament: Coded with Strong's Concordance Numbers*. Peabody: Hendrickson Publishers, 1995. Print.
75. Thayer, Joseph H. and James Strong. "Strong's NT 2673" *Thayer's Greek-English Lexicon of the New Testament: Coded with Strong's Concordance Numbers*. Peabody: Hendrickson Publishers, 1995. Print.

76. Calvin, John. *Commentaries on the Epistle of Paul to the Philippians, Colossians and Thessalonians. Christian Classics Ethereal Library*, Calvin College Computer Science, 1 June 2005. Web. 11 July 2017. <https://www.ccel.org/ccel/calvin/calcom42.i.html>
77. *The Geneva Bible: A Facsimile of the 1599 Edition with Undated Sternhold & Hopkins Psalms*. Buena Park, Calif: Geneva Pub. Co., 1990. Print.
78. *The Matthew Henry's Commentary on the Whole Bible. Christian Classics Ethereal Library*, Calvin College Computer Science, 13 July 2005. Web. 11 July 2017. <https://www.ccel.org/ccel/henry/mhc.i.html>
79. Wesley, John. *Wesley's Notes on the Bible. Christian Classics Ethereal Library*, Calvin College Computer Science, 13 July 2005. Web. 11 July 2017. <http://www.ccel.org/ccel/wesley/notes.i.xv.iii.html>
80. *Englishman's Concordance*: entry for "katechon". *Bible Hub*. Biblehub.com. 2016. Web. 11 July 2017. <http://biblehub.com/greek/katechon_2722.htm>
81. Hamp, Douglas. *Corrupting the Image: Angels, Aliens, and the Antichrist Revealed*. Crane: Defender Publishing, LLC., 2011. Print.
82. *The Holy Bible, King James Version*. Cambridge Edition: 1769; *King James Bible Online*, 2017. Web. 12 July 2017. <http://www.kingjamesbibleonline.org>
83. *The Holy Bible, New King James Version (NKJV)*. Nashville: Thomas Nelson, Inc., 1994. Print.
84. Entry for "*Textus Receptus*". *Wikipedia*. Wikipedia.org. 30 June 2017. Web. 11 July 2017. <https://en.wikipedia.org/wiki/Textus_Receptus>
85. Entry for "*Byzantine text-type*". *Wikipedia*. Wikipedia.org. 31 May 2017. Web. 11 July 2017. <https://en.wikipedia.org/wiki/Byzantine_text-type>
86. Entry for "*Codex Vaticanis*". *Wikipedia*. Wikipedia.org. 28 May 2017. Web. 11 July 2017. <https://en.wikipedia.org/wiki/Codex_Vaticanus>

About the Authors

Douglas Hamp earned his M.A. in the Bible and its World from the Hebrew University of Jerusalem and his PhD in Biblical Studies from Louisiana Baptist University. He is the author of numerous books, articles, and DVDs, and has appeared on national and international programs. He is Senior Pastor of the Way Congregation in Wheat Ridge, CO.

Chris Steinle is a former minister who began his professional career as a CPA. Many Christian theologians and prophecy scholars have backgrounds in law, accounting, and business. For Christians who believe the Bible to be God-breathed, the ability to gather information and draw correlations is crucial for rightly dividing the Word of God.

We hope the reader has appreciated the depth of research and thoughtful presentation of the authors' discoveries.

In today's Internet community, book reviews posted at booksellers' book pages are a meaningful way to provide feedback, and to guide the authors in future publications.

Please take a moment to rate and review this book.

www.ingramcontent.com/pod-product-compliance
Lightning Source LLC
LaVergne TN
LVHW041541070426
835507LV00011B/861